Cross-Disciplinary Perspectives on Regional and Global Security

Paweł Frankowski · Artur Gruszczak
Editors

Cross-Disciplinary Perspectives on Regional and Global Security

palgrave
macmillan

Editors
Paweł Frankowski
Jagiellonian University
Kraków, Poland

Artur Gruszczak
Jagiellonian University
Kraków, Poland

ISBN 978-3-319-75279-2   ISBN 978-3-319-75280-8 (eBook)
https://doi.org/10.1007/978-3-319-75280-8

Library of Congress Control Number: 2018933051

Cover credit: © KARI/ESA

Printed on acid-free paper

This Palgrave Macmillan imprint is published by Springer Nature
The registered company is Springer International Publishing AG
The registered company address is: Gewerbestrasse 11, 6330 Cham, Switzerland

CONTENTS

LIST OF TABLES

INTRODUCTION

Abstract   Introduction provides a theoretical framework on how global, regional and national actors, differ in their management approaches, capacity levels, and how these differences translate into cross-regional cooperation on security issues. The chapter focuses on three intertwining elements that should constitute the approach to regional security challenges, i.e. ideas, interests and institutions. The triad of these terms refers to the process of formulating and implementing security policy agenda in different regions, but also reflects political interests of every involved actor. A proper understanding of the role and importance of these elements in the analysis allows, in subsequent chapters, to seek answers to the basic research question, namely the meaning of policies related to contemporary security issues and challenges in particular regions.

The comprehensive analysis of key issues in the global security demands variety of approaches, perspectives and questions, before closer look onto regional security problems. This book provides an overview of how global, regional and national actors, differ in their management approaches, capacity levels, and how these differences translate into cross-regional cooperation on security issues. In order to come to terms of ongoing development of regional security arrangements, this book presents a comprehensive account of different solutions for contemporary security challenges in different regions.

In particular, our authors analyze three intertwining elements, that should constitute the approach to regional security challenges, i.e. **ideas, interests and institutions**. The triad of these terms refers to the process of formulating and implementing security policy agenda in different regions, but also reflects political interests of every involved actor. This triad constitutes interactions on the regional level but also between regional actors, and shapes the processes of developing the instruments for regional security, while pursuing an independent and holistic approach to contemporary challenges. A proper understanding of the role and importance of these elements in the analysis allows, in subsequent chapters, to seek answers to the basic research question, namely the meaning of policies related to contemporary security issues and challenges in particular regions.

The main question that the present book addresses is the following: What does it mean regional security in twenty-first century, and more specifically how to expound role and functions of specific actors on regional level. Because every security challenge and problem emerges and exists within a wider context of events, long-standing perceptions and norms allow to craft a specific framework of analysis for every single chapter in order to make them comparable, but with cross-disciplinary angle. Every chapter will consist of **four parts**, and every part reflects constitutive elements of the editorial team approach to contemporary security in particular regions as indicated above. The **first part** of every chapter is devoted to **ideas** underlying the inclusion of security in regional policies. A study of the **idea of security** will be based on the analysis of existing regional policies, adopted positions of third countries and the content of current legislation as part of important societal institutions. Ideas, as some authors suggest (Campbell 2004), may be cognitive or normative, and above all, they are often taken for granted and deemed to underpin debates on political decisions. This assumption is relevant also in the case of security issues, and in order to determine which entities play the most important role in shaping the idea of security, the editors decided to refer to the concept of framing, and agenda setting. The process of setting the agenda and framing (Goffman 1986; Daviter 2011; Rhinard 2010) is the result of manipulation of information and ideas, but also requires relying on existing frames. In this case, it will be essential to consider the ideas of normative power, regional hegemony, core states and merits of regional integration. In addition, the idea of security should be also analyzed from the perspective of expanding state competences. Moreover, the editors believe that the idea of the market, as important for any kind of security works as a strategic idea of building a repertoire of innovative political strategies used by any actor who adopts market ideas to compensate for a lack of power and political resources. The idea of the market or market ideas are designed to transform existing security institutions, but also have a normative element, assuming competition and efficiency for the benefit of citizens of particular region. Market ideas embrace also the promise of development, welfare and economic prosperity; the members of editorial team argue that security issues are subordinated to market ideas, even logic of political actions stem from the idea of deeper integration. The **second part** of every chapter is devoted to **interests** pursued by regional actors, including security issues in particular policies. The concept of interest is based on the assumption that the state is a system whose purpose is control and efficiency, which is acceptable from normative and empirical point of view. Interests, important for understanding regional security are analyzed from the perspective of active players redefining the borders of security and political spaces. Apart from states, three types of actor are particularly important: supranational institutions, subnational actors and private actors interacting in regional and global scale. All three actors act in a stream of changes in global security, and with their actions emphasize a pursuit for global common goods. For the purpose of this book, all three actors will be analyzed in detail, and regional interests in promoting the security issues are of primary importance. Nevertheless, when the regional systems are considered as strategic constellations, there are a good number of interests and ideas behind the proposed policies on security issues.

Since aforementioned actors operate in a real world their ideal goals cannot be fully realizable, and are constrained by regional powers, but also by preferences declared by actors themselves. It is remarkable that from 1945 onwards traditionally accepted instruments of security, as preventive war, lost their place in a dictionary of international relations. Absence of such conflicts provides the basis for new preferences, where perceptions of regional security have been embedded into domestic orders and preferences of particular governments. Therefore, interests will be analyzed in terms of the preferences of participants, which are dealt with in **three different dimensions**. **Subjective** dimension of preferences allows to indicate who are the actors declaring and implementing their preferences regarding security. In this group following actors will be examined: international institutions, states, civil society and private actors pursuing economic interests. The second dimension will be related to **nature of preferences**, whether they are exogenous, i.e. do not result from current and ongoing processes of regional integration, or endogenous, as result of previous actions, and, therefore, path-dependent. The **third** dimension will assume **ideological and material preferences** associated with the perception of the aim of integration as creating of ideas and identities, or the desire to acquire or expand resources. This dimension of interest will be based directly on first part of every chapter.

The **third part** of every chapter takes an **in-depth analysis of institutions** related to security issues in every region and will focus on the practical implementation of these provisions as well as relations between states—non-state actor and international organizations. Because the reason for any political decision is to change political reality, any critical assessment of policy-making should focus on the consequences of decisions taken. Such assumption results in an analysis of institutional structures that are responsible for agenda setting and which, under favourable circumstances, introduce new policies. In this part actors active on the regional level are perceived as actors who take core functions of the state. Therefore, in some parts of the world, regional integration actually refers to the key functions of the state, resulting in covert integration. Moreover apart of vertical integration (e.g. from states to EU level) horizontal transformation at the level of regional institutions is also important. The assumption that the transfer of powers relating to security takes place only from states to regional institutions diminish the importance of inter-institutional disputes and attempts to maintain or expand institutional power established regional actors.

The **fourth part** of every chapter traces back **interactions** and **instruments** triggered by the very nature of analyzed regions themselves. First, the emergence of actual interactions has been consolidated by geographical and geopolitical characteristic of analyzed regions, particularly in the case of Europe and Americas, which constitute limited number of actors who pool common resources like energy security, or space security. Second, pre-existing common historical and political heritage of analyzed regions serve as a useful narrative to understand interactions and choice of possible instruments.

This book applies cross-disciplinary perspective on regional security in the context of regional challenges and problems as well as foreign relations on the regional level. The establishment of common understanding of three intertwined elements following chapters address selected security issues in given regions. With these main questions on the role of ideas, interests and institutions, Chapter "EUROscepticism and Monetary Security in Europe" (Rafał Riedel) addresses monetary security, and substance of Euroscepticism as a negative attitude towards monetary integration in the European Union. Subsequently, Riedel presents and organizes evidence of monetary security and EUROscepticism, revealing a trend in Euroisation in selected countries.

Chapter "European Space Security and Regional Order" (Irma Słomczyńska) tackles the space security, and takes into account peculiar problem of space debris, where the European Union, through widening of its goals moved from being a regional organization towards a provider of global common goods. When institutions for space security are still in nascent phase, with this is mind Słomczyńska points out that interests of EU member states are still of military nature, and institutions are nested in a set of five key ideas for space affairs, established in Europe.

Chapter "Role of Sub-national Actors in North American Security" (Paweł Frankowski) addresses regional cooperation in the North America between sub-state actors on the ground of paradiplomacy, as an idea of cooperation between non-central governments. Despite constitutional constraints on plurality in international representation, some transborder security issues can be tackled by lower level of government, and finally security institutions have appeared.

Chapter "Regional Security in the Twenty-First Century's South America: Economic, Energy, and Political Security in MERCOSUR and UNASUR" and Chapter "The Distinctiveness of the Latin American Security System—Why Is It so Different? Public International Law Perspective", respectively systematize security arrangements in South America. When Katharina L. Meissner systematizes various concepts of regional organizations as security providers, Agata Kleczkowska highlights the role of international law, as an overreaching institution based on regional norms and interests.

Last part of this book tackles security issues in Africa, where variety and plurality of actors, interests and ideas co-exist, compete and have been congruest. In this part, Lola Reich, Blessing Onyinyechi Uwakwe, Buhari Shehu Miapyen, Douglas Castro, Sabrina White and Anna Cichecka account for the fact that in Africa the importance of law, intentional cooperation, human rights and environmental protection is appreciated very differently, and the role of great powers in Africa should not be neglected. When Lola Reich (Chapter "Security at the Centre of Post 2000 Eu–Africa Relations") emphasizes the role of exogenous factors for stability in Africa, Blessing Onyinyechi Uwakwe, Buhari Shehu Miapyen (Chapter "Boko Haram and Identity Reconstruction in Lake Chad Basin Region") focus on centrifugal forces on the regional levels and explore how better understanding of ideologies may contribute to understanding of security in Western Africa. Sabrina White (Chapter "Peacekeeping in the African Union: Gender, Women and the Battle Against Sexual Exploitation and Abuse") addresses the question of actors involved in United Nations Peace Operations, pointing out that institutions created to perform a security role in their efforts could evolve into stumbling blocks on the road to lasting peace. When Chapter "Peacekeeping in the African Union: Gender, Women and the Battle Against Sexual Exploitation and Abuse" focuses on negative aspects of women's role in peace keeping operation, Anna Cichecka (Chapter "Women's Participation in Peace Processes in East Africa—Selected Aspects") addresses women in the East Africa as important actors for peace building in the region. Final chapter (Douglas de Castro) responds to fundamental challenges by asking the questions on environmental security by analyzing the case of Okavango River Basin.

Reasons for selecting aforementioned cases vary. Instead of simply comparing certain regional arrangements by juxtaposition of institutional structures or treaties, we asked our contributors to adopt historical institutionalism (Pierson 2000, 2004) and explain case by case how ideas and interests coming from various sources shape, constrain and support institutions. This context is above all marked by the quest for security, broadly defined and understood. When institutions are widely presented as ultimate solution for stability, and a matter of utmost importance to keep lasting order in the region, we argue that normative stance behind any institution is always and by nature, political. Given the objectives of any analyzed institution, i.e. to provide security, one should not forget that institution reside in a political space, when variety of concerns, legal, outspoken or primordial raised by states and other actors play a crucial role and make an important reference point for any analysis of regional orders. National objectives and interests, as well as fear of regional hegemony, are not new, and there is no need to create a new paradigm to understand contemporary international security. There is, however, a need to rethink institutions in new circumstances, when links between global and regional problems are much closer than before. Therefore, to get and maintain regional security there is a need to strengthen collective structures and translate them into ideas and norms, when a belief into collaborative endeavour would be a universal idea, based on theory of justice (Sen 2009), protection of human rights and global commons. Adopting this perspective, where institutions, real processes and interactions between people and institutions will be treated as equally important elements of analysis allows us to understand that very idea of regional security is always for someone and for some purpose (Cox 1981). By unveiling linkages to particular historical circumstances, ideas of justice and role of institutions our contributors offer a rich variety of perspectives to think critically about security and regional orders.

Paweł Frankowski
Artur Gruszczak

REFERENCES

Campbell, John L. 2004. *Institutional Change and Globalization*. Princeton: Princeton University Press.

Cox, Robert W. 1981. Social Forces, States and World Orders: Beyond International Relations Theory. *Millennium—Journal of International Studies* 10 (2): 126–55. https://doi.org/10.1177/03058298810100020501.

Daviter, Falk. 2011. *Policy Framing in the European Union*. Palgrave Studies in European Union Politics. Basingstoke and New York: Palgrave Macmillan.

Goffman, Erving. 1986. *Frame Analysis: An Essay on the Organization of Experience*. Boston: Northeastern University Press.

Pierson, Paul. 2000. The Limits of Design: Explaining Institutional Origins and Change. *Governance* 13 (4): 475–99. https://doi.org/10.1111/0952-1895.00142.

Pierson, Paul. 2004. *Politics in Time: History, Institutions, and Social Analysis*. Princeton: Princeton University Press.

Rhinard, Mark. 2010. *Framing Europe: The Policy Shaping Strategies of the European Commission*. Dordrecht and Boston: Republic of Letters and Martinus Nijhoff.

Sen, Amartya. 2009. *The Idea of Justice*. Cambridge: Harvard University Press.

EUROscepticism and Monetary
Security in Europe

Rafał Riedel

Introduction

The objective of the paper is to investigate the correlations between the phenomenon of EUROscepticism (understood as a negative attitude towards the monetary integration on a supranational level[1]) and the monetary security in Europe. By doing so this study sees EUROscepticism both as dependant and independant variable, which positions itself very well in the most recent trend of the European studies. The so called third generation of Euroscepticism studies postulates to treat it not only as an explanatory variable but also as an explaining factor—not just a phenomenon which needs to be explained, but also

---

[1]Which is an element of a broader concept of Euroscepticism—the negative attitude towards the European integration as a whole or some of its aspects or ideas. These two terms are conceptualised more in details in the further parts of this article. See also Zuba and Riedel (2015).

R. Riedel (✉)
University of Opole, Opole, Poland
e-mail: riedelr@icloud.com

© The Author(s) 2018   1
P. Frankowski and A. Gruszczak (Eds.),
Cross-Disciplinary Perspectives on Regional and Global Security,
https://doi.org/10.1007/978-3-319-75280-8_1

a determinant of other important processes and phenomena. Such a turn in scholarly treating Euroscepticism is connected with the growing Eurosceptic views in Europe in real life politics—Euroscepticism is not any more a marginal aberration but became an element of the mainstream politics. This real life phenomenon spills over to the scholarly work which puts it in the centre of the research process.

This contribution follows the logic of the edited volume focusing on the ideas, interests and institutions related to monetary security in conjuncture with EUROscepticism. The chapter starts with the introduction into the concept of EUROscepticism and its relations with the classical Euroscepticism. Then the second key term of the paper is defined, which is the monetary security—nested in the general understanding of the economic security. Here, not only the author provides his own understanding of the monetary security, but also discusses its main levels, dimensions, functions and determinants. In the last part, the correlations between the two phenomena are discussed with the illustration of the selected EU member states representing Eurozone members and non-members.

EUROSCEPTICISM AS AN IDEA

Euroscepticism is generally and conventionally understood as a negative attitude towards the European Union, European integration process in general, some of its aspects or just the idea of uniting the continent in any respect. More specifically EUROscepticism is defined as a negative attitude towards the Eurozone, monetary integration on the supranational level, some of its aspects or ideas and concepts related to it.

Such conceptualising of EUROscepticism and Euroscepticism positions these two terms/categories in a rich scholarly literature, which became even more important in the context of the economic crisis that hit Europe in 2008 as well as the so called "Brexit" referendum (2016) and its consequences. Therefore the deep understanding of the phenomenon, its determinants, mechanisms, effects and side-effects is central in contemporary research on the European Union. Euroscepticism is not any longer just an aberration of the mainstream politics in the EU. It has become an element of the mainstream, at least, after the most recent elections to the European Parliament (2014) and the "Brexit" referendum (2016). As a result, also scientifically, it is not any more a contextual variable only, but it gained the attention as a central phenomenon to be explained.

Noteworthy, EUROscepticism as a scholarly concept is treated neutrally here, without any evaluative connotations attached. One can identify both negative and positive aspects of EUROsceptic argumentation, but this study is not evaluative. Its objective is not to judge if the EUROsceptics are right or wrong. It is rather to describe and explain the problem of EUROscepticism and to explain other phenomena and processes through EUROscepticism as an explanatory vehicle. The second variable of this research design is monetary security. This concept is also relatively multidimensional and the third part of this study is dedicated to it—unpacking the idea and the concept more in detail.

In the past, Euroscepticism was found on the margins of the political and societal system—it was more often the extreme right, less frequently the extreme left that expressed anti-EU feelings and general opposition to the European integration project (Holmes 1996). Today we identify the Eurosceptic views in mainstream politics as well. More importantly, together with the extensive growth of the European Union, it became natural. No more can it be treated as an aberration—on the opposite, total and unquestioned acceptance of every single aspect of today's European integration project would seem infantile. EU became a complex (multi-level governance) system in which some elements meet more whereas others seriously less acceptance. Additionally the economic crisis in Europe generated winners and losers also along the monetary integration lines. Such a situation requires scientific inquiry which will describe and explain the new developments and new contexts in the Euroscepticism evolution.

So far the scholars have explained the fluctuations in support or opposition for the EU through a number of theories, including cognitive mobilization (Inglehart 1970a), postmaterialist values (Inglehart 1970b; Inglehart et al. 1991), economic calculus and utilitarianism (Gabel and Palmer 1995; Gabel 1998), popular evaluations of national politics (e.g. Franklin et al. 1994), the importance of party political cues (Hooghe and Marks 2005), domestic factors including government and system support used as a proxy (Anderson 1998), satisfaction with EU democracy and representation (Rohrschneider 2002) or perceived cultural threat (McLaren 2002). In the real life, the factors hidden in these theories overlap and aggregate in the generalized acceptance or opposition towards the monetary integration and its developments.

The point of departure is usually the classical work by Taggart or by Taggart and Szczerbiak (2002), providing both the definition and the basic categorisation of major variants of Euroscepticism (hard and soft differentiation). The early definitions of Euroscepticism by Taggart (1998) conceptualized it as 'the idea of contingent or qualified opposition, as well as incorporating outright and unqualified opposition to the process of European integration'. This definition was further sharpened over the years with the distinction between 'hard' and 'soft' Euroscepticism (Taggart and Szczerbiak 2001). 'Hard' Euroscepticism referred to 'principled' opposition to the EU—namely a rejection of the entire project and a wish for withdrawal or not accessing the block. 'Soft' Euroscepticism, on the other hand, was characterized by 'qualified' or 'contingent' opposition to European integration, which may include opposition to specific policies or national-interest opposition (Beichelt 2004). Kopecky and Mudde (2002) advanced the literature by conceptualizing Euroscepticism based on Easton's (1965) differentiation between diffuse and specific support for a political system. They produced four categories: Euro-enthusiasts, Europragmatists, Euro-sceptics and Eurorejects. Other definitions include Flood's (2002) six-point continuum of rejectionist, revisionist, minimalist, gradualist, reformist and maximalist, Conti's (2003) five-point continuum of hard Euroscepticism, soft Euroscepticism, no commitment, functional Europeanism and identity Europeanism, Rovny's (2004) differentiation between magnitude and motivation, or Vasilopoulou's (2011, 2013) rejecting, conditional and compromising categories.

At the beginning Euroscepticism was treated as a marginal phenomenon in European politics. The term itself was coined (outside of academia) in Britain in 1980s. But it is vital to understand that its pedigree is at least as long as the history of the European integration process itself (or even longer—its idea). However, more than a decade later, this original concept does not encompass the broadness and complexity of the phenomenon.

In general the periodization in Euroscepticism studies shadows the various stages of European integrations. Therefore the natural milestone is the Maastricht treaty (the moment of *communitarising* a number of important policies) after which the scholarship in Europeanisation has entered a dynamic phase. From that moment it changed in nature, scope, content and impact. Apart from it, an important milestone in the development of Euroscepticism was the economic crisis that hit Europe in 2008/9 which brought Eurosceptic views higher on the political agenda. No more can Euroscepticism be located at the periphery of mainstream politics. Not only because of the most recent success of the Eurosceptic parties in 2014 EU Parliamentary elections,[2] but predominantly due to the fact that the Eurosceptic views are a regular part of everyday democratic process and there is not anything special about it. No more can it be treated as a populist margin of the political spectrum.

As regards the EUROscepticism concept, it has not been addressed directly as such in a systematic way. Certainly the monetary aspects of integration appear in many analysis of general Euroscepticism but they are not treated in isolation and with the dedicated scholarly attention that they require. The first paper which defines and conceptualises the term itself as well as its content, context, determinants and others is "EUROsceptycyzm – próba konceptualizacji" (Zuba and Riedel 2015, see also Riedel 2015).

Predominantly EUROscepticism is treated as dependent variable. It is operationalized as the expressed negative attitude towards the monetary integration (or some of its important fragments) by the public opinion, socio-economic elites, political leaders, official party positions, experts, media discourse and other elements of the general public debate.

The independent or explanatory variables are related to the most important determinants explaining the support for the monetary union, among them there are: economic, political, historical/ideational/identity—related ones (Risse 2003).

Like the *permissive consensus*, Euroscepticism (locating itself however in the opposite camp), initially was predominantly—but not exclusively—elite-driven. Later it became more and more democratic reaching a point in which one of its major arguments is the questionable political legitimacy of the European integration project. In twenty-first century we observe more critical discourse in the European public sphere, which cumulated in the times of the economic crises (it is questionable whether the EU or EMU are directly responsible for it though). Therefore it requires refreshed academic reflection of descriptive, explanatory and interpretative nature. The crisis not only generated tensions among the member states, their economies and societies. It sparked new European debates inside the member states' societies with new dynamics, new division lines and new implications.

---

[2] The scholarly analysis of Euroscepticism focuses on various aspects, predominantly however on party politics and public opinion.

MONETARY SECURITY—BETWEEN IDEAS AND INTERESTS

In this part of the text, the monetary security is defined as well as the following elements are identified and discussed: its constitutive elements, levels, dimensions, functions and determinants. It follows the logic from the more general concept of security in general, towards more detailed definitions of monetary security, as a consequence, the term is also contextualised in the broader understanding of the economic security.

Security, as a scholarly concept, is one of the most frequently debated and contested terms. Depending from the disciplinary perspective—political science, economy, international relations and others—it may be understood differently, even within the family of the social sciences. The problem is not only the number of definitions and approaches, but also the concept of security evolves due to the changing nature of the real life developments. As a consequence, security is a multifaceted, ambiguous and dynamic concept.

Its basic understanding sees it as a lack of threats. Classically in international relations security is defined in relation to the state and is a situation in which a state is not and does not feel threatened by military, political or economic pressure now and in a foreseeable future which allows the country to exist and develop in a desired direction. Therefore security is a state but also a process, it can be also understood as an objective, a value or a need at the same time. Optionally, and closer to the economic dimension of it, it is also a set of public policies that protect the safety or welfare of a nation's citizens from substantial threats (Murphy and Topel 2013). One may say that uncertainty and risk is a permanent element of the capitalist world. They are the other side of the same coin marked by freedom and choice (Cable 1995, p. 306).

Traditionally security referred predominantly to the military threats and risks. Nowadays more and more attention is given to the non-military aspects of security, like energy, climate or food security. This is a result of the post-Cold War developments in which the massive East-West military confrontations became less probable. The next part defines the monetary security, identifies its elements, levels, functions and determinants as well as positions it in the broader economic security concept. Economic security is a nest in which the monetary security is imbedded and is constituted of a number of elements to which the monetary security is correlated.

Monetary security is a state of the economy that guarantees the stable dynamics of the value of the currency both domestically and on international markets. Secure monetary policy generates targeted and predictable inflation as well as stable exchange rate against other currencies, especially from the major economic partners. Monetary security allows foreign trade, budgetary policy, debt roll-on on the state level, it also allows individuals and companies to function without turbulences in a stable monetary environment (as consumers, debtors, trade partners and in many other socio-economic functions).

As such it is determined by a number of other inter-related economic policies, like fiscal policy for example. It affects also many spheres of the economic policies, like the interest rates policy. The elements that constitute the monetary policy are:

- Price stability (according to the central bank target)
- Supply of money (balanced)
- Exchange rate (stable fluctuations)
- Monetary reserves policy (threatening potential speculators).

Monetary security will be perceived in a totally different way from the various points of view. The traditional, realist state-centric perspective will see the security being determined predominantly by the state and its authorities. In case of the monetary security this is still very much true in many nation-states, where the monetary policy is performed independently. In the case of Europe however this picture is much more complicated, due to the monetary union among some of the member states of the European Union. At the same time it is important to note here, that it is not only the Eurozone participating economies that are affected by this phenomenon, but indirectly also the other EU members and economic partners of the Eurozone countries. The impact of the European Central Bank goes far beyond the borders of the monetary union participating economies.

In this situation monetary security is not defined on the nation-state level but at the supranational level. Its conjuncture with other economic policies (and dimensions of economic security) still performed at the national level make the Eurozone a rich mosaic of various versions of the economic and monetary security outcomes. In the uniting Europe, monetary security should be observed on the community level, in most other cases it is the nation-state level that is adequate. We also cannot forget about some other sub-national levels which are subjects to the monetary security, for example individuals and companies.

An individual cannot create his or her own monetary security by creating monetary policy, but still is affected by the monetary security of the economy of residence. Individuals' savings may be denominated in more or less stable currencies, his/her debt can be denominated in a currency coming from an economy entertaining lower interest rates—these and many other examples show that an individual, by its economic behaviour and decisions, can generate a more or less secure individual economic situation—dependent on the monetary-related instruments.

However contemporary security formulas refer to the concept of collective security. Collective in the scale of the national economy (usually in case of monetary security) or even in a supranational scale. Due to its specifics of monetary concerns the international dimension is critically important in the case of this type of security (Huntington 1993). The stability of a currency depends also on the exchange rate fluctuations that are very often outside of control of the national governments. Speculative attacks may bring risk and turbulences to the national economy and its participants and not always the reserves appear to be efficient neutraliser to this kind of threats.

Therefore, taking into account the above mentioned deliberations, the levels of monetary security are:

- state (national economy as classically the primary level of monetary policy)
- individual (an individual in his/her socio-economic roles functions in an environment which stability is determined to a large extend to the various elements of the monetary security, for example; savings security)
- company (with the process of enhanced globalisation, both small and large scale companies operate transnationally and as a consequence also across different monetary systems. This generates a set of threats and risks dependent on the stability of a specific monetary system and its relations to other monetary systems. Companies' development and even their basic existence are determined by the changing value of money and its stability both domestically and in international scale)
- supranational (European Union's example shows that the common supranational monetary policy is one of the key steps in the

process of ever-closer economic integration. Apart from bringing numerous anticipated benefits, it also unveiled many side effects and unintended consequences. Predominantly due to the economic crisis, the shortcomings of the European monetary union architecture became clear and sharply visible).

By combining the defined elements of the monetary security with the above mentioned levels of it, it is possible to the identify various dimensions of it:

- economic dimension
- social dimension
- political dimension.

The economic dimension—due to the monetary security being predominantly an economic concept, the economic dimension of it is a substantial one and refers to the successfully targeted inflation policy, allowing for a balanced money supply, and in the international dimension of it also stable exchange rate fluctuations (in the equilibrium sphere acceptable by importers as well as by the exporters) with a safeguard in the form of money reserves discouraging potential speculative attacks. In the societal dimension, it is the individuals and groups and the society as a whole that are influenced by and meet the consequences of a good or bad monetary policy. The social dimension translates to the political one. The monetary policy is usually not directly accountable (in a democratic sense) to the electorates—it is one of the consequences of the central banks independence paradigm. Indirectly there is however a number of connections between the will or satisfaction/acceptance of the citizenry and the monetary policy (including the monetary security). This creates a complex system of correlations between the political and social sphere at the one side and the economic dimension of the monetary security on the other.

One could certainly identify numerous functions and spill-overs of the monetary security. In order to organise them, it is possible to group them into two categories which correlate also with the above mentioned levels of the monetary security:

- domestic functions and
- international functions.

Domestically, the monetary security provides a stable environment for individuals, companies and any other participants and actors of the economic system. It can be understood as a fundament of many other economic functions and stabiliser of the other social (like political) sub-systems. It is usually provided by the monetary policy of the central banks in conjuncture with other economic policies provided by the government. In different states/economies its level of independence can vary significantly in relation to the international environment. The primal function of stability spill-overs to some other sub-functions, like debt level (depending on the debt denomination), import/export competitiveness and others.

Internationally, monetary security provides stable conditions for economic exchange and protects the domestic actors (very often acting also transnationally) from external shocks. It can also be understood in terms of international economy scale. International monetary markets are linked and interdependent. Therefore the stability and predictability of one monetary system provides stable conditions for some other monetary system. Turbulences of one monetary system generate imbalances, risks and threats for some other monetary system. The exchange rate fluctuations play an important role in the international trade and determine the price competitiveness of international markets participants. As it is shown by the European example, the elimination of exchange rate mechanisms by participation in the monetary union, eliminates some group of negative factors, however at the same it generates another group of threats and risks (for example limiting the crisis-escape/way-out options).

STRUCTURAL AND INSTITUTIONAL FRAMEWORK

Monetary security is determined by as well as it determines a great many of inter-related elements, levels, dimensions of the economic system. Undoubtedly it is determined by the central bank's monetary policy, but also by other economic policies provided by the government. It remains under pressure of the international markets (especially but not exclusively currency markets) and just the inflationary pressures may have their origin domestically (for example: the increased domestic demand) and internationally (for example: the imported fossil fuel prices increase). The above-mentioned determinants illustrate that some of the determinants are controlled whereas others remain outside of the reach of the decision makers. Worth mentioning—their strength can differ depending from the scale of the economy in question, its healthy state and openness to the international economic exchange.

The monetary security, in turn, also constitutes an important determinant for many other economic policies, processes and outcomes. It is an important factor of the import-export competitiveness of a given economy (and its sub-units). It allows the predictability of the economic operations (due to the inflation targeting), which is specially important in strategic (medium- and long-term) planning at various levels. By defining the money supply, it determines the availability of the credit and create or discourage bubbles in different spheres and (sub)markets. Successful monetary security policy guarantees the money reserves, which determine the stability of the exchange rate fluctuations.

Monetary security is an element of a broader concept of the economic security, which is—in turn—a dimension of any other forms of security, including the energy, climate, food security, etc. Economic security requires some more attention since the concept of monetary security is built on it and deeply rooted in it. All in all, economic security sums up to satisfying the socio-economic needs, including health, education, social protection and inclusion as well as other work-related elements of economic security. This term however is used, and misused, by many scholars in various circumstances and contexts generating conceptual confusion. For some scholars, the economic security refers to these aspects of trade and investments that are related to the strategic sectors of economy, like for example the military or energy ones. For others the economic security consists of specific policy instruments which are used in international economic relations. In this case, the security of supply seems to be the key concept—no matter if it deals with the energy, raw materials, strategic minerals or intellectual property. Another way of defining the economic security, a geo-economic one, sees the state of economy as a modern weapon in international power balancing. The arsenal of such a definition of economic security consists of policies like: protectionist practices, isolationist behaviour, embargoes, boycotts, mercantilist approach in general. The last, but not least concept of economic security which focuses on the threat of global or regional (region understood as EU for example) instability which creates economic, social, ecological and other risks and threats (Cable 1995, pp. 306–307).

The *market failure* literature admits that to some extent, insecurity is a constitutive element of the capitalist economy, it is almost a precondition for a well functioning free market. At he same time some measures need to be taken in order to avoid the potential market failures (including the financial markets) as well as malformations of the economic system grown on corrupt practices like oligarhisation, syndicates or monopolism. If we connect these threats with some other risks like climate change or demographic challenges we discover a complex and puzzled picture of inter and intra dependencies within and among economic, social, political and ecological systems. The above stated risks and challenges show that the economic security is a complex and multidimensional concept. At the same time the economic development produces well-being but also political power. In the post-Cold War Europe it is clearly seen that the economy constitutes one of the major sources of power. It is expected to be increasingly important in a world where the military conflict is less and less probable. The competition race positions itself in the economic sphere (struggle for economic competitiveness, current account (im)balances, indebtedness, investment, innovation—struggle for supremacy) and the national security is won in an "economic war" (Cable 1995, pp. 306–308).

Depending on the scale of analysis we may define economic security—similarly to the monetary security—on various levels: an international one, state one, sectoral one, in a company's scale or even at the level of an individual citizen—participant of the economic system, as a tax-payer, consumer, product/service provider, etc. On an individual level the economic security is the state of having stable incomes enabling to sustain the standard of living now and in the foreseeable future. It consists of: solvency, predictability of the future financial flows, also employment security.

The same with the monetary security—it can be seen from the perspective of international economic relations, but also (and maybe predominantly) from the point of view of a national economy and its interests, a specific company or entrepreneur as well as from the individual perspective. Even when seeing the monetary security from the same (for example an individual's) perspective, it may look differently, depending the geographical localisation. An individual citizen of the United States of America, on every day basis using the US dollar (an international currency), may have a different perspective on the monetary policy and security than, the Swiss citizen, on everyday basis using the currency which is a safe haven in times of crisis (almost equal to gold), compared to the Polish citizen, using the Polish zloty, a currency which is stable (by central European standards), but at the same time exposed to the potential shocks originating outside of the Polish economic system (speculative attacks, devaluation risks, external inflation/deflation pressures, etc.).

Central European perspective is incredibly interesting in this regard, due not only Poland but also Hungary and other states from the region, have suffered from the exchange rate fluctuations in unprecedented way (with the noticeable exception of Slovakia after its 2009 entry into the Eurozone). Hundreds of thousands of households are indebted in Swiss Frank (for the low interest rates reason), and therefore dependent not only on the Schweizer National Bank, but also on the Swiss Frank exchange rate. Earning in one currency and paying the bills in another one is a natural source of risks—expanded into decades, taking into account the standard length of a hypothec credit. Still many individuals decided to take up this risk, and cumulated into hundreds of thousands of households, they created a source of potential instability for the whole national economy, when the exchange rate becomes turbulent.

All the above mentioned risks are directly connected with the monetary security of individual citizens, which is an element of the economic security in general. The demarcation lines between monetary and other dimensions of economic security are blurred, debatable and flexible. Some of the concepts of the economic security are based on the idea of protecting the domestic supplies, technologies and markets and therefore are seen in a more confrontational then cooperative perspective (Cable 1995, p. 305).

Before 1989 the world seemed (supposedly) less complicated—the security and economic objectives were not fundamentally in conflict. In today's world it is much more difficult to define who or what is the source of the threat, if it is real or potential, who is the enemy and what the security involves. Globalisation also does not help in this regard. The economic interdependence stimulates a growing integration in formal and informal settings. No economy is free from external influences and dependencies. They have become substantive elements of each and every economy, both creating opportunities and generating threats. Increased and intensified trade exchange, capital markets integration, labour mobility and many others stipulate, as a side-effects, also some enhanced organised crime, cyber attacks exposure, international economy sabotage, trans-border climate risks, money laundering and so on.

INTERACTIONS AND CORRELATIONS

To identify the correlations between the EUROscepticism and monetary security it is necessary to ask the question how the two influence one another. In what way the monetary security in Europe (as perceived by the EU citizens) influences the EUROsceptic views and how the EUROscepticism, as a phenomena, has an effect on the monetary security. In both cases, it is unavoidable to apply diversified variables since the European states and economies differ very much in both dimensions. Firstly, there is no one type of EUROscepticism and it evolves. Secondly, the monetary security is different (not to mention its perceptions) in specific countries and economies no matter if they remain under one umbrella of a common monetary policy, European Union or the European Economic Area. However, taking into account the scale of this chapter, it is possible to tackle only upon a narrow part of this diversified and dynamic picture. Therefore the author choses some exemplifications from states that are part of the Eurozone, both from the reach North (exemplified by Germany) and from the relatively poor South (exemplified by Greece) as well as countries that remain outside of the Eurozone. Here, a perspective from the so called old member states (exemplified by Great Britain), and new member states (exemplified by Poland) is delivered. There is a number of other optional explanatory variables possible to be applied, for instance the size of the country, its economic conditions and parameters, positioning in the core vs. peripheries of the European economy, etc. For illustrative reasons also some non-EU states' perspective will be presented, here: Swiss perspective (outside of the Eurozone, EU and EEA) of a "stubborn European" with a stable currency and privileged economic situation and the Ukrainian perspective—of a country aspiring to join the European integration process, in a handicapped political and economic situation.

The first question is how EUROscepticism affects the monetary security. Growing EUROsceptic and Eurosceptic views undermine the legitimacy of the European monetary union and the EU integration process as such. By doing so they may weaken the monetary security. Here it is important if it is the public EUROscepticism or the elites' EUROscepticism. If we consider different countries (with diversified both EUROscepticism and monetary security), we receive a very rich picture of Europe in this regard. Inside of the Eurozone, both in German and Greece, the general audience has by majority a positive attitude towards the euro, however for various reasons. Still in both countries the vast majority of the populations treat the common currency as a guarantee of stable prices and the whole system as functional. Outside of the Eurozone—the opposite, especially after the economic crisis. In countries like Poland or UK, the perception of euro is negative and both the populations and the elites in general prefer to stay outside of the supranational monetary setting. The trust invested in the common currency by the EU citizens who use it is an asset of itself serving the credibility and the stability of the whole system.

As noted above, one very important differentiation is the position inside or outside of the Eurozone. In the case of the Eurozone members the level of EUROscepticism affects their willingness to enhance the monetary integration process (supranationalisation of banking supervision, sanctions for breaking the rules of the monetary union, further institutionalisation, spill-overs into fiscal and other economic policies, leading to the political union—federalisation of Europe). For the non-Eurozone states (EU members), the question is whether to join or not to join the Eurozone, and the EUROscepticism as a factor plays far more important role here. Entering the monetary union requires wide spread consensus in the political system[3] which is very rare in todays' Europe. EUROsceptics act in such circumstances as veto players or blocking minority which gives them extra-proportional power in the decision making process. EUROsceptic opinions may keep a country out of the monetary union, which is directly connected with the monetary security.

If we consider that the sources of EUROscepticism are very often non-rational—stemming from political (tactical) or ideological sources—it is important to realise that EUROsceptic arguments can be reasonable or not. Monetary security is—on the opposite—much more reality-grounded. To a far less extend, compared to EUROscepticism, it is emotional. Lack of political will may result from a misperception of the subjectively interpreted facts. It may be objectively rational to join the monetary union, in the interest of the society, at the same time, the political momentum may be very much against this step. In such a case, EUROscepticism acts against the monetary security of the society and economy. Certainly the other way around it is equally possible—the

---

[3] Joining the Eurozone very often requires the change of the constitution which is not possible without building super-majority in the parliaments or decision in the form of a nation-wide referendum.

EUROsceptic views protect some society from making the mistake of joining the Eurozone, in times when it is better to stay outside of it. Now, if we connect the knowledge that we have about the positive and negative consequences of the monetary integration in Europe (and what kind of economies are more destined to participate than not) with the monetary security concept, it becomes clear that small, open, competitive economies should be members of the Euro-club—especially when surrounded by economic partners operating in one currency. Why Switzerland is not a part of the Eurozone and not even a part of the European Union? The answer is—because it is the Swiss Euroscepticism that keeps them outside of it. What builds the Swiss Euroscepticism? Ideational and political reasons. Pure economic calculations are much more in favour of Switzerland joining the EU and Eurozone, then the non-economic deliberations (traditional neutrality, specific political system, direct-democratic methods of decision making, position of Eurosceptic SVP—Schweizerische Volks Partei, etc.).

In both cases the EUROsceptic views of the citizenry may influence the behaviour of the decision-makers. Therefore they may be—by democratic procedures—encouraged or discouraged to implement or oppose some type of reforms which are correlated with the economic and monetary security. Both by taking action and by lack of action they may increase or decrease the objective or perceived (or both) security of their citizens and the whole economy.

How the changing monetary security influences EUROscepticism?

It could be speculated that in the case of the Eurozone, the more monetarily secure the citizens feel—the less EUROscepticism there should occure. The more economic turbulences connected with the Euro, the more EUROscepticism. That's inside of the Eurozone. Outside of it, the picture may look totally different. Participants of the economies enjoying stable monetary situation, taking all the advantages of having own currency are much less likely to pull towards adopting the common currency. Here the probability of EUROsceptic views are much more likely. Whereas in economic systems that lose much more then win from staying outside of the common currency block (currency devaluations, speculative attacks and external shocks), the participants' opinions do not gravitate towards the EUROsceptic camp.

The Greek case also shows an interesting phenomenon. Even though the Greeks received a great deal of austerity measures which are economically and socially painful for the society, and even though they perceive the crisis as the Eurozone crisis, they are not very much eager of leaving the Eurozone. True, the Eurosceptic as well as the EUROsceptic views are present in Athens, still the Greeks are aware that outside of the Eurozone (returning to the own currency—Drahma) is not an option. This would worsen their economic situation dramatically and this "Greek tragedy" situation (there are only bad and worse solutions) keeps them inside the Euro-block. This exemplification reveals another important aspect of the monetary security, which is its relational nature. It is not only the indefinite condition of the economy, but it should be estimated in relation to some real (not imagined or illusive) alternatives that are in a certain moment at the disposal. In a given geographical location, specific moment in time and particular economic situation there is some optimal monetary security available.

When identifying the potential influences of the monetary security on the EUROsceptic views, one should refer to the specific components of the monetary policy and security, predominantly the price stability, supply of money, exchange rate fluctuations, and the monetary reserves policy. All the above mentioned components are important for the monetary security, however for specific social groups their perceived salience will be defined differently. The depositors will pay special attention to the price stability and the low inflation index will be a crucial element for them. Therefore the losses related to the higher inflation will influence their level of EUROscepticism. On the other side the debtors (both individual and institutional) will be more or less satisfied with the monetary policy if there is more or less supply of money on the market. With the interests rates low and the beneficial conditions of rolling-on the debt, they will feel more secure economically. Those who trade internationally and are affected negatively by the exchange rate fluctuations will opt for a stable currency with stable exchange rate (Baldwin 1989). This will build their monetary security. The same in the scale of the whole economy as regards the monetary reserves, which guarantee the stability of the currency in international financial markets.

CONCLUSIONS

When deliberating on the correlations between the monetary security and the EUROsceptic views of the European citiznery and elites, it is important to recall and reconstruct the historicity of the monetary integration project in Europe. The introduction of euro was motivated by two important objectives directly related to the monetary security—one: to insulate Europe from the vagaries of the dollar, and second: to address the problems faced by the European Monetary System, that is, speculative attacks on the currencies of peripheral Europe and regional hegemony of a sovereign currency, the Deutsche Mark (Faudot 2015, p. 52). Noteworthy, from the very beginning—at the very cradle of the supranational monetary policy in Europe—there were the monetary security arguments on the agenda.

Two decades after the Euro introduction we dispose a much better knowledge and understanding of the monetary union functioning. When it solved some of the above mentioned problems, at the same it generated some new ones. Before the economic crisis, the Euro was treated as a major success (European Commission 2008), the majority of economists argued that the monetary union served positively in anchoring macroeconomic stability, promoting cross-border trade, increase financial integration and investment. In the global scale, the Euro was perceived as a pole of stability and a new pillar in the international monetary system. After the economic crisis it became obvious that the necessity to coordinate the monetary policy with a multiple fiscal policies (of the Eurozone member states) under one umbrella of the European Central Bank (one size fits all monetary policy) poses a serious problem. The need for real convergence (of the business cycles) was overshadowed by the so called convergence criteria of the Maastricht Treaty (inflation, interests rates, budgetary deficit, public debt, exchange rate fluctuations stability). Not to mention the structural differences between and among the member states—current account imbalances, diversified inflation, labour markets, banking systems, housing market, educational systems, welfare systems and so on.

Additionally, the economic crisis brought about some further enhancement of the debate about the fiscal federalism in Europe. Similarly to the nineteenth century America, Europe started to think seriously about fiscal transfer exceeding the modest 1% of the cumulated EU Gross Domestic Product. The solidarity mechanisms under discussion would finalise the economic union in integrating Europe by creating a community of fate. The Europeans, united under one debt, would finally dispose measures to answer the assymetric shocks, which correlates very well with the claims of the Optimal Currency Area Theory.

There are however a number of countries that—for monetary security and other reasons—prefer to adopt the Euro with or without full and legal participation in the monetary union. These are the most commonly identified reasons behind the Euroisation decision:

- stability of the exchange rate which stimulates international investment,
- elimination of speculative attacks risks,
- lower exchange risk for the reserves,
- lower interest rates,
- lower inflation,
- lower transaction costs,
- the option of re-establishing the domestic currency (as recreating an independent national central bank is theoretically possible exclusively in the case of unilateral Euroisation) (Komarek and Melecky 2003, p. 78).

On the other side however, there is also a number of reasons not to decide on the Euroisation:

- the disadvantage of not disposing own interested rates policy
- the higher risk of runs on the commercial banks in the absence of a "national" central bank acting as a lender of last resort
- the lack of foreign reserves (Komarek and Melecky 2003, p. 78).

The balance of advantages and disadvantages of positioning under the umbrella of a common currency should be complemented with the following argument: all countries (except for the so called centre, that is USA and EMU), when using their own currencies in trade, face a continuous struggle between internal and external balances (Moore 2004, p. 632). At the same time, it is logical that all countries collectively in the global economic system cannot have surplus in any period. There are winners and losers in this game, and so there are winners and losers in the struggle for more economic and monetary security.

SOURCES

Anderson, Christopher J. 1998. When in Doubt, Use Proxies: Attitudes Toward Domestic Politics and Support for European Integration. *Comparative Political Studies* 31 (5): 569–601. https://doi.org/10.1177/0010414098031005002.

Baldwin, R. 1989. The Political Economy of Trade Policy. *The Journal of Economic Perspectives* 3 (4): 119–135.

Beichelt, T. 2004. Euro-scepticism in the EU Accession Countries. *Comparative European Politics* 2 (1): 29–50.

Cable, Vincent. 1995. What Is International Economic Security. *International Affairs* 71 (2 April): 305–324.

Conti, N. 2003. Party Attitudes to European Integration: A Longitudinal Analysis of the Italian Case. European Parties Elections and Referendums Network Working Paper No. 13.

Easton, David. 1965. *A Systems Analysis of Political Life*. New York: John Wiley.

European Commission. 2008. EMU@10 Successes and Challenges After Ten Years of Economic and Monetary Union. *European Economy* 2. Luxembourg: Office for Official Publications of the European Communities 2008, xiv, 328 pp. ISBN 978-92-79-08384-6.

Faudot, Adrien. 2015. An International Invoicing Currency. *International Journal of Political Economy* 44: 51–70.

Flood, Chris. 2002. Euroscepticism: A Problematic Concept. Paper presented at UACES 32nd Annual Conference and 7th Research Conference, Queen's University Belfast, 2–4 September.

Franklin, M., M. Marsh, and L. McLaren. 1994. Uncorking the Bottle: Popular Opposition to European Unification in the Wake of Maastricht. *Journal of Common Market Studies* 32 (4): 455–472.

Gabel, M. 1998. Public Support for European Integration: An Empirical Test of Five Theories. *The Journal of Politics* 60 (2): 333–354.

Gabel, Matthew, and Harvey D. Palmer. 1995. Understanding Variation in Public Support for European Integration. *European Journal of Political Research* 27 (1): 3–19. https://doi.org/10.1111/j.1475-6765.1995.tb00627.x.

Holmes, M. (ed.). 1996. *The Eurosceptic Reader*. Basingstoke: Palgrave Macmillan.

Hooghe, L., and G. Marks. 2005. Calculations, Community and Cues: Public Opinion on European Integration. *European Union Politics* 44 (6): 419–443.

Huntington, Samuel. 1993. Why International Primacy Matters. *International Security* 17 (4): 72.

Inglehart, R. 1970a. The New Europeans: Inward or Outward Looking? *International Organization* 24 (1 Winter): 129–139.

Inglehart, R. 1970b. Cognitive Mobilization and European Identity. *Comparative Politics* 3 (1 October): 45–70.

Inglehart, R. (with Karlheinz Reif). 1991. *EuroBarometer: The Dynamics of European Opinion*. London: Macmillan.

Komarek, Lubos, and Martin Melecky. 2003. Currency Substitution in a Transitional Economy with an Application to the Czech Republic. *Eastern European Economics* 41 (4 July–August): 72–99.

Kopecky, P., and C. Mudde. 2002. The Two Sides of Euroscepticism: Party Positions on European Integration in East Central Europe. *European Union Politics* 3 (3): 297–326.

McLaren, Lauren M. 2002. Public Support for the European Union: Cost/Benefit Analysis or Perceived Cultural Threat? *The Journal of Politics* 64 (2): 551–566.

Moore, Basil J. 2004. A Global Currency for a Global Economy. *Journal of Post Keynesian Economics* 26 (4): 631–653.

Murphy, Kevin, and Robert Topel. 2013. Economics of National Security. *American Economic Review: Papers & Proceedings* 103 (3): 508–511.

Riedel, R. 2015. EUROskepticismus der Eurooptimisten. *Polen Analyse* (162): 2–17.

Risse, T. 2003. The Euro Between National and European Identity. *Journal of European Public Policy* 10 (4): 487–503.

Rohrschneider, Robert. 2002. The Democracy Deficit and Mass Support for an EU-Wide Government. *American Journal of Political Science* 46 (2 April): 463–475.

Rovny, J. 2004. Conceptualising Party-Based Euroscepticism: Magnitude and Motivations. In *Does Euroscepticism have a Passport?* ed. Marc Vuijlsteke, Anja Fiedler, and Pierpaolo Settembri, 31–48. Belgium, Collegium, No. 29.

Taggart, P.A. 1998. A Touchstone of Dissent: Euroscepticism in Contemporary Western European Party Systems. *European Journal of Political Research* 33 (3): 363–388.

Taggart, P., and A. Szczerbiak. 2001. Parties, Positions and Europe: Euroscepticism in the EU Candidate States of Central and Eastern Europe. SEI Working Paper 46, Opposing Europe Research Network Working Paper 2.

Taggart, Paul, and Aleks Szczerbiak. 2002. The Party Politics of Euroscepticism in EU Member and Candidate States. SEI Working Paper 51, Opposing Europe Research Network Working Paper 6.

Vasilopoulou, Sofia. 2011. European Integration and the Radical Right: Three Patterns of Opposition. *Government and Opposition* 46 (2 April): 223–244.

Vasilopoulou, Sofia. 2013. Continuity and Change in the Study of Euroscepticism: Plus ça change? *Journal of Common Market Studies* 51 (1): 153–168.

Zuba, K., and R. Riedel. 2015. *EUROsceptycyzm – propozycja konceptualizacji.* Przegląd Europejski 3 (37): 26–48.

European Space Security and Regional Order

Irma Słomczyńska

Any given idea in European Union (EU) is situated within a preestablished historical path. As a consequence path-dependent environment creates a two-fold effect: it limits the perception of problems and it shapes available strategies for decision makers of every level. Thus specific perception of space security in Europe also follows this logic, and the very term "security" for members of European Space Agency (ESA), members of EU, and European Commission has different meaning, regarding time, topic, and composition of decision-making body. European Space Policy, in line with the working document proposed in 1972, was based on two principles: (1) the creation of a strong European potential in the scientific, economic and/or political areas of interest; (2) the need for cooperation with the United States, the Soviet Union and the other, for the technologically strong Europe (European Space Conference 1972c, p. 1). However in the ESA convention and further activities five main themes could be distinguished—(1) quest for autonomy in space affairs (as prerequisite for European security); (2) international cooperation,

I. Słomczyńska (✉)
Maria Curie-Sklodowska University, Lublin, Poland
e-mail: Irma.slomczynska@poczta.umcs.lublin.pl

© The Author(s) 2018
P. Frankowski and A. Gruszczak (eds.),
Cross-Disciplinary Perspectives on Regional and Global Security,
https://doi.org/10.1007/978-3-319-75280-8_2

23

as a fundamental rule for every action undertaken by ESA and EU; (3) cooperation between member states instead of collaboration (permanent and coordinated, not occasional or unplanned); (4) cooperation for peaceful and scientific purposes; (5) global reach of EU. These five elements are clearly visible in the history of ESA but also in European space policy, established with the Lisbon Treaty. Moreover these elements compose strategic repertoire of ideas, which have been used in every activity, referred in every discussion, and maintained through institutional structure of European Space Policy.

The analytic framework for analyzing the functions of space security of regional order isolates two primary dimensions of the EU actions namely external and internal functions. Given the nature of EU activities, regulatory, commercial and normative actions, are important for both areas, space security can be used as an instrument of integration. However, for the purpose of this book the structure of this chapter is organized as follows. In the first part brief analysis of space security has been presented, as well as its origin and ideas important for ESA and the EU. Then, in following part, main five themes will be discusses, based on historical archives of European Space Research Organisation (ESRO), ESA, European Parliament (reproduced by ESA), and Western European Union (WEU). Finally, discussion over main elements of space security in latest documents prepared by the European Commission, reveals driving forces for regional order, when challenges and problems in outer space could be used as a transmission belt for domestic and regional preferences to the global level. These preferences are mostly of military nature and institutions of space security, that have been created by the EU, will be analyzed from the perspective of defense and military goals.

ORIGINS OF SPACE SECURITY

The most important goal for any state is survival and then security. Security is one of the vital interests of collective entities, but the caveat is that the concept of security becomes multidimensional and not only of military, but also economic, cultural and social security. Since possession and maintenance of space resources is the goal and instrument of security, it is worth considering the place of the concept of security in European space policy. Systematization of the challenges and threats of space security is not an easy task given the multitude of definitions of the very concept of space security, which is largely due to the fact that these definitions are derived from the national interests of states in relation to space, their activity in outer space, foreign policy goals or legal and/or technological constraints that do not allow for specific space resources. Furthermore, the specific nature of the current geostrategic environment should be taken into account, as the emergence of new actors in space as private companies, new technologies and further deepening dependence on space-based services makes reliable analysis of space security threats based on simple extrapolation of assumptions based on the experiences of the Cold War (Robinson 2015). Traditionally, space security, as Michael Sheehan correctly points out, refers to the military dimension of security, and the continued military dimension is a fundamental element in the definition of space security. However, the concept of space security should be extended by three further dimensions, such as economic, social and environmental security (Sheehan 2015, pp. 7–8). Since space policy is related to the implementation of public policies in other areas such as the environment, transport, agriculture, science, telecommunications, and entertainment, the definition of what is the space security also needs to be taken into account. The existing definitions of space security can be divided into two groups, the first of which includes definitions that raise the need to protect outer space, especially space orbit, in order to be able to undertake activities in space and to protect civil, military and commercial space resources from natural and man-made disasters. This area also includes the protection of terrestrial infrastructure necessary for the control and telemetry of objects in space. It is also worth emphasizing that the usefulness of space around the globe is limited by the laws of physics and technological capabilities, and certain orbits (such as geostationary orbit) are particularly vulnerable to space safety (Remuss 2015; Cooper 2003). The second group of definitions refers to the use of space for security on Earth, which is used for space resources such as telecommunications satellites, satellite navigation systems, satellite remote sensing and remote sensing, and maritime security or border control (Słomczyńska and Frankowski 2016). Thus, security of space, space through security through space can be distinguished. Such an approach covers not only material resources in space but also technological capabilities, international legal regulations as well as a set of ideas relating to the concept of space use. Therefore, I argue that space security should be defined as: (1) security in outer space, i.e. referring to all systems and objects deployed in outer space;

(2) the security of space, i.e. the avoidance of militarization of outer space or the use of space weapons through the regulation of the possible use of space for military purposes; (3) security through outer space, i.e. the use of space systems and objects for non-military activities such as transport safety, the environment, social security. The first dimension of space security is particularly evident in the actions taken by the EU and ESA Member States. For example during the meetings of the ESA Working Group on Satellite Navigation, the French side returned to the issue of security of the future Galileo system—both in terms of system security and the use of Galileo for security (European Space Agency 2001, p. 9).

Referring to existing space security definitions, it is worth pointing to the definition of James Clay Moltz, which, in its view, saves space from human activities, but also natural ones. He believes that space security can be defined as "the ability to place and use resources in space outside the Earth's atmosphere without interfering with the outside, damaging or destroying these resources" (Moltz 2008, p. 10). In addition, Moltz distinguishes four schools of There are four main schools of thought concerning space security: (1) space nationalism; (2) technological determinism; (3) social interactionism; (4) global institutionalism (Moltz 2008, p. 23), which determines the way in which space exploration is involved. Moltz's assumptions, however, are appropriate when analyzing the activities of the space powers, as they are based on a central-state perspective, largely due to the fact that this concept was born when the EU did not have both space resources and space strategy. On the other hand Jean Francis Mayence defines space security as three interrelated areas, as outer space for security, security in outer space, security from outer space (Mayence 2010, p. 35). For Mayence security in outer space, dominated by public actors, as space faring nations or ESA, is also complemented by the commercial stakeholders. However private actors, apart from assessing political risk of possible destructions their satellites on the orbit, rather focus on reducing any financial impact on space business. Broader understanding of "space security" encompasses issues concerning "more than just activities occurring beyond Earth's atmosphere" but all the elements of ground stations, and communication channels (Sheehan 2015, p. 12).

However after the end of the Cold War boundaries between strictly military and civilian approach to space, as well as the military space sector and civilian actors largely have been blurred, when military commanders use civilian satellite systems to gain strategic information or use commercial telecommunication links for health services directly from a battlefield. For example during the Gulf War international commercial satellite provided services field commanders and leased mobile satellite terminals used in the theatre of war connected communications systems with headquarters facilities in Florida (Elliot 1991).

Nevertheless, apart from positive examples of cooperation between private and public actors Sheehan argues that outer space can produce security and insecurity, therefore private companies active in outer space could apart of providing security with space assets can generate threats in outer space, from outer space, and also through outer space (Sheehan 2015, p. 15). Possible threats may include, among others, disruption of satellite signal, creation of space debris, potentially dangerous influence on Earth (destruction of object on Earth), but also protection of private data gathered from satellite imagery.

Last approach to space security, multidimensional, but clearly built in specific terms of private activity has been provided by the Space Security Index and the Project Ploughshares, who identify seventeen factors namely orbital debris, radio frequency (RF) spectrum and orbital positions, natural hazards originating from space, space situational awareness, access to and use of space by various actors, space-based global utilities, priorities and funding levels in civil space programs, international cooperation in space activities, growth in commercial space industry, public-private collaboration on space activities, space-based military systems, security of space systems, vulnerability of satellite communications, reconstitution and resilience of space systems, earth-based capabilities to attack satellites, space-based negation-enabling capabilities, outer space governance, national space policies, multilateral forums for space governance, and other initiatives, also provided by private actors (Space Security Index 2015). According to the researchers of Project Ploughshares, space security is "safe and sustainable access and use of space and freedom from space threats" (Abeyratne 2011, p. 15), and four areas can be distinguished: (1) the state of the space environment and its knowledge; (2) access and use of space by various entities; (3) security of space systems; (4) space management. The first area contains the issues related to space-related junk, the use of radio spectrum, the threat of natural origin from space and the knowledge of the situation in space. The second area includes space resources, priorities and levels of funding for civil space programs, international space cooperation, commercial use of outer space, private-public cooperation in space activities, and military use of space. The third area refers to the sensitivity of satellite communications, satellite links and ground stations, the resilience of space systems, and the ability to rapidly rebuild after possible attack, ground antisatellite resources, and space systems that limit the use of space resources (such as ASAT). Space national space policy, multilateral space management, such as PAROS and Committee on the Peaceful Uses of Outer Space (COPUOS), and other regional initiatives (Space Security Index 2015).

EUROPEAN SPACE SECURITY

Roger Bonnet and Vittorio Manno point out that the development of European space research started after World War II was due to several reasons of an economic, political and social nature. Firstly, the creation of an international organization on a European scale, with the aim of organizing research in the field of space exploration allowed Europe to formulate a unified position at time when the two superpowers were focused on the development of competitive space programs. Secondly, it prevented brain drain, because there was a risk that Europe's best scientists will leave for the United States (Bonnet and Manno 1994, p. 3). The alternative would be a situation in which European countries began to compete among themselves, and in the light of the limited resources, efforts of individual countries will be condemn to failure. Another possible solution would be cooperation, within the framework of NATO, which, however, excludes the possibility of cooperation with scientists from the Soviet Union. Therefore, the focus on international cooperation and emphasizing every step of disabling the peaceful nature of the activities and research conducted by European researchers gathered in ESRO and European Launcher Development Organization (ELDO) and then in ESA.

Economic incentive to start cooperation in the field of space research was the belief that these studies will translate into technological progress, much needed for the development of the European economy after World War II. As noted above, absence of a European military space research program, which would be comparable to the programs American or Soviet made that the European aerospace industry was not in a state to develop, and the solution to this situation was a civil space program (Bonnet and Manno 1994, p. 3). Some authors believe that the development of a European space program was also part of the construction of Europe's prestige in the international arena, and the pursuit of European autonomy in technology and space research was an important element of European identity in this dimension. At the same time, on should not underestimate the strategic choices made by researchers working in ESRO and ESA, whose aim was to achieve complete autonomy and independence from cosmic powers. Despite declared by ESRO and ESA "development for peaceful space research and international cooperation", it is obvious that one of the objectives of the European Space Policy has been to change the position of Europe and the abandonment of the role of the client in dealing with space powers.

The effects of the decision on the creation of ESRO and giving the organization strictly scientific character and independence as soon as possible from government influence can be seen even today in the activities undertaken by ESA. Striving for depoliticisation of space research also resulted in the next step, which was to create ELDO—European Launcher Development Organization. For policy makers and European researchers was obvious that satellites into orbit around the Earth will also have a military purpose.

Establishment of European Space Policy should be seen as a result of three converging and partially overlapping political processes, running on different levels and characterized by a different level of institutionalization. Declared and performed roles of the main political actors, namely the ESA, the European Commission, the WEU and the Member States of the EU and ESA (including Norway and Switzerland) resulted in the shape of three main programs EPK, or Galilleo, Copernicus and MUSIS.

First distinguished political process is associated with the desire for *international cooperation* in the exploration of space, an example will be the relationship between ESA and other countries like Brazil, India, Canada, China, Russia and the United States. Cooperation declared and taken by the ESA includes the countries that are considered terms of the allied countries (such as Canada or the United States), potential customers and areas of influence (India and Brazil), but also states competitors in the international arena (such as Russia/USSR and China) (Peter 2007). This allows to argue that in the case of exploration and exploitation of space strategic decisions may have long-term economic consequences for ESA, and regional security depends to far extent on broad cooperation. Cooperation, as main element of European space policy has been visible in changes made in official documents. For example during negotiations of ESA convention a word "collaboration" had been replaced by "cooperation", to strengthen institutional design, coherence and durability of new institution (European Space Conference 1975). It translates into **cooperation between member states** instead of collaboration (occasional unplanned, uncoordinated). Ideas of European cooperation in space affaires appeared during the negotiations, but also in letters of ESRO and ELDO officials. For example E.A. Plate, Chairman of Committee of Alternates in a letter to the President of the European Space Conference stressed that ESRO is an example of how international cooperation can be organized and shows that this cooperation can be effective "although the limited role of Europe in space is simply a fact".[1] It is worth noting that the official report presented at the Conference does not include observations made in a letter to the President. It highlights the fact that while the signing of agreements with Canada, the USSR, Japan and India. In the case of the USSR exchange of information was conducted in accordance with the contents of the report, with the Soviet Academy of Sciences (European Space Conference 1972a, p. 5). It means that in 1972 European countries were able to cooperate against political differences, rising above traditional game of big powers. It resulted further cooperation in ISS programme.

Analysis of the text of the Convention gives reasons to believe that its stakeholders primarily were trying to develop a document that would allow for the overall coordination of the activities of Member States in order to create a coherent European space policy. Consistency was to be achieved not only at the level of goals and ideas, but mainly through the coordination of national programs in order to create a single European program, with particular emphasis on the development of satellites utility. However, the final text of the Convention does not reflect the intentions that guided individual countries. To understand how clashing national interests and institutional during the process of negotiations on the final version of the Convention should look at sketches of the Convention and the changes that introduced delegations of different countries, as well as officials ESRO (European Space Conference 1975). The final text differs in a sketch in a few important details that indicate the influence of individuals on the nature of the adopted document, as well as the implementation of these guidelines in the future.

---

[1] European Space Conference, "New European Space Organization. Ha Michael Heseltine—Minister of Aerospace and Shipping of United Kingdom," September 11, 1972, RFP/sk, ESC-1457, Historical Archives of the EU.

But security through cooperation refers also to international activity of ELDO/ESRO and ESA. From the very beginning of space endevours European delegates were active at UN fora, working on peaceful uses of outer space (European Space Research Organisation 1964, pp. 4–6). As consequence the EU, is in the position of a strong participant in international relations occurring in the area of international space policy. Some authors noted that such actions are a manifestation of a specific attitude of the EU to build identity in the international arena, where the principle of cooperation promoted by the EU is essentially unique (Cornell 2012). However this idea has been strongly embedded into European minds, and on various occasions European delegations emphasize the need of international cooperation, as essential for any European activity. For example on the second meeting of Space Debris Working Group German delegation concluded "*with surprise*", lack of any references to international cooperation in summary of draft report on space debris (European Space Agency 1989b, p. 2).

The second political process, processes associated with accepting the fact that the European Space Policy will apply not only to activities related to research and peaceful use of space, but also will refer to a broad sense of security, both external and internal. Thus, it becomes apparent the military's influence on the direction of the strategic decisions taken by the EU in the area of space policy, while the impact of the Member States which have such systems, satellite intelligence and work together under bilateral or multilateral agreements.

Ideas promoted by ESA were not uncontested neither by other international institutions nor member states. For example in a recommendation adopted at the meeting of the Parliamentary Assembly of the WEU in 1984 for military use of space has been found that, "believing that capability in space will be a key determinant of warfare in the future and that in with the military point of view, differences in potential between the nations having the ability spacecraft, and others will just as big as today the difference between nuclear states and those that do not have nuclear weapons—Europe must simply take this into account (…) and the WEU is a valuable forum for debate and analysis of the impact for the defense of Western Europe using the latest military space technologies as well as the institutional structure unfettered political constraints ESA Convention to begin by leading countries of Western Europe's defense space European military space program" (Draft Recommendation on the military use of space WEU 1984).

In the report accompanying the recommendation of the parliamentary rapporteur emphasized both the fact that ESA has been created only for peaceful purposes, as well as the fact that the ESA Member States can develop their own programs and the WEU is the forum where such activities can be analyzed. In addition, also highlighted the concern actions of the Soviet Union, where publication of the secret Soviet military thought on it was concluded that "domination in space is essential to winning the war" (Explanatory memorandum (submitted by Mr. Wilkinson) Western European Union 1984, p. 5). Because members of WEU Assembly were delegates of national parliaments it could be argued that some member states of ESA treated its convention and rules rather as an obstacle for national interests. Therefore ESA has had mitigating effect during the last decade of Cold War, as peaceful and non-political body. However, as Lorenza Sebesta concludes, since the creation of the ESA, despite the declaration of a strictly scientific purpose of cooperation, political, economic and industrial interests are visible in the functioning of European cooperation in space (Sebesta 2003, pp. 294, 300).

Adopting realistic vision of world affairs and space activities (Creola 1999, 2008), another clement of European security could be distinguished—a need of *autonomy* in space affairs. Good example of different meaning of "autonomy" for European delegates could be opening address of Chairman of the Ministerial Conference Theo Lefevre in on 8th of November 1972, who drew attention that the choice between an autonomous European space policy and cooperation with the United States is not properly constructed alternative, because the focus should be on cooperation, so that the benefits to Europe were the greatest. In his speech there is also a reference to the "Europeanization" of space activities, which would be the basis for the structure to ensure effective cooperation. However Lefevre also pointed to the danger of "de-Europeanization" resulting from a limited number of Member States delegates participating in the conference. Therefore urged to save a "truly European program" (European Space Conference 1972b).

Country that particularly seeking for giving autonomy to European space activities has been France, hence French government decided to develop, with its own funds, a program of missiles capable of cargo into orbit with a weight of one ton. French Minister Charbonnel in a letter to the chairman of the Ministerial Conference announced that France intends to propose to the participating countries develop missile system, and France would be the main supplier and bear most of the costs of program development rocket (European Space Conference 1972d). This letter was met with a positive response participants who received on 20th of December 1972 Resolution of the appointment of the ESA to be established through a merging of ELDO and ESRO. The priority of the new institution was to participate in the post-Apollo program and the development of the French launcher, along with this program will be abandoned as Europe III (European Space Conference 1972e). French position was maintained for the next conference in July 1973, when the French representative stated that the suspension of a European rocket program means that Europe "has become vulnerable in comparison with those who have launchers and who may, for any reason, refuse us to use them (…) the concept of satellite navigation program is threatened by the pressures of private American interests, acting against the will of the American administration, which is not able to present us particular form of policy cooperation with Europe" (Annex 1 European Space Conference 1973).

In the statements by individual delegations were visible political divisions, as well as pressure from national governments to reduce spending on the construction of an independent system of missile launchers, as economically unprofitable. British delegation sought to dispel fears that the proposals of Americans who share their launchers proposed European customers "will force us too deeply in the hands of our American colleagues across the Atlantic." The arguments presented by the British delegation were purely economic, as it believed that the European market is so important for the United States, that will not mean a political advantage, but only a commercial transaction (European Space Conference 1969, p. 3).

As noted by John Krige there was a concern that Americans could dominate Europe, and missile development program will be abandoned. Such fears were particularly strong in France, whose representatives repeatedly hinted that the American position is not acceptable. This resulted, among others, from the fact that the decisions and negotiating positions formulated by French ministers associated with Gaullism, seeing in the proposal of the United States a clear goal which was to "establish and maintain dominance, which would give the United States an instrument of influence and political action for the rest of the world" (Krige 2014, pp. 123–124). American position, clearly ignoring Europe as a negotiating partner was seen during the negotiation of INTELSAT, where as one of the participants stressed the negotiations chief negotiator American eavesdropping meeting national delegation considering it natural. This resulted in protests, for example, the Swedish delegation, whose representative protested openly against the "methods as the Warsaw Pact" (Krige 2014, pp. 125–126).

When the space security and security as such has been provided by ESA rather in a covert way than openly in the form of political decision-making, the EU adopted entirely different stance on that. ESA delegates stress in various documents that ESA in not a political body, and its primary goal is to "focus on research and development" (European Space Agency 1994, p. 1). Even ESA has been cooperating very closely with United Nations and European Commission, working on issues such as space debris (European Space Agency 1989a), global navigation (European Space Agency 1983, 1996; Wakker et al. 1987), and global development (European Space Agency 1994, 1995a, b), and contributing to global security as such it avoids being treated as "security actor". It gives some level of autonomy for ESA, but also raises some questions about future activities, when the EU becomes more active, and European Commission is planning to put ESA under the control of the EU, as element of establishing appropriate relations between the EU and the ESA.

EUROPEAN INSTITUTIONS AND INSTRUMENT FOR SPACE SECURITY

As mentioned above different areas space security could be distinguished, and various perspectives on space problems play an important role in contemporary space security. Nevertheless when it comes to institutions and instruments for space security, space resources are first and foremost created and used for military purposes. When definitions of space security broaden the meaning of space affairs, and virtually everything is about security, all European space assets have been created for military purposes. Without Copernicus and Galileo, it would be impossible to develop transport policies and common agricultural policy and, above all, the EU's security and defense policy (Oikonomou 2012; Slijper 2015).

Support for the defense industry in the space sector has been signaled in the Commission Communication "Towards a more competitive and efficient defense and security sector" (European Commission 2013b), where the Commission has shown a very pragmatic approach to the sharing of space competence between Member States and the EU. This is one of the few examples where the Commission, unlike in the vast majority of cases, does not intend to take over the powers of states and even defends the right to maintain exclusive control over space resources. In the Commission Communication we can read, "some space capabilities have to remain under exclusive national and/or military control, a number of areas exist where increased synergies between civilian and defence activities will reduce costs and improve efficiency," which means that there are resources for which the Commission is not even attempting to apply the Community model, leaving it at the sole disposal of the Member States. However, if one analyzes carefully this Communication and compares with the inventory of EU space resources, it is obvious that only one of the EU member states that has "space capabilities", which is France. No other European country has the capacity to send any payload to Earth orbit, does not have space port, a network of satellites for optical reconnaissance and surveillance. Nevertheless, the Commission points out in the Communication that "there are many areas where increasing synergies between civil and military activities would reduce costs and improve efficiency." In this case, this applies to Galileo and Copernicus projects, where contributions are made both by the EU and the Member States through the ESA in the development and testing phase of the system.

The document also pointed to the need to build a unified strategy that would involve civilian and military space in the space, since "Most space technologies, space infrastructures and space services can serve both civilian and defence objectives. However, contrary to all space-faring nations, in the EU there is no structural link between civil and military space activities." According to the Commission, changes are necessary because it generates economic and political costs that Europe can no longer bear. The Action Plan outlined in the Communication covers three areas of significant space activity from the point of view of defense applications, and (1) the first place indicates the need to protect the space infrastructure. Galileo and Copernicus have been recognized as elements of space infrastructure, to support key EU policies. In order to protect these systems, the Commission proposes the creation of a European SST space tracking system, as "Space debris has become the most serious threat to the sustainability of our space activities." It was stated that "At present there is no SST capability at European level; satellite and launch operators are dependent on US data for anti-collision alerts." It is worth emphasizing here that the discussion on the system of observation and cataloging of objects appeared in the late 1980s and autonomous European capabilities in the form of coordinated measures still do not exist.

In a report presented in 1989, the ESA indicated that both ESA and ESA Member States do not have the necessary facilities to determine the amount of waste and that Europe is dependent on data provided by NASA (European Space Agency 1989a, p. 1). It has also been stressed that space debris is a global problem, which requires concerted and coordinated action on a global scale. International cooperation and relevant agreements should include: exchange of information on general research results on space debris conducted by other actors; agreements on reducing the amount of space debris; changes in orbit of geostationary satellites; coordination of satellites located on the same longitude; limited ability to send nuclear-powered satellites only to interplanetary missions; change and strengthen the meaning of the Convention on the Registration of Objects Released into Space; introduction of an open information policy by entities placing objects in space (European Space Agency 1989a, pp. 4–5). Effective control of space debris in orbit around the Earth must be based on international consensus and supported by international and national law. This is due to the need to create the obligation to remove potentially hazardous objects and to create rules for international liability for damage caused by space objects. While in principle the need to remove space debris is supported by many states (e.g., the Bogota Declaration), the United States is opposed to adopting any legally binding declaration as a result of internal determinants, as well as the unwillingness to bind the records. International law. It is worth noticing that space debris have been not taken seriously on the ESA forum. Although the problem of space debris was perceived by ESA experts, individual Member State delegations raised the issue of environmental issues as well as the need for a rational approach to the problem and not to overly hasten the issue of legal instruments when there is no scientific and technical data (European Space Agency 1989b, p. 5).

This does not mean, however, that individual European states do not have sufficient means to track objects in space, which is also highlighted in the Communication. It has been assumed that there are two possible solutions, i.e. support for a European Space Observation and Tracking System based on networks of existing Member States' systems or an agreement with the United States on the construction of a common system. However the second solution, considering the failure of the global navigation system, is unlikely. But if we analyze five key ideas of European space activity, such agreement would be an expected and welcomed, because idea of international cooperation in space affairs is one of the most appreciated values. This provided the basis for action by the Commission to define the objectives and areas of European SST capacity, as set out in Commission Communication, adopted on 1 March 2013, containing a draft decision establishing a Space Observation and Tracking Program (European Commission 2013a). However, as with other European space programs, the analysis of the solutions proposed by the Commission and the adopted decision points to the far-reaching conflict of ideas and interests in many areas. The first problematic area was the determination of the actual purpose of building and operating the SST, i.e. whether the system was to serve military purposes or to protect widely understood support for the sustainable use of space. As mentioned above only one from 28 EU member states has real space capabilities. Does it mean that cooperation between member states, and joint undertaking to create global security system on the regional level entirely for security purposes in fact serves interests of one country? Surely, other EU member states have space assets, such as satellites, and are dependent on space resources, but for military purposes, future SST system will be usable only for France. The second issue is related to the institutional structure of the SST and the role of the European Commission as a keystone of European space policy. Since the resources and data obtained from the SST are particularly sensitive to the Member States, as this allows not only the tracking of space junk but also military space objects, delegation of management powers to the Commission level would significantly affect the perception of sovereignty in the Member States. Third, and finally how to deal with an idea of global cooperation and space autonomy, when space debris is truly global problem but to large extent politicized. There are some similarities with space tracking and control over air-space, however the fundamental difference lays in the potential impact of loss of control over space resources, as a collision in orbit of large objects can trigger a chain reaction known as Kessler syndrome, which threatens the common goods i.e. outer space (Weeden and Chow 2012; Abiodun 2013). As in the case of two other European space systems, Copernicus and Galileo, the existence of the SSA system is linked to political choices around security issues and the autonomy of European space capabilities.

The question of the autonomy of European space policy came at the end of the 1980s, when action was taken to reduce the problem of space debris. It was then pointed out that the cost of construction of an autonomous European radar system for the detection of space debris would be exorbitant. There were doubts as to whether these costs could be justified by the need for European autonomy, while an agreement with the North American Aerospace Defense Command would limit costs (European Space Agency 1989b, p. 3). While discussing the construction of the space-based radar detection system, it was stated that European space autonomy would not be maintained "at all costs", but at the same time it was pointed out that the data collected by the United States were military and not always available to the European side. In addition, the US authorities treated the problem of space debris in political terms, and although they knew the significance of this problem, they were not willing to give it international significance, based on bilateral and multilateral agreements. In the case of SSA systems, the issue of international cooperation in space is extremely important, due to the specific nature of the threats and the environment in which space activities are carried out. This is visible both at the COPUOS level as well as the various regional and global initiatives such as the European Code of Conduct for Space Debris Mitigation, the ESA Space Debris Mitigation for Agency Projects, the IADC Space Debris Mitigation Guidelines, and the ITU Recommendation ITU-R S.1003.2 (Committee on the Peaceful Uses of Outer Space 2014). The pursuit of international co-operation, even in the face of disagreements between the space powers, is of utmost importance for the whole of European space policy, and this is evident not only in the activities undertaken recently, but also in discussions on the problems that have been addressed by the ESA. For example, at the second meeting on space debris, representatives of the German delegation "were surprised to find that there is no reference to international cooperation in the summaries," suggesting that the co-operation factor is a fundamental determinant of European action in the space dimension (European Space Agency 1989b, p. 2).

CONCLUSION: FOR WHOM THE SST TOLLS

Particular attention should been paid to the three elements constituting European space policy and space policy, i.e. ideas, interests and institutions. The triad of these concepts refers to the process of formulating and implementing the agenda of the European space security. It has been assumed that the interests and values promoted by participants in international relations are constantly changing and transforming, but that part of the idea remains unchanged because they are institutionalized and serve the goals of the strongest actors in international relations. Therefore space security, created and controlled on the regional level is always for someone and for some purpose. Even that space debris, along with nuclear proliferation, is one of really global problems, scale of distrust on the global level, and profound national interests limit possibilities of cooperation. This there is an urgent need to for adoption of new instruments on the global level, and far-reaching regulations, before any serious events happened. EU foreign policy objectives represent entrenched aspirations on the global level, also is outer space. However these global ambitions, depicted in documents issued by the Commission are marked by an ambiguity, especially when interests and ideas are intertwined. Regional European space security reflects traditional perspective of the international order when space faring powers are able to command and control outer space. However, this vision of security neither reflects real balance of power in space affairs nor establish any power to act in outer space. In terms of inability to act effectively, and create regional and then global order the EU offers a set of ideas and solutions for space surveillance that oterh space faring powers can adopt to tackle the problem of space debris. By invoking the principles of cooperation, peaceful purposes, and autonomy, the EU creates a possibility for all forms of space community, that would include inevitable invocation to common goods. However, with this normative stance, and a need of protection of humanity against itself, well crafted institutions are necessary to regulate space order on the basis of normative grounding.

REFERENCES

Abeyratne, Ruwantissa I.R. 2011. *Space Security Law*. Heidelberg: Springer.

Abiodun, Adigun Ade. 2013. We Must Harness Space for Sustainable Development. *Space Policy* 29 (1): 5–8. https://doi.org/10.1016/j.spacepol.2012.11.009.

Bonnet, R.-M., and Vittorio Manno. 1994. *International Cooperation in Space: The Example of the European Space Agency*. Cambridge, MA: Harvard University Press.

Committee on the Peaceful Uses of Outer Space. 2014. Compendium of Space Debris Mitigation Standards Adopted by States and International Organizations, A /AC.105/2014/CRP.13, 10.06.2014.

Cooper, Lawrence. 2003. The Strategy of Responsive Space. *Astropolitics* 1 (3): 44–62. https://doi.org/10.1080/14777620312331269999.

Cornell, Ariane. 2012. Motivational and Cultural Conditions for Regional Space Collaboration: Is Europe an Irreproducible Model? In *European Identity Through Space: Space Activities and Programmes as a Tool to Reinvigorate the European Identity*, ed. Christophe Venet and Blandina Baranes, 80–92. Vienna and New York: SpringerWienNewYork.

Creola, Peter. 1999. Switzerland and Space—How a Small Country Succeeds. *Space Policy* 15 (1): 41–44. https://doi.org/10.1016/S0265-9646(99)00006-5.

Creola, Peter. 2008. *Chairman, Legal Working Group on ESA Convention, ESC 1974–1975*. Oral History of Europe in Space Collection. Historical Archives of the EU. http://apps.eui.eu/HAEU/OralHistory/pdf/INT649.pdf.

Elliot, Ronald. 1991. C3I Warfare Moves into New Era. *Defense News*, January.

European Commission. 2013a. *Proposal for a Decision of the European Parliament and of the Council Establishing a Space Surveillance and Tracking Support Programme*, COM (2013) 107 final.

European Commission. 2013b. *Communication from the Commission to the European Parliament, the Council, the European Economic and Social Committee and the Committee of the Regions*. Towards a more competitive and efficient defence and security sector, COM (2013) 0542 final.

European Space Agency. 1983. *World System of Civil Navigation Satellites (NAVSAT)*. ESA/C(83)76, ESA-7013. Historical Archives of the EU.

European Space Agency. 1989a. *Implementation Proposal—Special Meeting of Space Debris Experts*. ESA/C(89)10, ESA-12956. Historical Archives of the EU.

European Space Agency. 1989b. *Space Debris Working Group—Second Meeting*. ESA/C/WG SPACE DEBRIS(89)OJ/2, ESA-13053. Historical Archives of the EU.

European Space Agency. 1994. *A World Wide Approach: ESA Linking to Developing Countries*. ESA/IRC(94)46, ESA/IRC(94)46, ADD.2, ESA-18504. Historical Archives of the EU.

European Space Agency. 1995a. *Resolution on ESA's Programmes and Activities Which Could Assist in Fulfilling the Needs of Developing Countries*. 116th Council Session: Paris on 22/02/1995. ESA/C/MIN/116, ESA/C/CXVI/RES.1(FINAL), ESA-18505. Historical Archives of the EU.

European Space Agency. 1995b. *Cooperation with Developing Countries*. The COPINE Project. ESA/IRC(95)28, ESA-19037. Historical Archives of the EU.

European Space Agency. 1996. *Satellite Navigation*. ESA/IRC(96)29, ESA-19980. Historical Archives of the EU.

European Space Agency. 2001. *European Space Agency—Program Board on Satellite Navigation*. 10th Meeting, Draft Minutes. ESA/PB-NAV (2001) MIN 10. Historical Archives of the EU.

European Space Conference. 1969. *Statement by the RT. Hon. A. Wedgwood Benn, Minister of Technology (UK)*. CSE/CM (November 68) P/1 ESC-36. Historical Archives of the EU.

European Space Conference. 1972a. *Report by the Secretary General of the European Space Conference on the Status of European Space Programmes*. CSE/CM (October 72) WP 1 ESC-116. Historical Archives of the EU.

European Space Conference. 1972b. *Ministerial Meeting*. CSE/CM (November 72) 4 ESC-120. Historical Archives of the EU.

European Space Conference. 1972c. *Elements of a European Space Policy*. CSE/CM (December 72) WP/1 ESC-131. Historical Archives of the EU.

European Space Conference. 1972d. *Letter Form the French Minister, Mr Charbonnel, to the President of the ESC*. CSE/CM (December 72) 7 ESC-129. Historical Archives of the EU.

European Space Conference. 1972e. *Resolution*. CSE/CM (December 72) 8 ESC-130. Historical Archives of the EU.

European Space Conference. 1973. *Minutes of the Ministerial Conference Held in Brussels on 12 July 1973*. CSE/CM (July 73) PV/1 ESC-132. Historical Archives of the EU.

European Space Conference. 1975. *ESA Convention: Tables Showing the Various Amendments to the Draft Convention Together with Alternatives Discussed, with 1. and 2. Revision*. CSE/CS/ESA(74)WP/15; CSE/CS/ESA(74) WP/15, REV.1, REV.2, ESC-1071. Historical Archives of the EU.

European Space Research Organisation. 1964. *Collaboration ESRO/ELDO*. Correspondence and Notes on Participation of ESRO/ELDO to UN Work in Peaceful Uses of Outer Space. ESRO/C/52, ESRO-6916. Historical Archives of the EU.

Krige, John. 2014. *Fifty Years of European Cooperation in Space: Building on Its Past, ESA Shapes the Future*. Paris: Beauchesne.

Mayence, Jean François. 2010. Space Security: Transatlantic Approach to Space Governance. In *Prospects for Transparency and Confidence-Building Measures in Space Report*, ed. Jana Robinson, Matthew Schaefer, Kai-Uwe Schrogl, and Frans G. von der Dunk, 35–36. Vienna: ESPI.

Moltz, James Clay. 2008. *The Politics of Space Security: Strategic Restraint and the Pursuit of National Interests*. Stanford, CA: Stanford University Press.

Oikonomou, Iraklis. 2012. The European Defence Agency and EU Military Space Policy: Whose Space Odyssey? *Space Policy* 28 (2): 102–109. https://doi.org/10.1016/j.spacepol.2012.02.008.

Peter, Nicolas. 2007. The EU's Emergent Space Diplomacy. *Space Policy* 23 (2): 97–107. https://doi.org/10.1016/j.spacepol.2007.02.007.

Remuss, Nina-Louisa. 2015. Responsive Space. In *Handbook of Space Security*, ed. Kai-Uwe Schrogl, Peter L. Hays, Jana Robinson, Denis Moura, and Christina Giannopapa, 131–155. New York: Springer.

Robinson, Jana. 2015. Space Transparency and Confidence-Building Measures. In *Handbook of Space Security*, ed. Kai-Uwe Schrogl, Peter L. Hays, Jana Robinson, Denis Moura, and Christina Giannopapa, 291–297. New York: Springer. http://link.springer.com/referenceworkentry/10.1007/978-1-4614-2029-3_57.

Sebesta, Lorenza. 2003. *Alleati Competitivi: Origini E Sviluppo Della Cooperazione Spaziale Fra Europa E Stati Uniti, 1957–1973*. GLF editori Laterza.

Sheehan, Michael. 2015. Defining Space Security. In *Handbook of Space Security*, ed. Kai-Uwe Schrogl, Peter L. Hays, Jana Robinson, Denis Moura, and Christina Giannopapa, 7–21. New York: Springer.

Slijper, Frank. 2015. The EDA's Inroads into Space. In *The European Defence Agency: Arming Europe*, ed. Nikolaos Karampekios and Iraklis Oikonomou, 241–259. London: Routledge.

Słomczyńska, I., and P. Frankowski. 2016. Patrolling Power Europe: The Role of Satellite Observation in EU Border Management. In *EU Borders and Shifting Internal Security*, ed. R. Bossong and H. Carrapico, 390–412. Cham: Springer. https://doi.org/10.1007/978-3-319-17560-7_4.

Space Security Index. 2015. Space Security 2015 | Space Security Index, October 20. http://spacesecurityindex.org/2015/10/space-security-2015/.

Wakker, K.F., B.A.C. Ambrosius, H. Leenman, and R. Noomen. 1987. Navigation and Orbit Computation Aspects of the ESA NAVSAT System Concept. *Acta Astronautica* 15 (4): 195–208. https://doi.org/10.1016/0094-5765(87)90001-4.

Weeden, Brian C., and Tiffany Chow. 2012. Taking a Common-Pool Resources Approach to Space Sustainability: A Framework and Potential Policies. *Space Policy* 28 (3): 166–72. https://doi.org/10.1016/j.spacepol.2012.06.004.

Western European Union. 1984. The Military Use of Space. In *Proceedings Vol. I, Thirtieth Session, First Part, June 1984—Assembly Document 976*. WEU-58.011. Historical Archives of the EU.

Role of Sub-national Actors in North American Security

Paweł Frankowski

No State shall […]enter into any Agreement or Compact with another State (U.S. Consitution, Article I, Section 10), but since the 1970s local governments have signed or entered into thousands of accords or compacts with national and subnational governments. This means that, despite the systemic obstacles and limits the states try to find their own specific role reserved to national states. State authorities establish overseas missions, meet officials from other governments, send special envoys to seek opportunities for foreign investments, vigorously emphasize their own opinion on human rights and security issues.

The goal of this chapter is to examine the nature and potential concerns and challenges of still unexplored phenomenon of sub-national actors' activity in the world politics with focus on the North America. The chapter finds that American non-central governments, even have clear agenda in foreign affairs, are more limited *by structured ideas* (U.S. Constitution and law), and *through structured institutions* (incentives from Congress, federal government, and the Supreme Court), than

P. Frankowski (✉)
Jagiellonian University, Kraków, Poland
e-mail: pawel.frankowski@uj.edu.pl

© The Author(s) 2018
P. Frankowski and A. Gruszczak (Eds.),
Cross-Disciplinary Perspectives on Regional and Global Security,
https://doi.org/10.1007/978-3-319-75280-8_3

43

through *interests*, agency and preferences on the states' level. Thus any success of their activity comes from *acceptance and consent* of federal government rather than from *disinterest* in Washington or power of governor's personal ambitions. The chapter also argues that to deal with the rise of states' activity in foreign affairs, more attention should be given to the question of change and continuity in relations between (1) central and non-central governments, and (2) between sub-national governments in the North America. Finally four models of interactions could be distinguished, and all transboundary activities should be analyzed through these models.

The chapter proceeds in the following manner. Part I deals with an idea of non-central governments activity in the world politics, assesses the main concerns with states' activity in foreign affairs due to constitutional constraints and federal structures, and identifies a number of variables that condition the emergence of sub-national diplomacy. Part II discusses interests of actors involved into sub-state activities in the North America. In Part III, I argue that, despite the given structure and limits, there is some room for sub-national activity for security, and existing models of interaction between central and non-central governments could be expanded by the model of coalescence.

The Constitution of the United States fifty times refers to the states, which confirms their crucial role in the American system. Their importance is guaranteed by the Tenth Amendment to the Constitution, but since 1930s, and the introduction of "New Deal" which has reinforced the federal government and, above all, the U.S. Supreme Court verdict in the case *the United States v. Curtiss-Wright Export Corp., 299 U.S. 304 (1936)*, the role of states has been reducing, including in the area of their international activity. This is due primarily to a very restrictive interpretation of the Supreme Court in cases which are internal and external policies. Some change in the approach to the position of states in the American system of government, aiming to re-acquisition of states' prerogatives, has appeared since the mid-nineties of the twentieth century. This can be seen primarily in the decisions of the Supreme Court, such as *United States v. Alfonso Lopez, Jr., 514 U.S. 549 (1995), Printz v. United States, 521 U.S. 898 (1997)* and *United States v. Morrison, 529 U.S. 598 (2000)*, which, however, seek to block further expansion of the federal government, than to the restoration of greater autonomy of the state governments.

The constitutional and legal constraints on state involvement in foreign affairs have been a subject of many scientific papers. As Louis Henkin points out "Foreign relations are national relations. The language, the spirit and the history of Constitution deny the States authority to participate in foreign affairs (...)" (Henkin 1996, p. 228). But he also notes that the detailed observation of the states' activity shows that constitutional interpretation fails to meet the reality posed of the present situation in the world politics. Despite the systemic obstacles and limits the states try to find their own specific role reserved to national states. State authorities establish overseas missions, meet officials from other governments, send special envoys to seek opportunities for foreign investments, vigorously emphasize their own opinion on human rights and security issues. Thus, despite the fact that the states have no international legal subjectivity, in the sense of being allowed to take action in foreign affairs as sovereign state, their political and international subjectivity allows them to act deliberately at the international arena.

The general principle limits the role of the states in foreign affairs, where the federal government is representative of the United States. This principle not only makes a clear differentiation between federal and state prerogatives, in the terms of external representation, but also point out that responsibility for foreign relations is in the hands of federal government. However, the context of foreign relations has been changed. Even as Peter Howard points out "from both a federalism and decision-making perspective, states have a *limited international role* and *minimal influence* in shaping the policies of the U.S. federal government toward other nations" (Howard 2004, p. 180), this role and influence shouldn't be ignored as irrelevant for political practice. Julian G. Ku argues that even many commentators presume the states' non-existence in the foreign relations, for example due to dormant preemption of states' activity in foreign affairs, they have a crucial role in American foreign activity. In many cases they are only institutions able to control the compliance when it comes to treaties and customary international law (Ku 2003).

But in the most case activity of non-central governments in foreign affairs is limited mostly to functional and regional issues, like attracting investment or tourism. Even the states have Constitutional right, called the Compact Clause, to enter into any agreement or compact, but with consent of Congress, these agreements, as Duncan Hollis points out, have "the mundane nature". For example level of attention to foreign-state agreements, like on firefighting cooperation or transboundary bridges suggests states' activity marginal to high politics, if not unimportant (Hollis 2010, p. 742). This "mundane nature" of states' activity results from structural limits. States' delegations cannot refer to national resources, because it might be a usurpation of federal prerogatives. Then everyday activities undertaken by the states, leads to the conclusion that states' activity is often marginalized and underestimated.

If one wants to find what kind of causes are for such situation, must consider, among many others, the structure of American political system, understood as the frames of Constitution, and idea of federalism (Elazar 1984; Verney 1995; Halberstam 2001; LaCroix 2010). Both elements are *embedded into* particular territory, which determines nature of the State and its sub-national units, and *embedded onto the nation*, as a ultimate determinant for every foreign activity. Thus the principles of exclusivity, where the federal government has an exclusive role to conduct the nation's foreign relations, and "speak with one voice" (Bilder 1989, p. 827; Spiro 1999, p. 1224) in the name of nation, is based on the strong conviction that federal premises are still the most important. This conviction could be found in the Federalist Papers, where John Madison stresses the necessity of uniform external representation, at the level of federal government, as "one nation in any respect" (Hamilton et al. 2007; Rakove 2007)

Some authors suggest that changes launched by "New Federalism", and tendency to shift financial responsibility to sub-national units to some extent explains tendency to take actions in the world politics. For non-central governments it has became clear that if they cannot find resources on the higher level, and local sources of possible incomes are depleted, the only strategy is to go abroad, and attract foreign investment. At the same time the constitutional framework has remained "remarkably intact" (Peters and Pierre 2004, pp. 79–80). Peters and Pierre argue that in a pursuit for international assets subnational authorities might violate the constitutional premises. But again, but it's worth adding that in all cases when federal superiority was questioned or undermined, the Supreme Court interpreted the federal-state balance in foreign affairs in favour of federal level (cf. Stumberg and Porterfield 2001; Swaine 2000; Trachtman 1998; Wilson 2007). Relations between federal government and state governments have place in the specific political climate, that create opportunities or challenges for effective cooperation. Even all these relations are limited by the constitutional framework, there is always some large margin for practical solutions in the form of joint committees, special programs or advisory commissions, which may have impact on the international affairs. For example U.S. Advisory Commission on Intergovernmental Relations (ACIR), created in 1959, had an impact on NAFTA during the negotiations (Gress 1996, p. 61). However ACIR was dissolved in 1996, partly due to lack of consensus between local, regional and federal officials (Kincaid 2011). Another body, National Governors' Association's Committee on International Trade and Foreign Relations, provided principles and guidelines for policies towards NAFTA and GATT, securing interests and of American states (Gress 1996, p. 58).

Federal government doesn't oppose to more formal states' activity as well. Some of these activities take shape of institutions which have formal structures, focusing on the international and transborder issues, as the Pacific NorthWest Economic Region.[1] Other forums, like Border Governors Conference[2] have form of annual meetings, but without formalized structure.

In that respect Peter Spiro, describing relations between the Constitution, ideas of federalism and foreign relations as such, points out that the *acceptance* of state *participation* in the world politics may result a fundamental change in the way how the US has been conceived in the international affairs (Spiro 1999, p. 1227). He points out that it might result a new form of Union in the future, however now we have a situation when the federal government *consents* to states' *involvement* in the international affairs. Nevertheless this consent might be revoked, when the states start to claim to the participation in the world affairs, with equal, or almost equal rights as the States. Ivo Duchacek aptly pointed out that the separation between foreign policy, traditionally understood as question of security and power, and domestic politics, has been blurred (Duchacek 1990, p. 7). Non-central governments, while predominantly focused on economic issues and state's welfare, occasionally voice their views on security, immigration, and human rights. It's not necessary a direct involvement in foreign affairs, but rather indirect

---

[1] Pacific NorthWest Economic Region consists of five American states (Alaska, Idaho, Montana, Oregon, and Washington) and five Canadian counterparts (Alberta, British Columbia, Saskatchewan, the Yukon, and the Northwest Territories).

[2] Border Governors Conference consists of Arizona, California, New Mexico, Texas, Baja California, Chihuahua, Coahuila, Nuevo León, and Tamaulipas.

action aimed to put pressure on the other states (Duchacek gives an example of state pension funds in 1980s, which were forced to divest their holdings in companies doing business with South Africa, Duchacek 1990, p. 8).

Thinking about the states' activity necessary limits our analytic capacities to methodological territorialism. However, that is territory which to large extent determines the states' challenges in the international affairs (Blatter 2001), and states' strategies are to large extent bounded to their place on the map. When the case of bordering states, like Texas, California or Arizona, and their "place on the map" determinants in the course of external activity is obvious, some states, trying to find their place on the map of international affairs, presumably have been adapting too far to the general course of American external activity. Even China and India represent enormous opportunities for many American states, Massachusetts should be more open to Europe, as Lawrence Summers points out (Pacheco 2008, p. 89). Thus, even territory and geopolitical position is not so important nowadays for foreign relations we should remember that international activities, to far extent, are conditioned through geographic proximity.

However, for bordering states, like Texas, California or Vermont, the foreign activity is a must, not a choice. Thus some authors suggested to study these bordering states not as state to state activity, but in the broader context of general US-Canada and US-Mexico relations, also on the federal level (Duchacek 1990, p. 23; see also Abu-Laban et al. 2007; Domínguez and Castro 2001). Paul Sharp quotes an example of relations between Canada and the US, where they have less and less a diplomatic character (Sharp 2009, p. 278). Nevertheless this tendency to lower the level of official relations, mostly at Canadian side, not necessarily corresponds with the same phenomenon at the other side of border. The Western Hemisphere Travel Initiative, a law of the United States that requires all traveling to United States from Western Hemisphere to show a valid passport, was adopted at the federal level, when local governments were not consulted.

Lastly, despite the persistence of grand ideas and structures the foreign activities of states are derivative of nationwide change, characterized by transition from limited to active action in the globalizing world. The emergence of new centers of political decisions, such as NGOs and transnational corporations makes these interactions with domestic and external environment more complicated and fuzzy. Conventional federalism's premises that interactions are horizontal or vertical, and dichotomous relationship between states and federal level seem to be no longer valid (Resnik 2009, p. 271). Moreover, the development of world politics during the twentieth century has brought a flourishing of organizations of members of local authorities (such as the National League of Cities and the National Governors Association), which consistently take actions at the meeting of domestic and foreign policy, which means that issues traditionally considered as international, have became subject of domestic policy.

In sum, regarding growing level of states' activity it's worth to think about its salience, permanence, and last but not least, place in the hierarchy of national interest. I elaborate recent changes in the hierarchy in the Part III of this chapter, but regarding the importance in the system, I propose three categories of states' activity: (1) regional transborder relations—which has become an ordinary behavior; (2) economic activity—becoming normal; (3) transborder relations—different than exclusively economic—an exception. These three categories of action differ in *range* (from regional to global), *rank* (from most important regional relations to marginal external policies), *area* of activity (from security, environmental protection, to economy, and cultural exchange), *frequency* of contacts, and *necessity* of relations (from regional matters, important for neighbouring countries to global, having less "mundane nature").

Depending on how interests and competences of the federal and state governments are defined four types of interaction between the two centers of power can be distinguished: (1) *coordination*, (2) *cooperation*, (3) *coexistence* and (4) *conflict*. Four types of relationships are derived from changes that are taking place in the American political system in accordance with the aforementioned typology by Jörg Broschek. It should be emphasized, however, that the change observed in the system can result in the emergence of a variety of responses from the participants of the system. Moreover, the typology proposed by Broschek refers to the ideal situation, while in reality we are dealing with the simultaneous superposition and conversion or denial and superposition. Therefore, the *type of change* will be of secondary importance, while the *type of interaction* will help to determine the function of sub-national governments and the hierarchy of preferences party political processes.

These types of interactions are determined by two types of variables: dependent, namely the interests and preferences of the parties involved and independent, that is, the structure of the system. The key question is therefore the extent to which the dependent variables can shape the independent variables and, therefore, how durable and possible is the change in the American political system. Analyzed following examples demonstrate the durability of the independent variables in the relative volatility of preferences and interests. The last element essential to the understanding of the relationship between external policies and foreign policy is the will of both parties to seize the opportunity of the process that gives them a specific institutional structure and the degree of articulation of preferences. This includes not only an attempt to coordinate the external action of American states from the federal level, but also the willingness to cooperate in the framework of the model of cooperation, the pursuit of their own preferences within the model of conflict or asymmetry in the degree of articulation of preferences in the framework of the model of coexistence.

STATES AS JUNIOR FOREIGN POLICY MAKERS

Taking into account above-mentioned discussion about change and preferences on the sub-national foreign activity I argue that changes in the American system, regarding foreign activity, are bi-directional by nature. In many respects states address their demands towards national level, and incentives coming from Washington might suggest slow evolution in the diplomatic statecraft. Due to recent development of state department's structure states' activity has started to be *normal, accepted and complementary* to efforts on the level of federal government (cf. Cornago 2010). Nevertheless sub-national governments are still less experienced and prone to influence. Non-central governments, profited by globalization and easier access to the world, would be also more vulnerable to its side effects. Opening to the world brings additional challenges, not only to sub-national governments, but also for foreign actors, trying to grasp the very nature of sub-national activity. But the most important threat would be possible interference on the state level, coming from other foreign governments or transnational corporations. Sometimes the states' governments in their pursue for foreign investment go too far with promises and tax exemptions, but it's not the most important problem. The major problem occurs when the states, trying to find the back door for foreign direct investment, multiply incentives for foreign companies to attract foreign investment. In some cases the process of making and implementing decision to lure foreign investors turns into cut-throat competition, where the results are dubious. It may undermines credibility of national economy system, because the national interest (more jobs) is a far cry from the state interest (more jobs but in the state) (Gardner Jr. et al. 2001). Moreover, the very notion of nation and national unity,[3] where "the peoples of the several states must sink or swim together" coined in the *Baldwin v. G.A.F. Seelig, Inc.*, should suppress ruthless competition between the states. Nevertheless since 1970s state governments have decided to offer hundreds of millions of dollars as an incentive package for foreign companies. Foreign investment, mostly in the car manufacturing, has been a clear example for competition between states on the global level (Fry 1990, p. 122). States, fighting for FDI, resorted to different methods, and in many cases it resulted a spill over effects in the state's economy. Foreign companies have been attracted not by the state as such, but positive example of predecessors. The clear example is city of Spartanburg in the South Carolina, where BMW invested in a manufacturing facility, and other companies followed (Maunula 2010).

COEXISTENCE

Coexistence, similarly to coordination, is characterized by a small number of interactions in relationships states—the federal government. In this case, however, preferences and interests are poorly articulated by only one of the parties, namely the federal government. This is due to two reasons. Firstly, the strong influence of the independent variable, i.e. the structure of the system; institutional constraints do not define clearly the scope of competence of the states and the federal government. Second, the perception of the activity of American states as an activity which does not affect the extension of the scope of authority, and thus maintains the institutional balance. Change can be characterized as layering, but also restitution, as indicated by the example of regional climate initiatives. The fact that restitution indicates a strong influence of the independent variable, where the structure of the federal system and the ability to experiment with the system also allows for the abandonment of ineffective solutions without involving the institution of the Supreme Court. Interactions, characterized as coexistence, encompasses for example, agreements with countries and sub-national participants and

---

[3] Baldwin v. G.A.F. Seelig, Inc., 294 U.S. 511, 523 (1935).

the possibility of concluding and negotiating treaties and regional agreements on climate change.

Duncan Hollis estimated that in the years 1955–more than 340 agreements with other countries or sub-national actors (as the Canadian provinces) were signed, and six agreements have been concluded by regional institutions such as the New England Conference of Governors. Forty-one states are party to the agreements, which shows that this form of activity in the international arena is relatively popular. Moreover, in recent years the number of concluded agreements has increased rapidly since, as Hollis estimated from the total number of agreements agreements over two hundred have been included in the last decade (Hollis 2010, p. 744). Although this suggests a relatively high activity, it is worth noting that some of the agreements are for a fixed term and have not been renewed. Such a situation occurs in the case of the Declaration on cooperation between Malopolska Voivodship and Stan Illinois, where the Declaration in accordance with the contents of the document in force for a period of three years from 2008 and was not renewed, and still works on the resumption of the revaluation forms and areas of cooperation. Among the agreements indicated by Duncan Hollis, there also agreements which despite the lack of formal expiration, are not performed.

Agreements concluded by the states taking the different names, have been referred to a number of areas, and the rules for their conclusion are also different for each state. In many cases, states entering into the agreement following the content and form of contract approved by Congress, which stems from the need to settle the issue of a practical nature. For example, as shown by R. Bruce Sackinger agreement to combat fires on the border between the United States and Canada take a different shape, although their scope and the essential purpose remains the same (Sackinger 2005). The differences relate primarily to the legal form of responsibility, as well as the distribution costs of the parties weights. In addition to bilateral treaties concluded between the United States and Canada, and agreements concluded between states with the consent of Congress, which allow the participation of Canadian provinces, there are also agreements between the lower-level centers such as state agencies. There are also cases where a compact concluded between states encompasses the entities located outside of the United States takes the form and the name of the compact and, therefore, in accordance with the Constitution, is subject to consent of the Congress, however, this agreement is not formally approved by Congress. Such a situation occurs in the case of The Great Lakes Forest Fire Compact (GLFFC) signed between state agencies involved in combating fires in forests (State Forest Fire Protection Agencies). According to the text of agreement the parties may also be Canadian territories or provinces bordering states which are party to the Agreement. According to the information on the website dedicated to the activities of the parties to the state agencies listed Michigan, Minnesota, Wisconsin and the Canadian provinces of Ontario and Manitoba. Why GLFFC is so important for coexistence model? Pursuant to the Agreement, Article 3 Agreement, the parties agree to appoint two persons to the board of Lake States Forest Fire Protection Board, and the board is responsible, under another article, for determining the methods, practices, and the prevention and control of forest fires. GLFFC can also provide the existence of the position of financial manager, who until 2008 was employed on a contract. This person is responsible for the coordination and implementation of an administrative nature related to the implementation of the agreement. The responsibilities of the financial manager is also filling in the relevant financial reports at the request of local, state and federal. This means that all levels of government recognize GLFFC a participant acting in the area of public policies, which include fighting fires. Another proof that GLFFC is considered an important element of the political system is to take into account the fact that GLFFC has been included as an official compact in relation to the National Interagency Fire Center (NIFC) which brings together eight different federal agencies with representation in each state. These agencies cooperate in fighting fires with their counterparts on the Canadian, Mexican and state authorities. The rules would be adopted in a document published by the NIFC provide that in the north- eastern area of the United States, there are four systems, which aim at fighting fires. Two of them include only U.S. states (Middle Atlantic Interagency Forest Fire Compact and the Big Rivers Forest Fire Management Compact) while the party Northeast Forest Fire Protection Compact (NFFPC) are also Canadian provinces. The above agreements have been concluded with the consent of the Congress, and GLFFC, as already mentioned, such an agreement does not have.

The federal level may exercise its functions in relation to the agreements concluded by states not only consent to the execution of the agreement, but also by supervising the arrangement, with strict administrative regulations setting out the action Parties to the Treaty in the dimension of federal law. An example of such surveillance may use the above-cited document setting out the terms of cooperation with the NIFC, where precisely defined legal requirements to firefighters operating within the individual systems. The existence of such regulation denies theses posed by Hollis, who claims that the actors at the federal level slightly interested in the agreements concluded by states with international participants, as they relate to the most insignificant issues. Rather argued that in place of the traditionally understood governance and the determination of the degree of dependence and acknowledgment of the primacy of the federal government and Congress, by applying the supremacy clause and preemption have been applied principles of multi-level governance (Hooghe and Marks 2003, 2013; Bache and Flinders 2004; Benz 2012), as selected technical or administrative form of regulation, devoid of political context, which turns out to be more efficient. At the same time, this form does not generate conflicts around the principles of federalism U.S., which in this case took the form of functional federalism, allowing solutions for the public good, where the parties focus on the function of the fully specified solution in the process of creating public good.

The situation associated with a particular treatment of GLFFC can serve as an example for other solutions, but the current state of research does not allow for separate type of interaction. However, if the solution adopted with GLFFC will be applied on a wider scale it would be reasonable to award a new type of interaction, coalescence in which the functions and powers of stakeholders coalesce, and their scope is determined by functional reasons, not political.

Promoting of certain values is the main prerequisite for further forms of cooperation, initiated within the model of co-existence, the system of regional agreements related to the reduction of carbon dioxide emissions. These agreements include not only the states of the U.S., but also the Canadian provinces and are an example of actions beyond the control and coordination of the federal authorities. Due to the lack of initiative on the side of the federal government's authority in each state decided to impose their own environmental standards, recognizing, however, that this initiative must include more states to actually have a significant impact on the environment. Barry Rabe notes that ostentatious lack of involvement of the federal government and the withdrawal of the findings of the Kyoto Protocol was the signal for the state governments to start experimenting with your own ideas related to the fight against global warming (Rabe 2011, p. 495). Decision of action under a coalition of several states, then states and provinces do not result solely from a desire to protect the climate and stop global warming, but also of economic calculations. Investments in green energy and reduce carbon dioxide emissions associated with costs that taxpayers must cover and entrepreneur. Therefore, an increase in environmental standards in one state would increase the competitiveness of the neighboring states. Only in the case of California such action was possible mainly because of the ambition of Governor Schwarzenegger's approach, a strong economy and the state have already undertaken efforts to limit emissions. Regional climate initiatives have focused special attention of researchers of international activity of U.S. states (Adelman and Engel 2008; Engel 2009; McAllister 2009; Kazazis 2012), as an example of clear action against the official position of the federal government. It should be noted, however, that these initiatives do not cause lasting institutional changes in the political system and the rising cost of implementation of these projects tend authorities part of states to withdraw from the agreements.

No formal response from the President and Congress on activity of state authorities and acceptance of the obligations resulting from international arrangements with a clear objection federal authorities gave grounds to believe that in this way the states tried to make the implementation of the Kyoto Agreement without the actual ratification. Voluntary adoption of liabilities treated as a set of good practices for the protection of the environment, by reducing pollution does not affect what is true formal powers of the Senate and the President to negotiate and conclude treaties (Article II, Section 2, para. 2 of the Constitution of the United States), but affect the ability of shaping foreign policy. Commitment of the authorities of U.S. states in terms of climate protection as equal participants in international relations indicates a gap in both the Constitution and the interpretation of the Supreme Court and is proof that the American system of state institutions cannot keep up this dimension of the changes taking place in an international environment. It also provides the basis for conducting analysis of the actions of state governments in terms of paradiplomacy (Eatmon 2009; Paquin and Chaloux 2012). On the other hand, however, failure of regional agreements concluded by states and Canadian provinces is an argument in favor of maintaining the existing solutions within American federalism, allowing political experiments, even if it includes participants from other countries. The inclusion of the entire state system of reducing carbon dioxide emissions would reduce the competitiveness of the economy and caused serious costs that would have to bear all the states. In the cited examples, the initial enthusiasm, even after the followers increase or regain state prerogatives in the area of international affairs, was not enough to bring about lasting institutional change.

***

Analysis of the impact of state policies on external U.S. foreign policy carried out based on the categories of foreign policy, federalism and the change indicates that, since *Curtiss Wright* there has not been a fundamental shift of power between American states and federal government. Preferences of both sides remain relatively unchanged. However some attempts to introduce such changes have been taken, but only area of dispute have changed. When *Curtiss Wright, Zschernig, Pink, Belmont* or *Franchise Tax Board* touched the regulation of the economy and the state law nowadays the area of dispute relates to human rights violations (Crosby), responsibility for war crimes (*Garamendi*), consular protection (*Medelin*) and immigration (*Arizona v. U.S.*). If states fail to enter the states in the area of activity reserved for the federal government in the area of foreign policy, it should consider whether they have an opportunity to articulate their interests in the international arena in such a way as not to be in conflict with the federal government.

Shift of power and change in institutions can be observed in the case of the initiatives undertaken by the states in the area of environmental policy and reduction of carbon-dioxide emissions. The creation of regional agreements restricting dioxide-carbon emissions, which also includes Canadian provinces could be an example of changes in the federal system to such an extent as it is characterized in Section I. However, failure of these projects and the lack of interest for the federal government may indicate that there is an area which would be subject to federal regulations. therefore it can be assumed that consent for such initiatives, as expressed by the lack of action from the federal level, was necessary to realize the ambitions of some governors, and they in this way get a substitute of prerogatives in the area of foreign policy. It is also an attempt to test the American political system for resistance to experiments carried out at conditions in this case, even regions.

In sum, it is clear that the impact of external policies of American states in the process of shaping U.S. foreign policy is a function of consent for such action by the federal government. Therefore, it is, in fact, the model of coordination, where level of power in the system remains unchanged and the decisions made at the federal level depends on the extent to which external policies will shape the policies implemented at the national level. The only element of the system, which could undermine the equilibrium is the Supreme Court, but in the light of the decisions taken in recent years, the thesis about the possibility of expanding the scope of state power seems to be farfetched. However possible scenario is the emergence of technical—administrative instruments, where particular solutions, developed at the level of states relating to the international environment, will be accepted, without the need for unnecessary politicization of issues resolved at the state level. because American states are increasingly dependent on federal grants, technical solutions will be supported by administrative and financial instruments. Therefore federal control of finance and goals at the states' level will be maintained, without having to resort to judicial review. This will allow to develop the coalescence model, which currently appears in the relations between the states and the federal government only to a limited extent.

BIBLIOGRAPHY

Abu-Laban, Yasmeen, François Rocher, and Radha Jhappan. 2007. *Politics in North America: Redefining Continental Relations*. Peterborough: Broadview Press.

Adelman, David, and Kirsten H. Engel. 2008. Adaptive Federalism: The Case Against Reallocating Environmental Regulatory Authority. *Minnesota Law Review* 92 (6): 1796–1850.

Bache, Ian, and Matthew Flinders (eds.). 2004. *Multi-level Governance*. New York: Oxford University Press.

Benz, Arthur. 2012. Yardstick Competition and Policy Learning in Multi-level Systems. *Regional & Federal Studies* 22 (3): 251–267. https://doi.org/10.1080/13597566.2012.688270.

Bilder, Richard. 1989. The Role of States and Cities in Foreign Relations. *American Journal of International Law* 83 (4): 821–839.

Blatter, Joachim. 2001. Debordering the World of States. *European Journal of International Relations* 7 (2): 175–209. https://doi.org/10.1177/1354066101007002002.

Cornago, Noé. 2010. On the Normalization of Sub-state Diplomacy. *The Hague Journal of Diplomacy* 5 (1–2): 11–36. https://doi.org/10.1163/187119110X12574289877326.

Domínguez, Jorge I., and Rafael Fernández de Castro. 2001. *The United States and Mexico: Between Partnership and Conflict*. New York and London: Routledge.

Duchacek, Ivo D. 1990. Perforated Sovereignties: Towards a Typology of New Actors in International Relations. In *Federalism and International Relations: The Role of Subnational Units*, ed. Hans J. Michelmann and Panayotis Soldatos, 1–33. Oxford: Clarednon Press.

Eatmon, Thomas D. 2009. Paradiplomacy and Climate Change: American States as Actors in Global Climate Governance. *Journal of Natural Resources Policy Research* 1 (2): 153–165. https://doi.org/10.1080/19390450902789275.

Elazar, Daniel. 1984. *American Federalism: A View from the States*, 3rd ed. New York: Harper & Row.

Engel, Kirsten H. 2009. Whither Subnational Climate Change Initiatives in the Wake of Federal Climate Legislation? *Publius: The Journal of Federalism* 39 (3): 432–454. https://doi.org/10.1093/publius/pjp008.

Fry, Earl H. 1990. State and Local Governments in the International Arena. *The ANNALS of the American Academy of Political and Social Science* 509 (1): 118–127. https://doi.org/10.1177/0002716290509001011.

Gardner Edwin I., Jr., Robert S. Montjoy, and Douglas J. Watson. 2001. Moving into Global Competition: A Case Study of Alabama's Recruitment of Mercedes-Benz. *Review of Policy Research* 18 (3): 80–93. https://doi.org/10.1111/j.1541-1338.2001.tb00196.x.

Gress, Franz. 1996. Interstate Cooperation and Territorial Representation in Intermestic Politics. *Publius* 26 (1): 53–71. https://doi.org/10.2307/3330756.

Halberstam, Daniel. 2001. Foreign Affairs of Federal Systems: A National Perspective on the Benefits of State Participation. *The Villanova Law Review* 46 (5): 1015–1068.

Hamilton, A., J. Madison, and J. Jay. 2007. *The Federalist Papers*. New Haven: Yale University Press.

Henkin, Louis. 1996. *Foreign Affairs and the Constitution*, 2nd ed. New York and London: W. W. Norton.

Hollis, Duncan B. 2010. Unpacking the Compact Clause. *Texas Law Review* 88 (4): 741–806.

Hooghe, Liesbet, and Gary Marks. 2003. Unraveling the Central State, but How?: Types of Multi-level Governance. *American Political Science Review* 97 (2): 233–243.

Hooghe, Liesbet, and Gary Marks. 2013. Beyond Federalism: Estimating and Explaining the Territorial Structure of Government. *Publius: The Journal of Federalism* 43 (2): 179–204. https://doi.org/10.1093/publius/pjs029.

Howard, Peter. 2004. The Growing Role of States in U.S. Foreign Policy: The Case of the State Partnership Program. *International Studies Perspectives* 5 (2): 179–196. https://doi.org/10.1111/j.1528-3577.2004.00168.x.

Kazazis, Alexander. 2012. Western Climate Initiative: The Fate of an Experiment in Subnational Cross-Border Environmental Collaboration. *The Brooklyn Journal of International Law* 37 (3): 1177–1214.

Kincaid, John. 2011. The U.S. Advisory Commission on Intergovernmental Relations: Unique Artifact of a Bygone Era. *Public Administration Review* 71 (2): 181–189.

Ku, Julian G. 2003. The State of New York Does Exist: How the States Control Complicance with International Law. *North Carolina Law Review* 82: 457–529.

LaCroix, Alison L. 2010. *The Ideological Origins of American Federalism.* Cambridge, MA and London: Harvard University Press.

Maunula, Marko. 2010. *Guten Tag, Y'all: Globalization and the South Carolina Piedmont, 1950–2000.* Athens and London: University of Georgia Press.

McAllister, Lesley K. 2009. Regional Climate Regulation: From State Competition to State Collaboration. *San Diego Journal of Climate & Energy Law* 1: 81–102.

Pacheco, Marc R. 2008. Going Global. *Commonwealth Magazine,* 87–89.

Paquin, Stéphane, and Annie Chaloux. 2012. Green Paradiplomacy in North America: Successes and Limits of the NEG-ECP. In *Sustainable Development and Subnational Governments: Policy-Making and Multi-level Interactions,* ed. Hans Bruyninckx, Sander Happaerts, and Karoline van den Brande, 217–236. Basingstoke, UK: Palgrave Macmillan.

Peters, B. Guy, and Jon Pierre. 2004. Multi-level Governance and Democracy: A Faustian Bargain? In *Multi-level Governance,* ed. Ian Bache and Matthew V. Flinders, 75–89. Oxford: Oxford University Press.

Rabe, Barry. 2011. Contested Federalism and American Climate Policy. *Publius: The Journal of Federalism* 41 (3): 494–521.

Rakove, Jack N. 2007. *James Madison and the Creation of the American Republic,* 3rd ed. New York: Pearson-Longman.

Resnik, Judith. 2009. What's Federalism for? In *The Consitution in 2020,* ed. Jack M. Balkin and Reva B. Siegel, 269–284. Oxford: Oxford University Press.

Sackinger, R. Bruce. 2005. Paradiplomatic Maneuvers on the Longest Undefended Border: National and Subnational Fire Protection Agreements between Canada and the United States. *Willamette Journal of International Law and Dispute Resolution* 13 (2): 319–350.

Sharp, Paul. 2009. *Diplomatic Theory of International Relations.* New York: Cambridge University Press.

Spiro, Peter J. 1999. Foreign Relations Federalism. *University of Colorado Law Review* 70: 1223–1276.

Stumberg, Robert, and Matthew C. Porterfield. 2001. Who Preempted the Massachusetts Burma Law? Federalism and Political Accountability Under Global Trade Rules. *Publius: The Journal of Federalism* 31 (3): 173–204.

Swaine, Edward T. 2000. Crosby as Foreign Relations Law. *Virginia Journal of International Law* 41 (2): 481–508.

Trachtman, J.P. 1998. Nonactor States in US Foreign Relations: The Massachusetts Burma Law. *American Society of International Law Proceedings* 92: 350–358.

Verney, Douglas V. 1995. Federalism, Federative Systems, and Federations: The United States, Canada, and India. *Publius* 25 (2): 81–97.

Wilson, Leanne M. 2007. The Fate of the Dormant Foreign Commerce Clause after Garamendi and Crosby. *Columbia Law Review* 107 (3): 746–789.

Regional Security in the Twenty-First Century's South America: Economic, Energy, and Political Security in MERCOSUR and UNASUR

Katharina L. Meissner

INTRODUCTION

Since the end of the Cold War, security in international relations has undergone significant transformations in two respects. Firstly, after the end of bipolarity, world regions and their regional powers have become central to international relations (Katzenstein 2005). They are a crucial component of world politics nowadays, and, next to states and international organizations, constitute actors in security governance. Secondly, the understanding of security and what it constitutes has transformed dramatically (Kacowicz and Press-Barnathan 2016, p. 298). Security aspects have widened from military issues to a more encompassing concept that includes non-traditional issues such as economics or energy.

K. L. Meissner (✉)
Institute for European Integration Research EIF, University of Vienna,
Vienna, Austria
e-mail: katharina.meissner@univie.ac.at

© The Author(s) 2018
P. Frankowski and A. Gruszczak (eds.),
Cross-Disciplinary Perspectives on Regional and Global Security,
https://doi.org/10.1007/978-3-319-75280-8_4

Taking into account the differentiation of actors—states, regions, and international organizations—managing these varying pertinent issues, scholars refer to security matters in the twenty-first century as *security governance* (see, for example, Flemes and Radseck 2012, p. 5).

Latin America as a world region is no exception: an increasing set of actors is involved in tackling both traditional and non-traditional security issues. Besides states and international organizations such as the Organization of American States (OAS), regional organizations with no focus on security per se engage more intensively in security governance in the twenty-first compared to the twentieth century (Kacowicz and Press-Barnatham 2016, p. 300). Two of these regional organizations are the Mercado Común del Sur (MERCOSUR) and the rather new Union of South American Nations (UNASUR) created in 2004. Originally envisaged as economic regional integration and infrastructure integration, respectively, both organizations engage in security governance more frequently (Oelsner 2009, p. 192). Security in twenty-first century Latin America encompasses multiple levels and a diverse set of issues. The broader region faces interstate disputes, domestic problems and transnational threats such as terrorism (Flemes and Radseck 2012, p. 7). Security issues are not restricted to the military dimension. Economic and energy security in regards to resource usage have gained increasing importance in Latin America over the past 17 years (Malamud 2003, p. 53; Valdivieso 2006, p. 86).

Since the turn of the millennium, increasing engagement of regional organizations such as MERCOSUR and UNASUR in security issues has led to overlapping regionalism in Latin America's security governance. This means that several systems of security governance on a unilateral, bilateral, and regional level exist at the same time and within the same region (Flemes and Radseck 2012, p. 6). In Latin America, international organizations such as the OAS coexist next to MERCOSUR and UNASUR. Additionally, regional core states such as Brazil or Venezuela invest in security governance both unilaterally and bilaterally together with external actors. These regional actors often invest in similar or the same traditional and non-traditional security issues. An outstanding example is overlap between the OAS and UNASUR's South American Defense Council (CDS) (Weiffen et al. 2013, p. 371). The expansion of issues in which UNASUR and its accompanying CDS invest thus leads to an increasing overlap with the OAS and MERCOSUR in terms of members and security aspects.

Yet, in both overlapping organizations, MERCOSUR and UNASUR, the key actor is Brazil besides Venezuela and the United States (US), which are influential players. Brazil is South America's regional power in several dimensions. The sheer size of its geography and population exceeds regional neighbors like Paraguay, Uruguay and Argentina by far. Brazil hosts huge amounts of energy and water reserves, and its economic power in the region compared to the rest of MERCOSUR's and UNASUR's member states is vast. The country is thus South America's core actor, both with a view to economic relations and security governance (Flemes and Radseck 2012, p. 14). MERCOSUR and UNASUR as regional organizations are largely driven by Brazilian needs (Krapohl et al. 2014), and, as this chapter argues, regional security governance in South America is no exception.

What is the extent to which South America's regional security governance through MERCOSUR and UNASUR is driven by Brazilian needs? This chapter explores economic, energy and traditional security in South America by focusing on overlapping regionalism of MERCOSUR and UNASUR. In doing so, it sheds particular light on Brazil and its interests with a view to regional security governance, partially drawing on and including data from the Brazilian National Defense White Paper (2012). The first part of this chapter examines the ideas of regional security in twenty-first century's South America by focusing on core underlying features of integration in that region and the shift from the common understanding of security as traditional, military aspects to non-traditional issues that include energy and economics. In the second part, the chapter pays attention to interests that revolve around regional security in South America with a particular emphasis on Brazil's preferences driven by the country's attempt to become an acknowledged global player. The third part analyzes the extent to which Brazil's interests feed into the regional institutions, MERCOSUR and UNASUR, which manage security in South America. This part shows the large overlap between Brazilian interests, on the one hand, and the design as well as competencies of these institutions in security affairs on the other hand. Before concluding and reflecting on security in twenty-first century South America, the chapter assesses the effectiveness of MERCOSUR and UNASUR in managing regional security, and sheds light on why Brazil established MERCOSUR and UNASUR as overlapping regional organizations next to the OAS.

IDEAS AND REGIONAL SECURITY IN TWENTY-FIRST CENTURY'S SOUTH AMERICA

Regional integration in South America always was and still is largely intergovernmental: heads of governments define and drive dynamics of cooperation and integration. Both organizations, MERCOSUR and UNASUR, were initiated by pairs of states with Argentina–Brazil sitting in the drivers' seat of MERCOSUR, while UNASUR was launched primarily by Brazil and Venezuela (Kacowicz and Press-Barnathan 2016, p. 303; Weiffen et al. 2011, 2013). Given the peculiar intergovernmentalism of South American integration, which is driven first and foremost by state presidents, Andrés Malamud (2003) coined the term 'presidentialism'. Although countries in that region started to set up supranational institutions, such as the parliamentary body Parlasur and a permanent judicial body in MERCOSUR, these institutions proved to be ineffective, and have, to a large extent, not been used by the member states Argentina, Brazil, Paraguay and Uruguay from the start (Meissner 2017). This gap of agreements, on the one hand, and de facto practice, on the other hand, has been a characteristic feature of South American integration since its initiation (Jenne and Schenoni 2015). In fact, it is mostly Brazil that sets the pace for integration both with a view to adopting agreements and encouraging compliance (Krapohl et al. 2014). This is also true for MERCOSUR's and UNASUR's regional security agenda which can be interpreted as an equation of Brazil's ideas and interests in that region (Kacowicz and Press-Barnathan 2016, p. 303). Apart from states and their presidents, especially private actors on the domestic level but also supranational bodies of regional organizations, have thus little room for maneuver in South American integration.

Most of the regional organizations in Latin America, especially MERCOSUR and UNASUR led by Brazil, started out as economic integration projects or inter-state cooperation on infrastructure and did not focus on security as such. They are multi-purpose regional organizations (Kacowicz and Press-Barnathan 2016) in the sense that they tackle a broad range of aspects revolving around economic and partly political integration. Security issues, especially traditional ones such as military or defense, were added later to these organizations. In MERCOSUR, member states started to integrate on security issues with the Political Consultation Mechanisms of Foreign Ministers (later also including ministers of defense) (Kacowicz and Press-Barnathan 2016). Increasingly turning to security issues, MERCOSUR aimed at preventing conflicts and maintaining peace and democracy rather than competing with other actors or regions in military or weaponry (Oelsner 2009, p. 197). UNASUR, in contrast to MERCOSUR, did not start with economic integration, but focused on issues of energy and infrastructure (Palestini and Agostinis 2015). Traditional security and defense aspects made it on the agenda of the organization explicitly with the creation of the CDS, once UNASUR had been established already. The earlier, relative absence of security and defense issues on the agenda of MERCOSUR and UNASUR is also due to the fact that South America is often seen as an area of peace with a remarkably low amount of inter-state violent disputes (Jenne 2016). Security issues in South America were thus rather subordinate to economic integration and in the case of MERCOSUR followed the creation of a customs union and in the case of UNASUR followed integration on energy and infrastructure.

One crucial motivation for Argentina and Brazil to set up MERCOSUR in 1991, with Paraguay and Uruguay acceding this dyad, was arguably economic interests. Two main concerns drove economic integration in MERCOSUR: improving domestic economic development and interdependence, on the one hand, and boosting the region's economic position in the global economy on the other hand. As part of the first rationale, MERCOSUR was a means for Argentina and Brazil to trade freely within and outside of South America, locking in the principles of the Washington consensus: deregulation, liberalization and privatization (Meissner 2017, p. 152). Economic development was seen as crucial for the region and its stability (Oelsner 2009). As part of the second rationale, which was much more important to the region due to its dependence on extra-regional trade (Meissner 2017), Argentina and especially Brazil feared marginalization in the global economy, which was increasingly characterized by globalization and global value chains (Buzan and Waever 2003, p. 325). Brazil repeatedly emphasized that MERCOSUR boosts the region's and its own country's global visibility, making the region more attractive to foreign investors and trade partners (Meissner 2017)—such extra-regional economic relations were and are still vital for South America. Therefore MERCOSUR's member states set up the customs union in 1994 which was supposed to lock in liberal reforms, attract investments and trade partners as well as improve the region's visibility and bargaining power on the international stage.

A second set of security ideas, next to economic concerns, revolved around domestic and transnational security in South America. These domestic and transnational threats subsume a large set of security aspects, including consolidation of democracy, the fight against corruption, trafficking of drugs, persons and weapons, terrorism as well as transnational organized crime (Oelsner 2011; Weiffen et al. 2013, p. 378 f.). Focusing on democratic stability, this was a crucial factor in the integration dynamics of MERCOSUR. When Argentina and Brazil initiated regional integration, consolidation of democracy was one of their major security concerns (Oelsner 2011, p. 192). As Andrea Oelsner (2015, p. 205 f.) argues, the issue of democracy became a matter of securitization with stabilizing democratic domestic systems as a top priority for Argentina and Brazil. The importance of and commitment to stabilizing democracy was expressed in the Protocol of Ushuaia (1998) that makes democratic domestic institutions a condition for MERCOSUR's regional integration (Oelsner 2011). In effect, this democratic clause makes democracy a pre-condition for being a full member state of MERCOSUR.

Next to domestic and transnational threats, South America increasingly turned to traditional security issues and its power projection in external relations. The region had and currently still has an objective: the modernization of its military and recognition as an important and responsible actor in world politics by the international community (Nolte and Wehner 2014; Oelsner 2011). Especially Brazil adopts the view that it should participate in international missions under a mandate by the United Nations (UN)—which it did during the United Nations Stabilization Mission in Haiti (MINUSTAH) (see Sect. "Institutions of Regional Security in Twenty-First Century's South America"). This was a notable change in Brazil's foreign policy agenda from the principle of non-intervention to assuming international responsibility (Malamud and Alcañiz 2017). UNASUR and its CDS were also established to strengthen regional identity, concerning defense and security issues (Weiffen et al. 2013, p. 383).

A fourth idea of security in South America revolves around energy and environment, especially the protection and usage of resources on the sub-continent. Energy security is mainly located at UNASUR that served regional integration in the areas energy and infrastructure. The idea of having closer collaboration on these issues was partly based on South America's overall vision of having a closer regional identity (Weiffen et al. 2013). UNASUR relied on the premise of political integration rather than economic collaboration, potentially encompassing a broad range of regional issues (Palestini and Agostinis 2015). Energy security has become a particular sensitive aspect to Brazil, as the next section will show, in part because it sees the US as a potential threat (Buzan and Weaver 2003) to its energy reserves.

REGIONAL SECURITY INTERESTS IN TWENTY-FIRST CENTURY'S SOUTH AMERICA

Brazil must have a capacity for defense that corresponds to its economic, political and strategic stature, in order to have its resources preserved, its voice heard, its position respected and its peaceful tradition safeguarded.
—Brazil's Defense White Paper (2012, p. 33)

Regional integration in South America is, by a large extent, driven by states through intergovernmentalism. As explained at the outset of the previous section, Andrés Malamud (2003) coined this as 'presidentialism' meaning state presidents determine the design and speed of regional cooperation. Actors on the domestic level, such as interest groups or sub-national regions, as well as actors above the nation-state, like the supranational bodies of MERCOSUR have far less influence on regional integration than in Europe. Among the states in South America, the regional power Brazil is by far the most important country in both MERCOSUR and UNASUR. Regional integration in South America, especially in MERCOSUR, can be seen as a function of Brazilian interests. This section explores Brazil's regional security interests.

Brazil's key interest in regional integration and regional security governance is to reach international recognition as a global player. As the country communicates itself in the Defense White Paper (2012, p. 15):

Brazil is a continental size country. It has the world's longest Atlantic coast and, with almost 191 million inhabitants[..], the planet's fifth largest population[..]. It is a great producer of renewable and non-renewable energy [...]. Rated as the world's sixth largest world economy by the International Monetary Fund (IMF)[..], Brazil has increasingly reached expressive levels of development [...]. Brazilian democracy is consolidated [...]. This heritage requires defense.

Table 1   Brazil's security interests (*Reference* Own illustration)

	Endogenous	Exogenous
Ideological	Regional identity	Global power status
Material	Domestic and transnational threats	Potential threat by the US
	Stabilizing democracy	Stability of economic integration

Brazil considers itself a big country. As such a big country, it assumes that it should have an appropriate role in world politics by constructively engaging in peaceful collaboration and effective multilateralism. As the Defense White Paper quote demonstrates, key aspects of its security agenda are its energy reserves, economic and political stability as well as a crucial role in regional and international defense of democracy. Attempting recognition as a global player, Brazil's core security interest is therefore ideological and exogenously driven (Table 1).

One of Brazil's key concerns is therefore to catch up militarily in accordance with the country's grand economic and political status, and to have a respected voice in international security architecture. The Defense White Paper (2012, p. 33) explicitly states that "Brazil must have a capacity for defense that corresponds to its economic, political and strategic stature, in order to have its resources preserved, its voice heard, its position respected and its peaceful tradition safeguarded". Part of this Brazilian agenda is to become more active and more influential in the UN and its peacekeeping missions. Brazil's long-term objective was and still is to reform the UN Security Council in order to make the regional power a permanent member (Defense White Paper 2012, p. 35). To this end Brazil also engages in peaceful conflict resolution and takes part in missions under the umbrella of a UN mandate (Wrobel 2009, p. 20 f.). Thus, one outspoken defense policy objective is Brazil's role in international peace and recognition as a powerful nation (Kenkel 2015).

Brazil's interest in reaching a great power status globally is inherently connected to its regional agenda of assuming a more important role in South America and uniting the region under one voice. To this end, Brazil follows a double strategy of strengthening regional cooperation and identity as well as representing the region to external partners (Merke 2015, p. 181). The exogenous interest of having global power status is thus linked to Brazil's intra-regional interest of strengthening

South America's regional unity. For Brazil, regional integration is part of a strategy to become a more influential player in world politics (Weiffen et al. 2013). This is why regional cooperation and stability is a top priority on Brazil's security agenda. It "gives priority to its immediate neighbors in South America" (Defense White Paper 2012, p. 16), so that regional stability is one core objective of its defense policy (Defense White Paper 2012, p. 27). Brazil's aim is to have stronger regional cohesion not only in economic, but also in political and military affairs. The country aims to represent the regional block—undividedly— on the global stage: it attempted to do so in the Doha Round negotiations through the World Trade Organization (WTO) (Hopewell 2013), and it aims to do so in defense and military matters (Defense White Paper 2012, p. 37). UNASUR's CDS was first thought of as a defense mechanism akin to the one of the North Atlantic Treaty Organization, and eventually the members agreed on consultation and prevention of conflict under the umbrella of UNASUR (Flemes and Radseck 2012, p. 14). With the launch of UNASUR and its CDS Brazil was thus trying to construct a South American identity in the area of military and defense cooperation (Defense White Paper 2012, p. 38).

Regional cooperation and stability is also crucial to Brazil in the area of economic integration. While UNASUR serves the purpose of creating a regional defense identity, MERCOSUR was supposed to unite South America under one umbrella in order to speak with one voice to external trade partners. This objective was both endogenously and exogenously motivated. The endogenous motivation targeted regional cohesion. Exogenously, Brazil wanted to make South America more attractive to external trade and investment partners (Meissner 2017). In spite of the financial crisis that hit the region hard at the turn of the millennium, Brazil tried to keep the regional bloc united in trade negotiations with the EU, US and WTO (Meissner 2016). Regional integration was a means for Brazil to enhance economic stability in South America and to prevent external partners from negotiating bilateral agreements with its immediate neighbors. The customs union was thus of high importance to Brazil since it ensured a united appearance in external economic relations (Duina and Buxbaum 2008). Brazil repeatedly leveraged MERCOSUR in negotiations with the US on the Free Trade Area Agreement and in negotiations with the EU on an Association Agreement. In these bargains, Brazil insisted on united negotiations rather than bilateral ones (Meissner 2016).

A further exogenously motivated, material security interest by Brazil, in particular, and by South America, in general, is the potential threat of the US and the region's wish to become independent from US influence. Countries in South America perceive the US as a threat potential militarily and as a threat to regional and national natural resources and energy reserves (Weiffen et al. 2013, p. 382). The creation of UNASUR's CDS can thus also be understood as a security alliance outside of the OAS and thus without the US (Weiffen et al. 2013, p. 382; Wrobel 2009, p. 22). Especially Brazil is weary of its natural resources in its maritime area. Along its maritime frontiers, Brazil found petroleum reserves in deep and ultra-deep water that are a major security interest of the country because of their crucial economic and strategic importance (Defense White Paper 2012, p. 17). This is why the regional power has a strong interest in sea defense and in controlling the Blue Amazon. Brazil's defense policy is therefore directed, to a large extent, at maintaining complete sovereignty over its jurisdictional waters and at protecting them from potential exogenous threats (Defense White Paper 2012, p. 26). Part of its *Brazil 2022 Plan* is, in consequence, the increase of naval power, including a nuclear submarine (Cope and Parks 2016; Wrobel 2009, p. 27). However, Brazil's vital national interest in protecting its energy reserves and especially the discovery of large oil reserves in ultra-deep water made the country hesitant to integrate substantially in the field of energy. The diverging interests of Brazil and Venezuela on energy integration became obvious over the course of further development of UNASUR (Palestini and Agostinis 2015, p. 17). Although energy integration was still on the agenda of UNASUR, Brazil's hesitation led to temporary stalemate on energy cooperation (Palestini and Agostinis 2015).

Besides the potential exogenous material threat by the US, Brazil also aims at preserving endogenous material security interests. These endogenous, that are intra-regional, security interests revolve around stabilizing national democracy and combating transnational threats. Stabilization of democracy was an inherent goal of regional integration in South America, especially in MERCOSUR (Kacowicz and Press-Barnathan 2016, p. 302). This led, in 1998, to the Protocol of Ushuaia which codified MERCOSUR's member states' commitment to democracy (Oeslner 2011, p. 196). Later, in the twenty-first century, transnational security threats became increasingly relevant to South American integration. One of Brazil's defense policy objectives was and is to contribute to national cohesion and to guarantee Brazilian sovereignty and territorial integrity

(Defense White Paper 2012, p. 27). Such threats to sovereignty and territorial integrity arise from organized crime, terrorism and armed groups that question national unity or the state's monopoly on legitimate violence (Defense White Paper 2012, p. 32). Especially after 9/11 in the US, MERCOSUR's agenda on traditional security issues laid emphasis on fighting terrorism and combating organized crime (Oelsner 2011, p. 193).

In sum, Brazil's security interests are both of an ideological as well as a material nature and they respond to endogenous, that is intra-regional, as well as exogenous, that is external, threats. The regional power Brazil shares material security concerns with its immediate neighbors. These concerns revolve around threats from within the region. The countries feel the need to maintain national sovereignty against domestic and transnational armed groups and organized crime, but they also stem from beyond the region. South America, in the shadow of American dominance, perceives the US as a potential threat to economic and energy security as well as to hard, military issues. Next to these material concerns, Brazil's interests are driven by the country's ideological desire to have a globally acknowledged grand power status. For Brazil, being a recognized regional power in South America and gathering its neighbors under one umbrella, is a step towards global power. Therefore, Brazil has a strong interest in establishing a regional identity in security issues and in representing the region beyond South America.

At the same time, Brazil's ideational values strongly correspond to national sovereignty, which aids its status as a rising power on the international stage (Hofmann et al. 2016). Regional organizations and establishing a regional identity serve as a means to strengthen national purposes. They are not supposed to cede sovereignty to supra-national bodies. Thus, Brazil's security interests and the role of MERCOSUR and UNASUR must be understood in the context of strong attachment to national sovereignty. The prevalence and importance of national sovereignty undermine deeper regional integration, so that horizontal rather than vertical cooperation prevails in both MERCOSUR and UNASUR.

INSTITUTIONS OF REGIONAL SECURITY IN TWENTY-FIRST CENTURY'S SOUTH AMERICA

Institutions of regional security in South America, that are MERCOSUR and UNASUR, can be understood as a direct translation of Brazil's interests in institutional design. Both, MERCOSUR and UNASUR, are deeply intergovernmental and decisions are taken by consensus. Due to Brazil's interest in gathering South American countries under one regional umbrella, it has a preference for horizontal integration, meaning enlargement, rather than vertical integration, meaning deepening. This is also reflected in Brazil's regular unilateral deviation from regional agreements resulting in trade disputes. This section will unfold these arguments by shedding light on economic, energy and security integration in MERCOSUR and UNASUR. It explains the organizations' institutional design and their competencies.

MERCOSUR mainly served economic integration and regional commercial stability in order to attract foreign direct investments and facilitate trade relations with extra-regional partners. This responded to Brazil's interest since it boosts economic relations with external partners like the EU or the US and makes the region more attractive from an economic viewpoint, thus ensuring economic security. Although there was notable influence from the example of the EU in the institutional set up of MERCOSUR (Lenz and Burilkov 2016), the regional organization was and still is intergovernmental. Decisions among Argentina, Brazil, Paraguay and Uruguay are taken by consensus and the regional organization lacks strong supranational bodies. MERCOSUR's most important bodies are the Common Market Council, the Common Market Group and the Trade Commission. They are strongly intergovernmental and consist of member states' governments' representatives whose decisions require consensus.[1] This positively reflects Brazil's preferences: Brazil has a right to veto decisions, and, given its asymmetric economic power in South America, has therefore strong bargaining power in MERCOSUR (Krapohl et al. 2014).

There is a clear divergence of preferences among Brazil, on the one hand, and its neighbors, on the other hand, regarding MERCOSUR's institutional design. While Brazil favors horizontal integration and thus enlargement, other member states continuously ask for vertical, deeper regional integration. This issue surfaced at the turn of the millennium when South America faced a severe financial crisis. In this situation, Argentina, Paraguay and Uruguay wanted deeper macroeconomic cooperation and collaboration on currency issues, but Brazil showed no such interest in deeper integration (Krapohl et al. 2014). Rather than

---

[1] This paragraph is based on Meissner (2017, p. 149 f.).

deepening economic integration, Brazil lobbied for Venezuela's accession to MERCOSUR. Venezuela announced its intention to join the regional organization as a full member in 2006, which Brazil appreciated (Rivera 2014). Eventually, Venezuela's membership was approved in 2012, but suspended in 2016 due to its failure to comply with MERCOSUR's requirements for trade integration and due to its domestic human rights situation. Brazil's approach of favoring horizontal integration also translated into association agreements with Bolivia, Colombia, Chile, Ecuador and Peru (Flemes and Radseck 2012, p. 20).

Compared to economic integration, institutionalization of regional security governance through MERCOSUR is significantly slimmer. Although Brazil and Argentina had a vital security interest in stabilizing democracy and rule of law, this did not translate into the MERCOSUR treaty, namely the Protocol of Ouro Preto (1994). Security issues and MERCOSUR's commitment to democracy were codified in the Protocol of Ushuaia. Furthermore, MERCOSUR set up a Democracy Observatory which works towards the objectives laid out in the Protocol of Ushuaia (Oelsner 2011, p. 199). Traditional security and defense issues are mostly dealt with on a bilateral basis rather than through MERCOSUR's regional governance: these bilateral avenues are, for instance, the Argentine-Brazilian Consultation and Coordination Mechanism and the Permanent Analysis Mechanism (Oelsner 2011, p. 200). In order to react to transnational threats, MERCOSUR's member states set up a number of initiatives to combat organized crime and terrorism such as the Triple Frontier's Tripartite Command, Conference of Home Ministers of MERCOSUR, a Regional Intelligence Center and a Permanent Working Group on terrorism (Oeslner 2011, p. 201). However, institutionalization in MERCOSUR is rather low in general, and particularly of security issues.

Similarly to MERCOSUR, UNASUR is strongly intergovernmental and focuses primarily on sectoral integration in infrastructure and energy. UNASUR's Constitutive Treaty was signed in 2008, integrating MERCOSUR and the Andean Community in one union (Kacowicz and Press-Barnathan 2016, p. 19; Nolte and Wehner 2014, p. 187). The regional organization's institutional bodies are a Council of Presidents and two bodies consisting of governmental representatives next to a General Secretariat: the Council of Ministers of Foreign Affairs and the Council of Delegates (Closa and Palestini 2015). UNASUR's institutions comprise additional councils on specific sectoral issues such as energy, infrastructure or defense policy. In line with the overall trend in South and Latin America, UNASUR is thus a typical intergovernmental regional organization where decisions are made among governmental representatives by consensus.

Security issues featured more prominently in UNASUR when Brazil proposed to establish CDS as a means to move towards regional defense integration. UNASUR's CDS has the objective of creating a regional identity on security issues, creating and consolidating a zone of peace in South America, and moving towards common positions on defense issues (Weiffen et al. 2013, p. 377). Based on the Brazilian wish to collaborate closer on defense and security in the region, UNASUR serves to mutually exchange information on military matters and to consolidate confidence within the region (Weiffen et al. 2013). Gathering South America together under UNASUR, the regional organization is supposed to make regional security governance more autonomous and independent from OAS and US's participation (Closa and Palestini 2015). Especially due to tensions between Colombia and Ecuador, regional security governance and hence the CDS gained importance in South America (Nolte and Wehner 2014, p. 187). An additional protocol following the establishment of CDS served as an official commitment to preserve democracy and combat unlawful armed groups (Closa and Palestini 2015). Thus, UNASUR became crucial as an organization of South America's regional security governance since the beginning of the twenty-first century.

UNASUR's understanding of regional security covers explicitly both traditional and non-traditional issues such as securitization of natural resources. Detlef Nolte and Leslie Wehner (2014, p. 188 ff.) point out that UNASUR adopted a multidimensional agenda of security in its Constitutive Treaty. This agenda goes beyond a traditional conceptualization of security that is focused on military issues. One of these non-traditional issues is preservation of natural resources such as energy or water supply. Oil and water reserves are understood as part of national sovereignty and thus require defense from potential threats. This was highlighted by Brazil, which has the specific objective of improving airspace and submarine military in order to ensure defense of its natural resources (Defense White Paper 2012). UNASUR mirrors Brazil's and Venezuela's interest in protecting oil and water reserves from potential threats such as the US (Nolte and Wehner 2014, p. 191). This led to the formation of UNASUR's sectoral council on energy, namely the South

American Energy Council (Closa and Palestini 2015). However, due to the divergence of interests between Venezuela, on the one hand, which lobbies in favor of deeper integration of the energy market, and Brazil, on the other hand, which favors limited integration, deeper cooperation in the direction of a possible Energy Integration Treaty is hindered (Closa Palestini 2015). This divergence of interests is consistent with dividing lines in MERCOSUR between vertical, deep integration and horizontal integration, with Brazil favoring the latter approach.

In sum, institutions of South America's security governance system mirror closely Brazilian security interests. These are rooted in economic, energy and traditional—defense—matters. According to Brazil's needs and based on its regional power status, both MERCOSUR and UNASUR are strongly intergovernmental institutions that promote horizontal rather than vertical integration in these three fields. Focusing on economic regional integration, MERCOSUR was enlarged by Venezuela (which is currently suspended), but Brazil was hesitant to concede sovereignty or to agree on deeper economic coordination. Focusing on energy and security, UNASUR is equally intergovernmental with Brazil determining the integration dynamics in South America. Based on Brazilian needs, UNASUR carved out the CDS which serves as a regional defense mechanism with a view to exchanging information and consolidating mutual confidence. Given Brazil's hesitation, energy integration in UNASUR is still rather limited with a clear divergence of interests over deepening collaboration in this field. In both institutions, MERCOSUR and UNASUR, and in all three dimensions, Brazil is the driving force that determines design and speed of regional security integration.

Assessing the Performance of MERCOSUR and UNASUR on Regional Security

How have MERCOSUR and UNASUR performed in the context of South America's regional security governance? What were actual measures taken by South America on regional security issues?

The most noteworthy development in the context of regional security is the Brazilian decision to live up to its commitments of multilateral security responsibility and to participate in an international mission under the UN umbrella in Haiti. The United Nations Stabilization Mission in Haiti (MINUSTAH) was a mission set up in 2004 to support recovery of Haiti after a devastating earthquake. Members of both regional organizations, MERCOSUR and UNASUR, were involved in that mission. Brazil assumed leadership of MINUSTAH's military arm and had the mandate to coordinate the demobilization of unlawful armed groups (Siman Gomes 2016). Besides all four members of MERCOSUR, other South American countries like Chile or Peru took part (Oelsner 2011, p. 202). UNASUR settled in Port-au-Prince with a technical secretariat in order to help on the ground (Nolte and Wehner 2014, p. 185). Managing South America's participation in this mission, the countries tried to demonstrate their regional cohesion on security and their regional capacity to coordinate on defense and military issues (Oelsner 2011). Since MINUSTAH in 2004, the participation of MERCOSUR's member states in international UN missions has been consistently high: MERCOSUR contributed around 37% of troops to these missions (Oelsner 2011).

Over the course of the twenty-first century, MERCOSUR has also increasingly turned towards cooperation in defense and military areas primarily at a bilateral level. Brazil set up defense policy working groups with South American states, and holds annual meetings with Argentina on the Consultation and Coordination Mechanism for International Security and Defense Issues (Oeslner 2011, p. 207). Also on a bilateral basis, South American countries try to make their defense expenditure more transparent based on bilateral agreements (Oelsner 2011, p. 207). In the military area, Argentina and Brazil agreed on safeguard provisions regarding nuclear materials in South America, thereby implementing the Common System for Accounting and Control of Nuclear Materials (Oelsner 2011, p. 207). MERCOSUR's members also carry out military exercises within the region. These encompass military exercises on a naval, air and land basis as well as peacekeeping, rescue, humanitarian aid and cross-border missions (Oelsner 2011).

MERCOSUR has become increasingly active on security issues also in its external affairs despite the fact that is has no security competencies per se. As analyzed by Diana Panke (2017), MERCOSUR as a regional organization regularly contributes to international security negotiations. From 2008 to 2012, it was among the most vocal regional organizations in several security negotiations, making 16 statements in total. This places MERCOSUR in the top four vocal regional organizations. In first place, the EU's statements amount to 100 in total. In comparison, UNASUR made just four regional statements although it has explicit competencies in the field of security (Panke 2017). In comparison to MERCOSUR though, UNASUR has been much more active on security issues within the region of South America.

Cooperation on defense and military issues is a core goal of UNASUR, which seeks regional cohesion in security affairs. Building on the bilateral agreement to calculate defense expenditure between Argentina and Chile, UNASUR set up a similar mechanism that facilitates the members' procedure of making these expenditures transparent (Nolte and Wehner 2014, p. 194). This was pushed by UNASUR in order to establish a methodology of measuring the amount member states spend on defense. This will lead eventually to a white book on defense expenditure (Nolte and Wehner 2014, p. 194). Furthermore, UNASUR's countries plan military exercises akin to the bilateral ones of MERCOSUR and try to facilitate domestic defense training (Weiffen et al. 2013, p. 380). These measures aim at building mutual confidence among UNASUR's member states and at promoting regional identity in security areas.

MERCOSUR and UNASUR both actively promote domestic stability of democratic institutions and engage against threats by domestic or transnational unlawful groups. Ensuring territorial sovereignty against domestic or transnational threats, MERCOSUR made use of its Democracy Observatory and established a number of initiatives for police cooperation. Supporting and maintaining democratic stability in South American countries, MERCOSUR used its Democracy Observatory several times. Since 2006, MERCOSUR has sent several missions to observe elections in member countries, first on an ad hoc basis and later under the umbrella of the MERCOSUR Democracy Observatory, for instance, the missions to monitor elections and referendums in Brazil, Bolivia and Venezuela (Oelsner 2011, p. 206). In order to combat transnational threats such as organized crime or terrorism, MERCOSUR also established a Center for Police Training as well as a System for the Exchange of Security Information which facilitate exchange of intelligence information between national police forces (Oelsner 2011, p. 208). These measures are rooted in MERCOSUR's plan to set up an institution similar to INTERPOL.

Despite UNASUR's short existence, its active involvement in supporting democratic stability is noteworthy. UNASUR acted as a mediator resolving domestic and cross-border crises on several occasions, which reinforced its legitimacy as an effective security institution. These crises covered political unrest in Bolivia (2008), Ecuador (2010), Paraguay (2012) and Venezuela (2013), border disputes between Colombia and Venezuela (2010), and the location of US military bases in Colombia (2009) which caused tensions with South American neighbor countries (Nolte and Wehner 2014; Weiffen et al. 2013).

During political unrest in Bolivia (2008), UNASUR reacted swiftly and effectively (Closa and Palestini 2015; Weiffen et al. 2013). Several provinces in the country—Santa Cruz, Beni, Pando and Tarija—threatened Bolivia's territorial sovereignty by demanding to be autonomous from the federal government. In the province of Santa Cruz, a referendum was held to approve its autonomy from Bolivia's central government. The tensions between those in favor and the federal government soon escalated, resulting in 30 casualties (Nolte and Wehner 2014, p. 193). UNASUR reacted immediately by calling for an extraordinary meeting under Chile's President Michelle Bachelet, then President *pro tempore* of UNASUR. In this meeting, Brazil used the chance to shape UNASUR's institutional design by making its participation at the meeting or any involvement of the regional organization conditional on the affected country's consent (Closa and Palestini 2015). This ensured and stabilized UNASUR's intergovernmental character signaling a clear preference for national sovereignty. UNASUR then sent a joint mission to Bolivia which proved to be highly effective (Nolte and Wehner 2014). This reinforced UNASUR's reputation as a legitimate and effective regional security actor in South America.

Similarly to Bolivia, UNASUR became active during political unrest or domestic crisis in Ecuador (2010), Paraguay (2012) and Venezuela (2013). When Ecuador faced a domestic threat to its democracy under the legacy of Rafael Correa, who, at the same time, was President *pro tempore* of UNASUR, the President of Argentina Christina Kirchner and her husband called for an extraordinary summit on the very day of the crisis (Weiffen et al. 2013, p. 381). They agreed that several foreign ministers of UNASUR's member states would travel to Ecuador in order to support the government (Closa and Palestini 2015). UNASUR used the same procedure during crises in Paraguay and Venezuela, thereby reinforcing the region's commitment to democracy as expressed in the organization's Constitutive Treaty.

In inter-state disputes, UNASUR also reacted promptly and mediated between conflicting parties. One dispute was caused by border tensions between Colombia and Venezuela due to leaders of the unlawful armed group FARC being located in Venezuela. Hugo Chávez, then President of Venezuela, asked for an emergency meeting of UNASUR's foreign ministers in order to discuss these border tensions. Chávez insisted that UNASUR shall be responsible for resolving the border dispute rather than the OAS due to Venezuela's concerns of US membership and American influence in the latter organization (Nolte and Wehner 2014, p. 196). Although UNASUR was initially unsuccessful in solving the dispute, it successfully acted as a mediator once Juan Manuel Santos took office as Colombian President (2010). Néstor Kirchner, husband of Christina Kirchner and UNASUR's secretary general, mediated between Colombia and Venezuela. Eventually the situation was resolved and led to renewed diplomatic relations between the two conflicting parties (Nolte and Wehner 2014, p. 196). UNASUR also supported the resolution of tensions between Colombia, on the one hand, and other South American countries such as Brazil or Venezuela, on the other hand, over the US military bases on Colombian territory (Weiffen et al. 2013, p. 381). In all instances, UNASUR's ad hoc procedure of intergovernmental conflict resolution proved to be remarkably effective and successful, thereby rendering the OAS less important in South America.

In brief, UNASUR and MERCOSUR have increasingly turned to traditional security issues—defense and military cooperation—over the course of the twenty-first century. While MERCOSUR initially focused on economic integration and added bilateral collaboration on defense and military issues later, UNASUR started out as a regional organization on energy and infrastructure but soon established a defense mechanism, the CDS. Both regional organizations became active on traditional security issues in external as well as intra-regional affairs. Externally, members of both MERCOSUR and UNASUR started investing in missions under the umbrella of the UN, a noteworthy example being MINUSTAH. Both organizations contribute to international security negotiations (Panke 2017). Intra-regionally, UNASUR reacted immediately and effectively to domestic and transnational tensions. Although UNASUR, like MERCOSUR, is strongly intergovernmental and these reactions were on an ad hoc rather than formally institutionalized basis, the organization was successful in mediating between conflicting parties.

OVERLAPPING REGIONAL SECURITY ORGANIZATIONS IN SOUTH AND LATIN AMERICA

The regional organizations MERCOSUR and UNASUR coexist next to other integration projects in South America with partly overlapping membership and policy competencies. Hence, the region is no exception to the global trend of overlapping regionalism. Out of 15 Latin American regional organizations in total one state on global average belongs to approximately four integration schemes (Panke and Stapel forthcoming). In South America, there is an overlap between MERCOSUR, UNASUR, the OAS and the Rio Group, which all contribute to traditional or non-traditional regional security.

The OAS is Latin America's oldest regional organization with a clear focus on traditional security issues, meaning peace and security on the continent. Its objectives are consolidating democratic stability, resolving inter-state disputes and tensions peacefully, promoting continental cooperation and limiting the availability of conventional weapons, among others. Its primary purpose is to promote regional cooperation in security affairs through exchange of information and a peaceful settlement of conflicts among Latin American countries. The OAS encompasses 34 countries next to the US, including Argentina, Brazil, Paraguay, Uruguay and Venezuela which are all members of MERCOSUR and/ or UNASUR (Venezuela's membership in MERCOSUR was suspended in 2016). Membership within MERCOSUR, UNASUR and the OAS clearly overlaps, and especially the latter two regional organizations have similar purposes, namely to maintain regional peace and security.

Besides the OAS, the Rio Group is an established institution among Latin American countries that seeks to coordinate the countries' foreign policies, enhance regional security and prevent the introduction of weapons of mass destruction in the region. The institution envisages a Latin America free of weapons of mass destruction and relies on security and confidence-building measures among its member states to establish and maintain mutual trust. Twenty three member states constitute the Rio Group, among them Argentina, Brazil, Colombia, Paraguay, Uruguay and Venezuela. Thus, the Rio Group also overlaps with the OAS and UNASUR regarding both membership and policy objectives. On the occasion of the unity summit of the Community of Latin American and Caribbean States (CELAC), the Rio Group was subsumed under CELAC. It seeks to gather all Latin American and Caribbean countries together in order to promote regional cohesion. Similar to the Rio Group and UNASUR, CELAC has an agenda of combating threats to security, especially transnational terrorism and nuclear weapons.

Why did South American states, especially Brazil, decide to establish UNASUR despite the already existing and overlapping regional security organizations OAS and the Rio Group? Research on overlapping regionalism is only in the making (Malamud and Gardini 2012; Panke and Stapel forthcoming), though one driving force of UNASUR was the region's desire to become more independent from the US. While the OAS includes the US as the clearly dominant power, UNASUR is an organization restricted to South American countries thereby excluding the American hegemon. This corresponds positively to Brazil's idea of strengthening regional identity and of being acknowledged as a rising power on the international stage with a pre-dominant status among its immediate neighbors. To Brazil, UNASUR constructs and defines its sphere of influence, namely South America, as separate to the one of the US (Malamud and Gardini 2012).

Conclusion

What are ideas and interests revolving around security in the South American region in the twenty-first century? To what extent are MERCOSUR and UNASUR driven by Brazilian needs as institutions of regional security, and how do these organizations perform on security in South America? This chapter set out to answer these questions and to provide an overview of regional security in South America in the context of traditional and non-traditional threats in the twenty-first century.

Regional organizations in South America are strongly intergovernmental with heads of states making decisions by consensus. Andrés Malamud (2003) coined this as presidentialism. Thus, crucial actors in South America's regional security governance are states and their presidents. Sub-national and supra-national actors only have a marginal role. In both organizations, MERCOSUR and UNASUR, Brazil is the regional power, and, given the intergovernmental character of these regional organizations, it is the most important player, determining design and speed of regional integration. Security cooperation is no exception to this: therefore defense and military collaboration within MERCOSUR and UNASUR can be seen as an equation of Brazilian ideas and interests.

Brazil's security interests focus on three areas that are both of traditional and non-traditional nature. Non-traditional security interests are economic and energy issues, namely making the region attractive to extra-regional investment and trade partners, preventing vulnerability to economic sanctions as well as protecting national oil and water reserves. Traditional security interests revolve around defense and military cooperation with a view to constructing regional identity. Hence, Brazil has an interest in constructing regional identity on a broad set of economic and security issues instead of regional identity being restricted to economic integration. These security interests encompass material as well as ideological concerns and respond to endogenous as well as exogenous threats. Materially, South America and Brazil perceive the US as a potential, exogenous threat to economic, energy and military security in the region. Endogenous material threats to security are domestic and transnational unlawful armed groups, organized crime and terrorism. They undermine national sovereignty and territorial integrity. Ideological concerns, however, are equally important to Brazil, because the country's objective is to be acknowledged as a rising power with regional and global player status. To this end of being recognized as an influential global actor, Brazil strengthens regional cooperation and stabilizes its role as a regional power in South America.

The regional organizations MERCOSUR and UNASUR mirror Brazilian ideas and interests regarding security. While MERCOSUR focuses on economic integration with defense and military cooperation being secondary to trade, UNASUR initially served energy and infrastructure collaboration but soon turned to a regional defense mechanism that is the CDS. With UNASUR, Brazil established a regional security organization independent of the US: it constructs and promotes a regional identity and unity on defense and military issues. UNASUR can be seen as a means to strengthen Brazil's regional power and to increase its global visibility. This is due to the organization's objective of mediating between conflicting parties in the region and consolidating peace and security independent of the OAS where the US is the most powerful member.

In conclusion, Brazil's role in South America's security governance can be seen as a 'reluctant regional power' (Malamud and Alcañiz 2017) that draws on soft, diplomatic means rather than hard measures, such as economic power or coercion, to contribute to regional peace and stability. National sovereignty is understood as a crucial component of regional peace and democratic stability in South America. Therefore, security interests revolve around maintaining and strengthening national sovereignty under the umbrella of regional cooperation. This underpins regional security governance through MEROCSUR and UNASUR where Brazil constructs a common, regional identity on security matters in order to strengthen its national self-perception as a global power.

REFERENCES

Buzan, Barry, and Ole Waever. 2003. *Regions and Powers: The Structure of International Security*. New York: Cambridge University Press.

Closa, Carlos, and Stefano Palestini. 2015. Between Democratic Protection and Self-Defense: The Case of Unasur and Venezuela. Robert Schuman Centre for Advanced Studies Research Paper, 2015/93, Florence.

Cope, John A., and Andrew Parks. 2016. *Frontier Security: The Case of Brazil*. Washington, DC: National Defense University Press.

Defense White Paper. 2012. *Livro Branco de Defesa Nacional*. http://www.defesa.gov.br/arquivos/estado_e_defesa/livro_branco/lbdn_2013_ing_net.pdf. Accessed 15 May 2017.

Duina, Francesco, and Jason Buxbaum. 2008. Regional Trade Agreements and the Pursuit of State Interests: Institutional Perspectives from NAFTA and Mercosur. *Economy and Society* 37 (2): 193–223.

Flemes, Daniel, and Michael Radseck. 2012. Creating Multi-level Security Governance in South America. In *Comparative Regional Security Governance*, ed. Shaun Breslin and Stuart Croft. Oxon: Routledge.

Hofmann, Stephanie C., Barbara Bravo de Moares Mendes, and Susanna Campbell. 2016. Investing in International Security: Rising Powers and Institutional Choices. *Cambridge Review of International Affairs* 29 (3): 831–851.

Hopewell, Kristen. 2013. New Protagonists in Global Economic Governance: Brazilian Agribusiness at the WTO. *New Political Economy* 18 (4): 603–623.

Jenne, Nicole. 2016. The Domestic Origins of No-War Communities: State Capacity and the Management of Territorial Disputes in South America and Southeast Asia. PhD dissertation, European University Institute.

Jenne, Nicole, and Luis Schenoni. 2015. Latin American Declaratory Regionalism: An Analysis of Presidential Discourse (1994–2014). Robert Schuman Centre for Advanced Studies Research Paper, 2015/53, Florence.

Kacowicz, Arie M., and Galia Press-Barnathan. 2016. Regional Security Governance. In *The Oxford Handbook of Comparative Regionalism*, ed. Tanja A. Börzel and Thomas Risse, 297–323. Oxford: Oxford University Press.

Katzenstein, Peter J. 2005. *A World of Regions: Asia and Europe in the American Imperium*. Ithaca and London: Cornell University Press.

Kenkel, Kai. 2015. Multilateralism and Concepts of Security in South America. *International Studies Review* 17 (1): 150–152.

Krapohl, Sebastian, Katharina L. Meissner, and Johannes Muntschick. 2014. Regional Powers as Leaders or Rambos? The Ambivalent Behaviour of Brazil and South Africa in Regional Economic Integration. *Journal of Common Market Studies* 52 (4): 879–895.

Lenz, Tobias, and Alexandr Burilkov. 2016. Institutional Pioneers in World Politics: Regional Institution Building and the Influence of the European Union. *European Journal of International Relations*. https://doi.org/10.1177/1354066116674261.

Malamud, Andrés. 2003. Presidentialism and Mercosur: A Hidden Cause for a Successful Experience. In *Comparative Regional Integration*, ed. Finn Laursen, 53–75. Farnham: Ashgate.

Malamud, Andrés, and Gian Luca Gardini. 2012. Has Regionalism Peaked? The Latin American Quagmire and Its Lessons. *The International Spectator: Italian Journal of International Affairs* 47 (1): 116–133.

Malamud, Andrés, and Isabella Alcañiz. 2017. Managing Security in a Zone of Peace: Brazil's Soft Approach to Regional Governance. *Revista Brasileira de Política Internacional* 60 (1). https://doi.org/10.1590/0034-7329201700102.

Meissner, Katharina L. 2016. Competing for Economic Power: South America, Southeast Asia and Commercial Realism in European Union Foreign Policy. PhD dissertation, European University Institute.

Meissner, Katharina L. 2017. MERCOSUR. In *Regional Integration in the Global South: External Influence on Economic Cooperation in ASEAN, MERCOSUR and SADC*, ed. Sebastian Krapohl, 147–179. Cham: Palgrave Macmillan.

Merke, Federico. 2015. Neither Balance Nor Bandwagon: South American International Society Meets Brazil's Rising Power. *International Politics* 52 (2): 178–192.

Nolte, Detlef, and Leslie Wehner. 2014. UNASUR and Regional Security in South America. In *Regional Organisations and Security: Conceptions and Practices*, ed. Stephen Aris and Andreas Wenger, 183–203. New York: Routledge.

Oelsner, Andrea. 2009. Consensus and Governance in Mercosur: The Evolution of the South American Security Agenda. *Security Dialogue* 40 (2): 191–212.

Oelsner, Andrea. 2011. Mercosur's Incipient Security Governance. In *The Security Governance of Regional Organizations*, ed. Emil J. Kirchner and Roberto Dominguez, 190–217. New York: Routledge.

Oelsner, Andrea. 2015. Articulating Mercosur's Security Conceptions and Practices. In *Regional Organisations and Security: Conceptions and Practices*, ed. Stephen Aris and Andreas Wenger, 203–223. New York: Routledge.

Palestini, Stefano, and Giovanni Agostinis. 2015. Constructing Regionalism in South America: The Cases of Sectoral Cooperation on Transport

Infrastructure and Energy. *Journal of International Relations and Development*. https://doi.org/10.1057/jird.2015.15.

Panke, Diana. 2017. Regional Actors in International Security Negotiations. *European Journal for Security Research* 2 (1): 5–21.

Panke, Diana, and Sören Stapel. (forthcoming). Exploring Overlapping Regionalism. *Journal of International Relations and Development*. https://doi.org/10.1057/s41268-016-0081-x.

Rivera, Salvador. 2014. *Latin American Unification: A History of Political and Economic Integration Efforts*. Jefferson, NC: McFarland.

Siman Gomes, Maíra. 2016. Analysing Interventionism beyond Conventional Foreign Policy Rationales: The Engagement of Brazil in the United Nations Stabilization Mission in Haiti (MINUSTAH). *Cambridge Review of International Affairs* 29 (3): 852–869.

Valdivieso, Patricio. 2006. Südamerika: Gefahren und Möglichkeiten für die Sicherheit. In *Transatlantische Beziehungen im Wandel: Sicherheitspolitische Aspekte der Beziehungen zwischen der Europäischen Union und Lateinamerika*, ed. Franz Kernic and Walter Feichtinger, 67–91. Baden-Baden: Nomos.

Weiffen, Brigitte, Matthias Dembinski, Andreas Hasenclever, Katja Freistein, and Makiko Yamauchi. 2011. Democracy, Regional Security Institutions, and Rivalry Mitigation: Evidence from Europe, South America, and Asia. *Security Studies* 20 (3): 378–415.

Weiffen, Brigitte, Wehner Leslie, and Detlef Nolte. 2013. Overlapping Regional Security Institutions in South America: The Case of OAS and UNASUR. *International Area Studies Review* 16 (4): 370–389.

Wrobel, Paulo. 2009. Brazil's Approach to Security in the Twenty-First Century. In *Global Security in a Multipolar World*, ed. Luis Peral, 15–31. Paris: EU Institute for Security Studies.

The Distinctiveness of the Latin American Security System—Why Is It so Different? Public International Law Perspective

Agata Kleczkowska

INTRODUCTION

Alejandro Alvarez in his famous article published in the *American Journal of International Law* in 1909, pointed out characteristics of international law in American continent, concluding that the set of characteristics he dealt with can be named as 'American International Law' (Alvarez 1909, p. 353). Even though many features of this 'American International Law' which Alvarez brought up do not match questions important for the contemporary international law (he referred e.g. to the colonial system, conquests etc.), it seems that this term could still find application to the current state both of international law and political relations. However, after the events of the twentieth century, which marked even more the distinctiveness of the Latin American States, one could claim that it would be even justifiable to use the term 'Latin American international law'.

A. Kleczkowska (✉)
Polish Academy of Sciences, Warsaw, Poland
e-mail: agata.kleczkowska@inp.pan.pl

© The Author(s) 2018
P. Frankowski and A. Gruszczak (eds.),
Cross-Disciplinary Perspectives on Regional and Global Security,
https://doi.org/10.1007/978-3-319-75280-8_5

The aim of this paper is thus to discuss the distinctiveness of international law as applied and formed by the Latin American States with regard to the security issues. Following the idea pursued in this book, the chapter will be divided into four parts, devoted to ideas, interests, institutions and interactions. Each of these parts discusses different aspects of the Latin American security system from the perspective of public international law. The thesis advanced in this paper is that Latin American security system is distinct from the universal one not only in terms of important security issues, history and pursued policies, but also because of the specific application and understanding of principles and institutions of international law, which underline the autonomy of the Latin American region from the rest of the international community.

IDEAS: PRINCIPLES OF NON-INTERVENTION AND COMMITMENT TO DEMOCRACY AS THE FUNDAMENTS OF THE LATIN AMERICAN SECURITY SYSTEM

This part of the chapter seeks to discuss the role of the two fundamental principles of the Latin American security system, that is the principles of non-intervention and the commitment to democracy. Obviously, these are not the only principles that can be invoked among those forming the identity of Latin America in international relations and under international law, since among others there are principles of States' sovereignty, the sovereign equality of States as well as the right to self-determination. However, these are the principles of non-intervention and commitment to democracy that focus the most important values of the Latin American system as the whole in terms of security, as well as influence mostly the actions of Latin America with regard to security. Thus, the aim of this part is to discuss the meaning of these principles, as well as the consequences of their application in Latin American States.

When it comes to the principle of non-intervention, A. van Wynen Thomas and A. J. Thomas, Jr. claim that the origins of this principle may be traced back to the birth of American States as independent entities and reflect both the history and experiences of these nations, as well as attitudes of American leaders and jurists (van Wynen Thomas and Thomas Jr. 1956, p. 3). As long as this statement is true, it seems that the most relevant period of time for the crystallization of the principle of non-intervention is the nineteenth century, since in the course of this époque, European powers intervened many times in affairs of Latin American States. Thus, the emergence of the principle of non-intervention was the reaction to the policy of interventionism pursued by foreign powers against the American States (Thomas Jr. 1959, p. 73).

The efforts of States of American continent towards making principle of non-intervention the fundament of their foreign policy can be characterized as two-fold. On one hand, American States sought to codify the principle in legal acts. As the very first attempts of such codification one should point out the conclusions of the Congress of Panama of 1826. Other significant developments include, but are not limited to the Montevideo Convention on the Rights and Duties of States, Additional Protocol Relative to Non-Intervention, Inter-American Reciprocal Assistance and Solidarity Act, as well as the Charter of the Organization of the American States (the Bogota Charter).

The latter legal act will be discussed in details in part III of this chapter. However, it is indispensable to mention here some of the provisions of the Bogota Charter in terms of the principle of non-intervention. It is reflected not only in those articles which refer directly to the non-intervention, such as Articles 15, 16, 8 and 11, but also in these provisions that concern the prohibition of the use of force (Articles 5 (f), 17, 18), recognition (Article 9) and the sovereignty and equality of States (Articles 6, 7). As a result, the meaning of the principle of non-intervention is underlined under the Bogota Charter in many contexts and constitutes a fundament of relations between the Members of the Organization of American States (OAS).

On the other hand, however, apart from the attempts to legally codify the principle of non-intervention, American States formed political and legal doctrines, which promoted non-interference. Among them, one needs to mention Calvo and Drago doctrines (1868, 1902), as well as the Monroe doctrine.

Calvo and Drago doctrines referred to the prohibition of armed interventions because of financial disputes, and at end were codified in the Second Hague Convention with respect to the limitation of the employment of force for recovery of contract debts. When it comes to the Monroe doctrine, the US President James Monroe, in his message to the US Congress on 2 December 1823 proclaimed the principle of non-intervention in intercontinental relations (Pearce Higgins 1924, p. 103). In his statement, the principle consisted of two parts: promise of non-intervention by the United States in European affairs and warning against interventions by Europe in the affairs of American States. However, one should observe that despite the fact that the doctrine promoted solidarity of the whole American continent against European interventionism, the USA did not attempted to prevent all European interventions (van Wynen Thomas and Thomas Jr. 1956, pp. 11–12, 15–17). Moreover, also the United States itself many times intervened in the affairs of the Latin American States, what will be further discussed. As a result, the United States attitude only deepened the significance of the principle of non-intervention for the Latin American States.

The second principle which will be discussed, that is the principle of democratic governance, was highlighted from the very beginning of the independence of American States.

Despite the lack of explicit requirement that only democratic States can be members of the OAS, many legal acts adopted within the American system, including the Bogota Charter, clearly favor democratic regimes (Duxbury 2011, p. 171).

When it comes to the Bogota Charter, initially, it mentioned 'democracy' only in two passages: in the preamble, as well as in Article 5 (d) on the principles of the Organization. However, the Cartagena Protocol of 1985 which amended the Charter, introduced some substantial changes to the initial articles of the Charter. Thus, in the revised version of the Charter, the reference to 'representative democracy' was made in Articles 2 (b), 3 (d), Article 30 and Article 45. That is how the representative democracy became both the purpose and one of the principles of the OAS. However, the Charter does not stipulate how the 'representative democracy' as the purpose of the Organization should be achieved; as it turned out, this ambiguity contributed to the conflicts within the Organization, with the most serious one that occurred in relation to the situation in Panama in 1989 (Vasiliki 2011, p. 689).

The importance of democratic values was also supported by the creation of the Rio Group in 1986, which during its functioning suspended twice its members because of breach of democratic rules (Panama in 1989 and Peru in 1992) (ibid.). In this context, one can mention also the Santiago Commitment to Democracy and the Renewal of Inter-American System (1991), the OAS General Assembly Resolution 1080 (1991), Protocol of Washington (1992), Declaration of Quebec (2001), as well as Inter-American Democratic Charter (2001).[1]

---

[1] Available at: http://www.oas.org/charter/docs/resolution1_en_p4.htm.

Article 1 of this latter instrument stipulates democracy both as a right of the peoples of the Americas, as well as the obligation of governments to promote it and defend it. The most interesting part of Charter in the context of this paper seems to be Chapter IV, titled 'Strengthening and Preservation of Democratic Institutions', which determines the competences of the OAS in situation when the democracy will be endangered in one of the Member States. Thus, it is not only when 'the government of a member state considers that its democratic political institutional process or its legitimate exercise of power is at risk' which may prompt the reaction on the part of the OAS (Article 17), but the Organization itself may also undertake certain steps. Nevertheless, as long as Article 18 mentions launching the competences of the OAS 'with prior consent of the government concerned', Articles 19 and 20 allow Organization to decide on its own if the reaction of the Organization is necessary. The most serious measures the Inter-American Democratic Charter mentions in reaction to the breach of democracy in one of Member States are 'diplomatic initiatives' and suspension from the membership in the OAS.

Until today, only one State, that is Honduras (Vasiliki 2011, pp. 702–709) was suspended from the OAS on the basis of the Inter-American Democratic Charter. However, recently, the OAS discusses also the suspension of Venezuela due to the situation in that State. The gravest charges pressed against the Venezuelan government after the political shift in 2004 are that the government rejects the separation of powers, the judiciary ceased to be independent, human rights are violated and the political opposition is prosecuted.[2] The Venezuelan government strongly opposed convening the meeting of the OAS Permanent Council which was supposed to discuss the situation in Venezuela without its consent, and referred to Article 1 of the OAS Charter, which prohibits the Organization from intervention in internal affairs of Member States.[3] Venezuela declared the actions undertaken by the OAS as 'an act

---

[2] Human Rights Watch. "Venezuela: OAS Should Invoke Democratic Charter." https://www.hrw.org/news/2016/05/16/venezuela-oas-should-invoke-democratic-charter. Accessed on 25 July 2017.

[3] Sanders, Ronald. "Commentary: OAS Dysfunctionality Requires Charter Review." http://www.caribbeannewsnow.com/headline-Commentary%3A-OAS-dysfunctionality-requires-Charter-review-33968.html. Accessed on 25 July 2017; Charles, Jeanette. "OAS Fails to Reach Consensus on Venezuela Suspension in Latest Extraordinary Session." https://venezuelanalysis.com/news/13009. Accessed on 25 July 2017.

of interventionism being planned against Venezuela that is in violation of international law'.[4]

The Inter-American Democratic Charter itself could not serve as grounds for military intervention. However, in its preamble, the Charter enumerates, inter alia, the above mentioned Resolution 1080 of the OAS General Assembly. The Resolution is described in the Charter's preamble as establishing 'a mechanism for collective action' in case of breakdown of democracy in one of the OAS Member States. The Resolution 1080 itself is quite short and very imprecise. The most controversial passage of the resolution states that in the situation of the 'sudden or irregular interruption' of democracy in one of the Member States, the Secretary General may call the ad hoc meeting of the Ministers of Foreign Affairs or the special session of the General Assembly 'to look into the events collectively and adopt any decisions deemed appropriate, in accordance with the Charter and international law'.[5] Potentially, it could become the basis of collective intervention, including also military intervention, in the Member States that left the path of democracy.

However, it should be underlined here that the attachment of the Latin American States to democracy was not always the reason to intervene in the affairs of the OAS Member States, not to mention military interventions. For example, right after the creation of the OAS, the Caribbean States experienced series of internal turbulences, because of multiple cases of overthrown of the local governments. Due to the regularity of similar cases, the problem started to gain more geographical dimension and could potentially threaten the security of the whole continent. Nevertheless, even then, the American States supported the principle of non-intervention in the Declaration of Santiago of 1959, as one pointed by one Author, 'even if toleration of dictatorial régimes had to be the price of integrity' (Macdonald 1963–1964, pp. 367–368).

The Member States of the OAS were ready to agree on the interventions because of the failure of democratic governments only when the continent was threatened by the introduction of communism, like it happened in case of Cuba (Duxbury 2011, p. 173). Resolution VI, expelling

---

[4] Telesur. "Venezuela at OAS: If US Really Wants to Help, Stop Attacking Us." http://www.telesurtv.net/english/news/Venezuela-at-OAS-If-US-Really-to-Help-Stop-Attacking-Us-20170328-0032.html. Accessed on 25 July 2017.

[5] AG/RES. 1080 (XXI-O/91), Adopted at the Fifth Plenary Session, Held on 5 June 1991.

'present government' of Cuba from the OAS, adopted by the Eighth Meeting of Consultation of Ministers of Foreign Affairs in response to the situation in Cuba in 1962, condemned Cuba for introducing communism as its political system, and invoked the principle of non-intervention; however, in the meantime, the resolution did not explain how Cuba breached the principle of non-intervention and why the political system it wished to introduce was wrong from the standpoint of the OAS Member States (ibid., p. 174). It seems that the rationale behind this critique was the collective security of the OAS Member States which deemed communism as a threat to its peace and security, since the Resolution claimed that the connections between the governments of Cuba and the USSR 'are evidently incompatible with the principles and standards that govern the regional system, and particularly with the collective security' as established by the Bogota Charter and the Inter-American Treaty of Reciprocal Assistance (the Rio Treaty). That was also the context of the declarations made during the Tenth Conference of American States in Caracas with regard to the intervention in case of establishment of the communist regime in one of the American States (Thomas Jr. 1959, pp. 76–77).

Summing up the considerations upon the principle of non-intervention and principle of democratic governance in Latin American States, one should refer to the universal security system. Thus, the UN Charter does not mention the principle of non-intervention explicitly in any of its provisions. It rather underlines the meaning of the prohibition of the use of force, understood only as a form of military coercion, using the world 'to intervene' only once, in relation to the competences of the Organization towards the internal affairs of member States. On the other hand, it also does not refer to democracy at all but rather prohibits the use of force against 'political independence' of Member States and underlines the validity of States' sovereignty and self-determination.

This brief description of the regulations of the UN Charter is sufficient to underline the most important differences the Latin American and universal security systems. Thus, the universal approach focuses rather on the prohibition of the military interventions and the States' right to choose their own political systems, leaving aside the question of indirect intervention and the most suitable political system. The regional approach adopted by the Latin American States is, on the other hand, the result of their history and experiences that indicate the need to defend their independence on the very first place. However, it is not free from inconsistencies, it does not clearly accommodate the principle of non-intervention with its preference for democracy, what has been, and potentially will be, the reason of major crisis within the Organization.

INTERESTS: LATIN AMERICAN STATES' SECURITY INTERESTS

The second part of the chapter discussed the current interests of the Latin American States in terms of their internal and external security. These considerations focus on two points, that is the security interests within the community of the Latin American States, and the relations between the Latin America and the United States. However, it should be underlined that all the remarks are of overall character and their purpose is to underline the specific situation of the Latin American States interests under international law and with regard to security issues, and not to discuss all these questions exhaustively.

Thus, on the first place, one should highlight the most important security matters that arise within the community of Latin America from the perspective of international law.

First of all, while many parts of the world are currently potentially endangered by armed conflicts, both of international and non-international character, including Europe, Far East and Middle East, it is very unlikely that inter-State conflict could burst out in Latin America nowadays. Contrary to most inflammatory parts of the world, there are no religious or ethnic-hatred conflicts in Latin America. This situation is also reflected in figures since Latin American States has the lowers rate of inter-state conflicts and the lowest military expenditure related to GNP (Sorj 2005, p. 47).

However, two reservations should be made regarding this state of affairs. Firstly, even though it is highly unlikely that the use of force could occur nowadays in Latin America, there are still some territorial disputes (e.g. between Costa Rica and Nicaragua, Bolivia and Chile) (Jácome, p. 1); that was also the reason behind the last interstate conflict in Latin America that occurred in 1995 between Ecuador and Peru. Secondly, despite the lack of danger of inter-state conflicts, it does not mean that Latin America is a safe and non-violent region, since the it has to face several serious internal threats (Sorj 2005, pp. 46–47). States with the highest criminality rates are Mexico, Venezuela, Honduras, Nicaragua etc. (Holder 2014). In order to fight with the current threats to security of American States, the OAS has founded Committee on

Hemispheric Security and the Secretariat for Multidimensional Security to struggle with drug trafficking and organized crimes (Jácome, p. 1).

The second highlight which should be made is that it is hard to point any concise and comprehensive military doctrine which could present either the approach of the whole region or at least particular States. The Latin American States military doctrines were probably most visible in 1960s and 1970s, when they proclaimed the duty of the armed forces to take over control over the State from the civilian leaders when the latter turned out to be incapable to effectively govern the State. However, the military doctrines in Latin America also had another component, that is interest in national security against indirect aggression (Fitch 1998, pp. 109–110, 115).

Nevertheless, in the context of military and political doctrines, the very recent phenomenon of ALBA needs to be mentioned. ALBA stands for the Bolivarian Alliance of the Americas, which refers to the idea of Simón Bolívar creating Gran Colombia (Hirst). The Alliance, which was founded in 2004 by Venezuelan president Hugo Chávez and the President of Cuba of that time, Fidel Castro, has currently 11 members. The Alliance declares i.a. that it 'inherits Bolivar's anti-imperialist legacy' and constitutes 'the FTAA's [Free Trade Area of the Americas] antithesis given how it defines itself in direct opposition the free trade ideology which underlies agreements such as the FTAA'.[6] In fact, ALBA seeks to replace the US influences in the region, 'with a toxic mix of anti-democratic values, massive corruption, and a doctrine that draws on terrorism and totalitarian models, including the justification of the use of weapons of mass destruction against the United States' (Farah 2015, pp. 92–93). Thus, the ALBA States promote values far from the Western concepts of sovereignty and protection of human rights, supporting Syrian regime or annexation of Crimea.

Finally, one needs to pay attention to the emergence of many subregional organizations in Latin America. As one Author put it, while the USA present hemispheric approach towards security issues, the Latin American States have more local vision (Sorj 2005, p. 48). Also A. Varas stays very critical towards the current state of security affairs in American continent as he claims that new developments in the context of global security requires 'moving beyond rigid, inefficient, obsolete

---

[6]ALBA Info. "What is the ALBA?" https://albainfo.org/what-is-the-alba/. Accessed on 25 July 2017.

institutionalization of security matters at the hemispheric level', as well as shifting the balance towards sub-regional Organizations, which are more appropriate, given the contemporary interests of American States (Varas 1998, p. 12). Among such sub-regional systems addressing the needs of States one should enumerate Andean Community, Mercosur, as well as Central American Integration System. These sub-regional initiatives deal not only with the economic issues, since they also developed their own security policies (for such purposed as fight with drug trafficking etc.) (Jácome, pp. 1–2).

When it comes to the relations between the Latin American States and the United States, as Donald T. Fox observes, even though American States share common values, it was 'the unique combination of circumstances which enabled the United States quickly to attain power, prosperity and political stability' (Fox 1968, p. 44). This characteristic very clearly illustrates the mutual relations between the Northern and Southern parts of the American continent—on one hand, integrated by common values, on the other—divided by the supremacy of the United States.

Thus, the US potential was the reason behind many attempts in the history of the continent when the United States tried to impose its policies on the Latin American States throughout interventions, including also armed interventions. As it was stated above, despite the Monroe doctrine, Latin American States were subjected to numerous interventions in the nineteenth century, not only on the part of the European States, but also the United States (Caminos 1988, p. 159) (just to mention the US intervention in Cuba in 1898).

The new époque did not bring any change of this attitude since it is even hard to enumerate all the examples of the United States interventions in Latin American at the beginning of the twentieth century; just to mention a few direct military interventions, one can invoke military occupation of San Domingo (1916–1924), Haiti (1915–1934), Nicaragua (1928–1933). The costs of the last of these interventions, that is the one in Nicaragua, outweighed the benefits, and contributed to the change in American policy, marked by the 'Good Neighbor Policy'. The Policy was subsequently codified in Article 8 of the Montevideo Convention and confirmed during Buenos Aires conference (Fox 1968, pp. 45–48).

During the Cold War, the major purpose for the US interventions was to establish or to maintain democracy and to prevent the instalment of communism in any of the Latin American States. Among the most widely discussed interventions, are undoubtedly the 'defensive quarantine' during the Cuban missile crisis, as well as the US interventions in the Dominican Republic and in Panama.

The former one took place in 1965 when the series of the coup d'état helped colonel Caemaño to took over the control of the major parts of the State's territory. Since the United States supported the junta which was overthrown by Caemaño, in April 1965 it started the intervention in the Dominican Republic (Doswald-Beck 1985, pp. 226–228). Among a few justifications for the intervention, the US invoked also the validation of the intervention by the OAS, since the Organization decided to support the establishment of the peacekeeping forces in the Dominican Republic in the aftermath of the US intervention. As the US explained, the OAS could condemn the intervention, but decided to endorse it. Moreover, the USA claimed that the UN Security Council (UN SC) was not competent to discuss the intervention since the problem which arose within the Dominican Republic was of regional character, so it should have been resolved by regional tools, including the OAS involvement (Kanakaratne 1965, pp. 107–108).

When it comes to the intervention in Panama, even though the situation in that State was deteriorating since 1987 (which, according to the US government, influenced also the situation of the US citizens in Panama who were allegedly persecuted by the authorities), the major crisis occurred in May 1989, when general Manuel Noriega attempted to overthrow the newly elected president Guillermo Endara. His efforts turned out to be successful since in September 1989 he formed a new government. In December 1989, the parliament of Panama adopted the resolution which declared that Panama is in state of war with the United States because of the aggression launched by the USA against the Panamanian nation; however, the resolution was reported in the USA as the declaration of war against the USA. Consequently, on December 20, 1989 the USA started the intervention in Panama (Henkin 1991, p. 301; Wedgwood 1991, pp. 610–617).

The Panama case illustrates also another phenomenon—the OAS condemned the Noriega regime labelled it as the threat for international peace and security but did not undertake any decisive actions. The condemnation encouraged the United Statesintervention which soon took over the initiative, starting the intervention. Thus, Panama case showed how the efforts to protect democracy can lead to the breach of the most fundamental principle of international law in American continent, that is the principle of non-intervention (Farer 1996, p. 14).

However, apart from direct military interventions, one needs to mention that the USA also intervened indirectly in few Latin American States, including probably the most widely discussed intervention in Nicaragua, which was assessed by the International Court of Justice in the case concerning military and paramilitary activities in and against that States. The ICJ determined that the US activities in Nicaragua included, inter alia, laying mines in Nicaraguan ports, conduct of high and low-altitude reconnaissance flights, financing contras, providing them with logistic support, the supply of information, radar coverage, information on the location and movements of enemies' forces etc. (Military and Paramilitary Activities in and against Nicaragua 1968, para. 80, 91, 95, 106). In its judgement, the ICJ ruled out that by 'training, arming, equipping, financing and supplying' paramilitary activities in Nicaragua, the USA were 'in breach of its obligation under customary international law not to intervene in the affairs of another State' (ibid., para. 292(3)).

The US interventions in Latin America were condemned by the Latin American States, even though not by all of them. The reason behind such attitude was that during the Cold War period, relations between the US and Latin American States were greatly affected by their relation towards the communist regimes emerging in Western hemisphere—those States that were willing to fight with the threat on the part of communism, established stronger ties with the USA (Varas 1998, p. 20).

However, it should be also observed that in recent years, the position of the USA in region is decreasing, leaving the vacuum, used by such powers as China and Russia (Farah 2015, pp. 91–92). Moreover, such States as Venezuela, take the USA as the aim for their attacks, just to refer to the ALBA example mentioned above. In 2012, it was announced that Venezuela seeks to strengthen its forces to prepare to the 'popular war' with 'the empire', so the USA, and to that end, reinforces the guerilla forces. By 2019, two million recruits are supposed to join Venezuelan forces to support fights during the prospective US invasion.[7]

Summing up, the major threats for the Latin American States are not the ones which are reason for concern for the majority of the international community, like the international terrorism, proliferation of

---

[7] "Venezuela Plans a Million Strong 'Guerrilla Army' against US Invasion". *The Telegraph.* http://www.telegraph.co.uk/news/worldnews/southamerica/venezuela/9471752/Venezuela-plans-a-million-strong-guerrilla-army-against-US-invasion.html. Accessed on 25 July 2017.

weapons of mass destruction or migration, but rather the American continent faces the threats that are specific for the region. Consequently, the tools and instruments that are available for the Latin American States should be suited for their particular needs and threats they face. On the other hand, the role of the USA as the hegemon is declining. The rationale behind it could the fact that in past the United States many times showed that despite the alleged solidarity and hemispheric approach towards security issues, these are the US interests that prevail and only occasionally they find support among Latin American States.

INSTITUTIONS: LATIN AMERICAN INSTITUTIONAL SECURITY FRAMEWORK

The aim of this part is to discuss the institutional framework of the Latin American system as reflected in the three treaty pillars of this system, namely, the Charter of the OAS, The Inter-American Treaty of Reciprocal Assistance and Treaty for the Prohibition of Nuclear Weapons in Latin America and the Caribbean. Thus, this part depicts the major finding of these treaties, their significance for the security system, as well as differences between them and the general international law. However, it should be beard in mind, that these three treaties are not the only ones that form the institutional framework for the Latin American security system, and they are completed by many other acts and not-binding declarations.

Discussion upon the institutional security framework in American continent needs to begin with spotlight on the Bogota Charter, the foundation of the most important regional organization.

The Charter is composed of twenty-two chapters, including Chapters I, II, IV, VI and XIX, which are of special importance for this chapter.

Chapter I declares 'Nature and Purposes' of the Organization, among which one needs to underline the defense of sovereignty, territorial integrity, and independence (Article 1), strengthening the peace and security of the continent, promotion of representative democracy, with due respect for the principle of nonintervention, as well as pacific settlement of disputes among the OAS Member States' (Article 2 (a)–(c)).

Chapter II includes "Principles" of the Organization, including the solidarity of the American States the need of the effective exercise of representative democracy, the right of Member States to choose, without external interference, its political, economic, and social system; the duty to abstain from intervening in the affairs of other States; condemnation war of aggression; as well as principle of collective self-defense.

Chapter IV, which refers to 'Fundamental rights and duties of States', underlines that 'States are juridically equal, enjoy equal rights and equal capacity to exercise these rights, and have equal duties' (Article 10). Moreover, Article 19 reiterates the principles of non-intervention, since it states that 'No State or group of States has the right to intervene, directly or indirectly, for any reason whatever, in the internal or external affairs of any other State', and underlined that it refers not only to armed interventions but also any other form of interference of political, economic or cultural character. Further, Article 22 refers to the prohibition of the use of force.

Bearing in mind that content of these first chapters of the Charter, one can make a few observations. Firstly, the Bogota Charter contains a very important difference comparing to the general international law—the principle of non-intervention prohibits explicitly all forms of intervention, not only by armed forces, while under general international law it is allowed for some non-military means of reaction against States responsible for violations of international law (Thomas Jr. 1959, p. 74). Moreover, contrary to the UN Charter, the Bogota Charter, does not leave any doubts as to whether the prohibition of intervention should be applied only to armed actions, what still remains controversial under the UN Charter. Secondly, the Bogota Charter does not refer to the protection of human rights, neither as the principle nor purpose of the Organization. It is so because Latin American States were rather focused on their sovereignty than the protection of human rights (Sorj 2005, p. 43), and the latter concept was deemed as idea that could be implemented only if it was not about to jeopardize the sovereignty of States (Duxbury 2011, p. 173). Thirdly, even though the UN Charter proclaims the sovereign equality of States, it does not mention 'judicial equality', promoted by the Bogota Charter as one of the foundations of the organization (S/25996, para. 13). What's more, the concept of the 'judicial equality of States' is not only declared as the right and duty of Member States, but also finds the factual application in the following chapters of the Charter and rules of functioning of the organs of the Organization—the OAS Charter does not privilege any Member States with the right to veto the resolutions adopted by the Organization, as well as all Member States are represented in all major organs of the

Organization. Finally, while the prohibition of the use of force was designated as the most basic principle of the UN Charter, the OAS Charter does not highlight the meaning of the prohibition that much, placing it as the last of the 'fundamental rights and duties of States'.

It should also be highlighted that the OAS has longer experience than the UN in terms of collective security and cooperation for peace and stability, and these were Latin American States that were promoting the idea of collective security during San Francisco conference, what eventually led to the inclusion of provisions of Chapter VII, as well as the regulation of collective self-defense in Article 51 in the UN Charter (ibid., para. 3). Not surprisingly, the OAS Charter also contains a chapter devoted to the collective security (Chapter VII).

The last chapter that should be mentioned here is Chapter XIX which concerns the relations with the United Nations organizations, declaring that 'None of the provisions of this Charter shall be construed as impairing the rights and obligations of the Member States under the Charter of the United Nations'. However, this formula is not only a mere repetition of Article 103 of the UN Charter but is much more meaningful bearing in mind that OAS is also a 'regional arrangement' mentioned in Chapter VIII of the UN Charter. Consequently, the OAS cannot undertake 'enforcement action' without the authorization of the UN SC. As the following subchapter on the Rio Treaty will depict, this provision can constitute sometimes an important limitation on the OAS actions and policy.

When it comes to the Rio Treaty its core provision is undoubtedly Article 3, which states that 'an armed attack by any State against an American State shall be considered as an attack against all the American States' and, consequently, will cause the reaction of the American States under 'the inherent right of individual or collective self-defense recognized by Article 51 of the Charter of the United Nations' (para. 1). However, this latter phrase does not mean that under the Rio Treaty, the notion of collective measures, as well as self-defense, are understood in the same way as under general international law, including the UN Charter.

The first major difference concerns the criteria of application of the right to collective self-defense. Under the UN Charter, the collective measures of self-defense may be applicable only when an armed attack occurred; however, this issue is not that clear under the Rio Treaty. Article 6 of the latter states that:

If the inviolability or the integrity of the territory or the sovereignty or political independence of any American State should be affected by an aggression which is not an armed attack or by an extra-continental or intra-continental conflict, or by any other fact or situation might endanger the peace of America, the Organ of Consultation shall meet immediately in order to agree on the measures which must be taken in case of aggression to assist the victim of the aggression or, in any case, the measures which should be taken for the common defense and for the maintenance of the peace and security of the Continent.

It stems from it that even when an armed attack did not occur, but the Member State of the OAS is 'only' endangered, already on that stage, the Organ of Consultation may undertake certain measures to preserve peace and security or assist the endangered State. Consequently, the collective measures of self-defense under the Rio Treaty may be undertaken also in case of an imminent threat of aggression or armed attack. This conclusion does not stay at variance with the restrictive interpretation of the right to self-defense, as applied by the Latin American States, which would allow self-defense only after an armed attack occurred, and not because of imminent threat. It is so since the Rio Treaty does not grant any rights to individual States but refers only to collective measures undertaken by the OAS as the whole (van Wynen Thomas and Thomas Jr. 1959, pp. 182–183). Moreover, the measures undertaken by the OAS not necessarily have to be of armed character.

The Rio Treaty serves both as the system of collective self-defense under Article 3, and as regional arrangement under Chapter VIII of the UN Charter. Consequently, under Chapter VIII of the UN Charter, any use of 'enforcement measures' require authorization on the part of the UN SC (ibid., pp. 177–178, 207). However, one needs to observe that majority of measures which may be undertaken under the Rio Treaty in order to repel the armed attack, as collective measures, are not of armed character since Article 8 mentions that:

For the purposes of this Treaty, the measures on which the Organ of Consultation may agree will comprise one or more of the following: recall of chiefs of diplomatic missions; breaking of diplomatic relations; breaking of consular relations; partial or complete interruption of economic relations or of rail, sea, air, postal, telegraphic, telephonic, and radiotelephonic or radiotelegraphic communications; and use of armed force.

Few doubts can be raised with regard to this provision. First of all, the right to self-defense amounts to the right to use force, not to use nonforcible measures. However, Article 8 of the Rio Treaty, among collective measures to be undertaken in case of an armed attack in exercise of the right to self-defense, enumerates five measures of not armed character and the use of force at the very end. As a result, one could pose a question whether the measures enumerated in Article 8 of the Rio Treaty still constitute self-defense and may be named as such (ibid., p. 186).

That is why, A. van Wynen Thomas and A. J. Thomas, Jr. claim that if the measures undertaken by the Organ of Consultation are of peaceful character, they do not require the authorization from the part of the UN, since Article 53 requires such authorization only in case of armed measures, as well as Article 52 (3) permits the use of peaceful measures by regional arrangements. According to these Authors, only if the Organ of Consultation would like to use military measures against the actions of Member States not of an armed character, the authorization of the UN SC is clearly required (ibid., p. 198).

A. van Wynen Thomas and A. J. Thomas, Jr. formed their opinions in 1959, so years before the most famous and broadly discussed case of application of Article 8 of the Rio Treaty, namely the Cuban missile crisis. After the US government discovered the construction of the missile facilities in Cuba, the National Security Council considered different scenario and different legal justifications for the prospective intervention aimed at destruction of the facilities. Eventually, the USA decided to apply the so called 'defensive quarantine', however, with no justification under international law (Munton, para. 1–7). That is why, the US legal advisors decided to turn to the OAS looking for legal grounds for the 'quarantine'. The US government called for a meeting of the OAS Council, which serving as the Organ of Consultation, under Articles 6 and 8 of the Rio Treaty, on 23 October 1962 enacted the Resolution 'on the adoption of necessary measures to prevent Cuba from threatening the peace and security of the Continent'. The major point of the resolution was paragraph 2, which stated that:

> to take all measures, individually and collectively, including the use of armed force, which they may deem necessary to ensure that the Government of Cuba cannot continue to receive from the Sino-Soviet powers material and related supplies which may threaten the peace and security of the Continent and to prevent the missiles in Cuba with

offensive capability from ever becoming an active threat to the peace and security of the Continent.

The United States claimed that the measures undertaken under the OAS Resolution were not enforcement measures but a recommendation, and Article 53 (1) of the UN Charter was not applicable; consequently, the authorization on the part of the UN SC was not required (Meeker 1963, pp. 521–522). Moreover, the US government explained that the measures introduced under the Resolution were legal since the UN SC turned out to be ineffective organ in similar situations in the past, and when the UN SC is paralysed by the veto of one of its Permanent Members, the alternative solutions are available. Within the UN framework, these alternatives include the measures undertaken by the UN Secretary-General and the UN GA; outside the UN, this role is performed by the regional arrangements, including the OAS (Chayes 1962–1963, p. 556). Nevertheless, despite these claims, the defensive quarantine constituted enforcement measure under Chapter VII and required the authorization of the UN SC on the grounds of Article 53 (1) of the UN Charter.

Summing up, it stems from that even if the OAS undertakes measures virtually of non-armed character, such as blockade of a State, they constitute enforcement measures and consequently, require the authorization of the UN SC. However, if the measures are of an armed character, but are undertaken in the exercise of the right to collective self-defence, do they still require the authorization of the UN SC or, as right to self-defence, may be exercised discretionally by the OAS until the UN SC 'has taken the measures necessary to maintain international peace and security' (Article 3 (4) of the Rio Treaty)? That issue can potential become in future another moot point.

Finally, despite these apparent contradictions between the interpretation of the Rio Treaty and the UN Charter, one needs to observe that the UN Charter completes the provisions of the Rio Treaty. It is apparent also from the terminology used under the Rio Treaty since some of the provisions of the Rio Treaty are addressed not only to 'High Contracting Parties', but refer to 'any American State'. However, it does not mean that the Rio Treaty imposes obligations on third parties, since the provisions addressing some obligations to non-member States are of general nature and fit within the framework of obligations connected with international peace and security as binding under the UN Charter. On the other hand, a Treaty can refer to third parties if it grants them rights; that is the case here, the more since these 'rights' under the Rio Treaty are connected with the collective self-defense, anyway recognized under the UN Charter (van Wynen Thomas and Thomas Jr. 1959, pp. 211–212).

Finally, as the last institutional pillar of the Latin American security system one needs to mention the Treaty for the Prohibition of Nuclear Weapons in Latin America and the Caribbean (Treaty of Tlatelolco) which created the first one nuclear-free zone in the populated area (Espiell 1978, p. 25). Thus, even though in the times of the Cold War the whole international community lived in fear of nuclear war, these were the Latin American States that as the first ones decided to proceed with the legal act in order to repel such threats. Certainly, the Cuban missile crisis, caused by the construction of facilities capable to launch missile with nuclear warheads, helped Latin American States to realize that the danger that Great Powers may use the American continent to start the nuclear conflict was serious and they should prevent similar attempts (Epstein 2001, pp. 157–158). Thus, the treaty of 14 February 1967 turned into reality concepts of withdrawing the whole continent from the nuclear race (Espiell 1978, p. 26), since in Article 1 (1) of the Treaty its parties decided 'to use exclusively for peaceful purposes the nuclear material and facilities which are under their jurisdiction'.

The legal and political meaning of the treaty is reinforced by few factors. First of all, all States of American continent are parties to the Treaty. Secondly, one of the parties to the Additional Protocol I and II is the United States. The ratification of the Protocol I by the USA is particularly significant since due to this, the Treaty is applicable also to the territories under the US jurisdiction, which are of utmost political and military importance, such as military bases located in Guantanamo, Virgin Islands and Porto Rico (Espiell 1977, p. 570). Thirdly, not only American States are parties to the free-nuclear zone created by the Treaty, but also such States as France, the United Kingdom, China, Russia and Netherlands signed the Protocols Additional to the Treaty. Finally, the Treaty fits into framework created by the UN GA resolutions on disarmament and denuclearization.

It is worth to underline, that in the face of constant failure of the United Nations to engage all Member States in denuclearization process, adoption of the Treaty of Tlatelolco helped to revive and encouraged similar developments in other parts of the world. These developments include, but are not limited to the adoption of following legal acts: South Pacific Nuclear-Free Zone Treaty of 1985, Treaty on the South-East Asia Nuclear-Weapon-Free Zone of 1995, African Nuclear-Weapon-Free Zone Treaty and Treaty on the Nuclear-Weapon-Free Zone in Central Asia, and as a result, creation of the denuclearized zones in respective parts of the world.

Neither parties to the Treaty of Tlatelolco nor third States ever attempted to diminish the significance of the Treaty or apply such an interpretation of the Treaty as to allow for instalment of nuclear weapon in Latin America.

Summing up, despite the restrictive regulation of Article 2 (4) of the UN Charter, as well as rigid requirements for self-defense under Article 51, the Latin American legal instruments tend to slightly change this framework, not only by adding the explicit prohibition of indirect aggression but also because of the whole range of nonmilitary measures which may be used to repel armed attack as the tool of collective self-defense. Even though introduction of such measures into the Latin American system not necessarily amount to contradiction with the UN Charter, it seems that the Latin American States attempted more to follow their traditions in terms of security issues than to fit itself into the framework imposed by the UN Charter. In the past, some situation occurred when the Latin American States opposed to the actions undertaken by the UN SC claiming that the issue at stake is of regional character, as well as undertook actions on their own, without the authorization of the part of the UN organs. However, one should bear in mind, that as long as differences between the universal and regional security systems are not surprising, these differences cannot prevent universal organs from safeguarding international peace and security.

Interactions: Security System in Latin America vs. Universal Security System—Internal Law Perspective

Due to its history and experiences of relations with the rest of the international community, the Latin American States created its own security system, specific and distinct from the universal one. It is visible both in terms of the principles most valuable for the Latin American States, including especially the principle of non-intervention, and in their approach towards security issues, which prompts strong reaction towards any attempts of imposing on them foreign will. However, this attitude is striking not only in relation to other regions of the world, but also within continent;

moreover, this latter statement refers both to the United States and relations within the Latin American States community. More than any other group of States in any other part of the world, Latin American States are very sensitive to any attempts of intervention into their domestic affairs, even though the system they created envisages the possibilities of intervention even in case of the change of political regime in one of the Member States. Thus, the clash between the principle of non-intervention and Latin American attachment to democracy is becoming more and more serious problem, as the example of Venezuela shows, and requires changes and further developments, not only in reaction to this particular case, but on the institutional level. Potentially, the system which favors one particular form of political regime could turned out to be more effective, also with regard to the preservation and reaction in case of political crisis, since it imposes concrete requirements on its members, but it seems apparent now that it cannot be reconciled with the principle of non-intervention.

On the other hand, the distinctiveness of Latin America is built up also upon the lack of potential sources of inter-State conflicts in Latin America and minimal threat of terrorist attacks, which endanger nowadays potentially any part of the world. Thus, paradoxically, it dismisses Latin American States from the problems shared by, e.g. Europe, North America, Asia and Africa. However, stabile situation and peaceful cooperation between Latin American States led to the creation of the first nuclear-free zone, as well as other serious developments in disarmament, what would be hard to achieve anywhere else in the world.

CONCLUSIONS

The paper discussed the Latin American security system in four dimensions: ideas, understood as principle of non-intervention and commitment for democracy; interests, including brief analysis of inter-State relations in Latin America, as well as their relations with the United States; institutions, with reference to three most important institutional pillars of the system; as well as interactions between this triad. Even though the paper makes only an overall assessment of the Latin American security issues, it highlights that the system that Latin American States created is distinct from the universal one and based on different values and experiences. However, it does not mean that it is deprived of any flaws, even if the problems the Latin American States have to face are different that the ones that plague the rest of the international community.

REFERENCES

Literature

Alvarez, Alejandro. 1909. Latin America and International Law. *American Journal of International Law* 3 (2): 269–353.

Caminos, Hugo. 1988. The Latin American Contribution to International Law. In *The American Society of International Law Proceedings of the 80th Annual Session*, 157–161, Washington.

Chayes, Abram. 1962–1963. Law and the Quarantine of Cuba. *Foreign Affaires* 41: 550–557.

Doswald-Beck, Louise. 1985. The Legality of Military Intervention by Invitation of the Government. *The British Year Book of International Law* 56 (1): 189–252.

Duxbury, Alison. 2011. *The Participation of State in International Organization: The Role of Human Rights and Democracy*. Cambridge: Cambridge University Press.

Epstein, William. 2001. The Making of the Treaty of Tlatelolco. *The Journal of History of International Law* 3 (2): 153–179.

Espiell, Hector Gros. 1977. U.S.A. e denuclearizzazione nell'America Latina. *Rivista di Studi Politici Internazionali* 44 (4): 565–578.

Espiell, Hector Gros. 1978. The Treaty for the Prohibition of Nuclear Weapons in Latin America (The Tlatelolco Treaty): Present Situation and Future Prospects. *AEA Bulletin* 20 (5): 25–34.

Farah, Douglas. 2015. The Advance of Radical Populist Doctrine in Latin America How the Bolivarian Alliance is Remaking Militaries, Dismantling Democracy and Combatting the Empire. *PRISM* 5 (3): 91–105.

Farer, Thomas. 1996. Collectively Defending Democracy in the Western Hemisphere: Introduction and Overview. In *Beyond Sovereignty: Collectively Defending Democracy in the Americas*, ed. Thomas Farer, 1–28. Baltimore and London: John Hopkins University Press.

Fitch, John Samuel. 1998. *The Armed Forces and Democracy in Latin America*. Baltimore: Johns Hopkins University.

Fox, Donald T. 1968. Doctrinal Development in the Americas: From Non-intervention to Collective Support for Human Rights. *New York University Journal of International Law and Politics* 1 (1): 44–60.

Henkin, Louis. 1991. The Invasion of Panama Under International Law: A Gross Violation. *Columbia Journal of Transnational* 29: 503–515.

Jácome, Francine. Security Perspectives in Latin America. *THINK PIECE 04: Friedrich-Ebert-Stiftung*, 1–6. www.library.fes.de/pdf-files/iez/12103.pdf.

Kanakaratne, N.T.D. 1965. US Intervention and the UN Charter. *Guild Practitioner* 24: 106–116.

Macdonald, Ronald St. J. 1963–1964. The Organization of American States in Action. *University of Toronto Journal* 15 (2): 359–429.

Meeker, Leonard C. 1963. Defensive Quarantine and the Law. *American Journal of International Law* 57: 515–524.

Pearce Higgins, Alexander. 1924. The Monroe Doctrine. *British Year Book of International Law* 5: 103–118.

Sorj, Bernardo. 2005. Security, Human Security and Latin America. *Sur— International Journal on Human Rights* 3: 39–55.

Thomas, A.J., Jr. 1959. Non-intervention and Public Order in Americas. In *Proceedings of the American Society of International Law at Its Fifty-Third Annual Meeting*, April 30–May 2, 72–80.

van Wynen Thomas, Ann, and A.J. Thomas Jr. (eds.). 1956. *Non-intervention. The Law and Its Import in the Americas*. Dallas: Southern Methodist University Press.

van Wynen Thomas, Ann, and A.J. Thomas Jr. 1959. The Organization of American States and Collective Security. *Southwestern Law Journal* 13 (2): 177–214.

Varas, Augusto. 1998. Cooperative Hemispheric Security after the Cold War. In *Regional Mechanisms and International Security in Latin America*, ed. Olga Pellicer, 10–44. Tokyo: United Nations University Press.

Vasiliki, Saranti. 2011. A System of Collective Defense of Democracy: The Case of Inter-American Democratic Charter. *Goettingen Journal of International Law* 3: 675–714.

Wedgwood, Ruth. 1991. The Use of Force in International Affairs Self-Defense and the Panama Invasion. *Columbia Journal of International* 29: 609–628.

Material Sources

Additional Protocol Relative to Non-intervention. In *United States Treaties and International Agreement, Compiled by Charles I. Bevans 3 (1931–1945)*. Washington: Department of State 1968.

The Caracas Declaration of Solidarity of March 28, 1954. http://avalon.law.yale.edu/20th_century/intam10.asp. Accessed on 25 July 2017.

Declaration of Principles of Inter-American Solidarity and Cooperation. In *Report of the Delegation of the United States of America to the Inter-American Conference for the Maintenance of Peace, Buenos Aires, Argentina, December 1–23, 1936*. Washington: U.S. Government Printing Office 1937.

Inter-American Reciprocal Assistance and Solidarity Act. In *United States Treaties and International Agreement, Compiled by Charles I. Bevans 3 (1931–1945)*. Washington: Department of State 1968.

International American Conference, Historical Appendix. The Congress of 1826, Panama, and Subsequent Movements Towards a Conference of American Nations: Reports of Committees and Discussion Thereon, Vol. IV. Washington: Government Printing Office 1890.

Letter dated 29 April 1965 from the Permanent Representative of the United States of America Addressed to the President of the Security Council/ Presidential Statement on the Dominican Situation, issued at 9 p.m., 28 April 1965, S/6310.

Military and Paramilitary Activities in and against Nicaragua (Nicaragua v. United States of America), Merits, Judgement, ICJ Reports 1986, p. 14.

Montevideo Convention on the Rights and Duties of States. League of Nations Treaty Series (1933): 165–119.

OAS General Assembly Resolution 1080, AG/RES. 1080 (XXI-O/91), Adopted at the Fifth Plenary Session, Held on June 5, 1991.

Report of Secretary—General: An Agenda for Peace: Preventing Diplomacy, Peacemaking and Peace-Keeping. Replies Received from Intergovernmental Organizations: The Organization of American States, S/25996.

Resolution on the Adoption of Necessary Measures to Prevent Cuba from Threatening the Peace and Security of the Continent, 23 October 1962 [w:] *American Republics Act to Halt Soviet Threat to Hemisphere: Text of Resolution*, The Department of State Bulletin November 12, 1962, Vol. XLVII, no. 1220.

Resolutions Adopted at the Eighth Meeting of Consultation of Ministers of Foreign Affairs, Punta del Este, Uruguay, January 22–31, 1962. http://avalon.law. yale.edu/20th_century/intam17.asp. Accessed on 25 July 2017.

UN Security Council, 1196th Meeting, Official Records, 3 May 1965, S/PV.1196.

Internet Sources

ALBA Info. What is the ALBA? https://albainfo.org/what-is-the-alba/. Accessed on 25 July 2017.

Central American Integration System. Historical Overview of SICA. http:// www.sica.int/sica/resena_sica_en.aspx. Accessed on 25 July 2017.

Charles, Jeanette. OAS Fails to Reach Consensus on Venezuela Suspension in Latest Extraordinary Session. https://venezuelanalysis.com/news/13009. Accessed on 25 July 2017.

Hirst, Joel D. What is the Bolivarian Alternative to the Americas and What Does It Do? *Americas Quarterly.* http://www.americasquarterly.org/HIRST/ ARTICLE#hirst. Accessed on 25 July 2017.

Holder, Frank. Public Insecurity in Latin America, March 2014. FTI Consulting. http://www.fticonsulting.com/~/media/Files/us-files/insights/reports/ 2014-latin-america-security-index.pdf. Accessed on 25 July 2017.

Human Rights Watch. Venezuela: OAS Should Invoke Democratic Charter. https://www.hrw.org/news/2016/05/16/venezuela-oas-should-invoke-democratic-charter. Accessed on 25 July 2017.

Munton, Don. Cuban Missile Crisis. In Max Planck Encyclopedia of Public International Law. http://opil.ouplaw.com.

Sanders, Ronald. Commentary: OAS Dysfunctionality Requires Charter Review. http://www.caribbeannewsnow.com/headline-Commentary%3A-OAS-dysfunctionality-requires-Charter-review-33968.html. Accessed on 25 July 2017.

Telesur. Venezuela at OAS: If US Really Wants to Help, Stop Attacking Us. http://www.telesurtv.net/english/news/Venezuela-at-OAS-If-US-Really-Wants-to-Help-Stop-Attacking-Us-20170328-0032.html. Accessed on 25 July 2017.

Venezuela Plans a Million Strong 'Guerrilla Army' against US Invasion. The Telegraph. http://www.telegraph.co.uk/news/worldnews/southamerica/venezuela/9471752/Venezuela-plans-a-million-strong-guerrilla-army-against-US-invasion.html. Accessed on 25 July 2017.

Security at the Centre of Post 2000 EU–Africa Relations

Lola Reich

Relations between the African and the European continents, albeit the colonial legacy, have remained close knitted. Starting with the provision within the Rome Treaties (1957), the tight partnership evolved through the Youndé Agreements (1964–1969) and Lomé Conventions (1975–2000). The two last Lomè agreements and their successor, the Cotonou Partnership Agreement (CPA), signed in 2000, introduced an increasing emphasis on political stability and security. Thus, while development policies have a long history, security issues gained salience, particularly as the conflicts, civil wars and interstate wars in Africa (especially sub-Saharan Africa) reached a peak during the 1990s and continued to remain a concern to the European Union (EU) also at the dawn of the new century.

The first part of this chapter will focus on how the foreign and security policy of the EU (and especially its strategic peace and security partnership with Africa/JAES P&S) was profoundly informed and framed within the paradigm shifts in the conceptualisations of security, development and regional integration. Concerning the security concept, around

L. Reich (✉)
University of Vienna, Vienna, Austria
e-mail: lola.raich@univie.ac.at

© The Author(s) 2018
P. Frankowski and A. Gruszczak (eds.),
Cross-Disciplinary Perspectives on Regional and Global Security,
https://doi.org/10.1007/978-3-319-75280-8_6

113

this time we observe the rapid salience of the human security (HS) concept as opposed to a traditional state-centric security as well as to the security-development-nexus both of which have made peremptory comprehensive and coherent policies that take into account the symbiotic interrelationship between security and development concerns. Another important paradigm has been that on regional integration and cooperation as an appropriate instrument in tackling security and instability in said regions. The EU has proved a weighty example in this matter. Concerning Africa, this last issue intensified and reached its peak with the creation of the African Union (AU) at the dawn of the new century, providing Africa with an important structure with which to present itself as a unified actor within the international arena. The analysis will show how the EU within said discourses managed to find niches that substantiated its claims as a to be taken seriously international security provider, while at the same time endeavouring to forward its (and its member states) explicit interests vis-á-vis the African continent.

The second part of the chapter will then focus on the inter-institutional interactions.

FRAMING OF SECURITY & PROMOTION OF INTERESTS

In 2000, the then EU Portuguese Presidency clearly stated the security concerns by interlinking them with development issues: 'Being realistic about development means thinking in an integrated manner about politics, security and trade as well as development aid itself' (Cardoso et al. 2000; Hadfield 2007, p. 45). At about the same time, the EU and Africa held their first ever summit on continental level, in Cairo, Egypt. The resulting Cairo Declaration together with an Action Plan highlighted the main issues of concern between the two parties. Security figured prominently in both the documents, due to the acknowledgement that: 'persistence of numerous conflicts, which continue to cause [...] loss of human life as well as destruction of infrastructure and property threaten peace, stability, regional and international security and hinder the aspirations of African peoples to peace, prosperity and development' (Cairo Declaration 2000)

Subsequent to the terrorist attacks on 9/11, the already ongoing debate on European security focused on the necessity to tackle terrorism adequately (Allen and Smith 2002, p. 97; Boer and Monar 2002, pp. 11–28). In 2003, the European Union's Security Strategy (ESS) furthered a close link between the new and the old security threats and underdevelopment by stating that 'security is the first condition for development'. It pointed out that 'conflicts can lead to extremism, terrorism and state failure [and] it provides opportunities for organised crime'. On state failure the ESS underlines that 'collapse of the state can be associated with obvious threats, such as organised crime or terrorism. State failure is an alarming phenomenon that undermines global governance and adds to regional instability'.

Despite the first steps undertaken through the Cairo Process towards a comprehensive EU Africa policy, there was still a wealth of sectoral and fragmented policies. The challenges to coordination for a more efficient and effective action, asserted the need for a new and comprehensive single approach, which evolved under the form of the 'EU Strategy for Africa' (ESA). The main objectives of this strategy were the provision of a single framework for all EU actors as well as the development of Africa, namely the attainment of the Millennium Development Goals (MDGs) as one of the EU's main political priorities. Peace and security again advanced as prerequisites to a sustainable accomplishment of MDGs. The greatest problem of ESA was that the African partners saw themselves excluded from it, since they perceived it as a strategy FOR rather than a strategy WITH Africa. In a second try, at the Lisbon Summit, the second between Europe and Africa, the EU–Africa relationship marked a real turning point. The agenda within the resulting document of the Joint Africa–European Union Strategy (JAES) was characterised by far-flung objectives and an all-embracing list of measures for future activities. Its Action Plan set out the steps for the EU in supporting the African peace building efforts. JAES defined the long-term policy orientation between the two continents, based on a shared vision and common principles: African unity, interdependence, ownership and responsibility, respect for human rights and democratic principles, right to development, strong political dialogue, burden-sharing, solidarity, common and human security, etc. The main objectives of JAES consist on improving the Africa–EU partnership, promoting peace, security, democratic and human rights, basic freedoms and gender equality, sustainable economic development, including industrialisation, regional and continental integration, ensuring that all MDGs are met by 2015, effective multilateralism and a people-centred partnership.

THE JOINT AFRICA EU STRATEGY—PEACE AND SECURITY PARTNERSHIP (JAESP)

The strategy's First Action Plan, jointly agreed by the European and the African parties, outlined eights areas for strategic partnership for the period of 2008–2010. The Second Action Plan for the period of 2011–2013 did have the same eight priority areas. The fourth summit ensued a Roadmap for the period 2014–2017 that saw an overhaul of the above and focussed on five priority areas, with peace and security agenda heading them.

The objective of the JAES P&S is to cooperate in enhancing the capacity of Africa and EU to respond timely and adequately to security threats and to join efforts in addressing global challenges. Priority actions foresee the enhancing of the dialogue on challenges to peace and security, the full operationalization of the African Peace and Security Architecture (APSA) and last but not least predictable funding for African-led Peace Support Operations (PSOs). The Roadmap 2014–2017 added three additional objectives: increased cooperation in addressing root causes of conflict and crosscutting issues of common interest such as terrorism and transnational organised crime; maritime security with special attention to counterpiracy, illegal fishing and toxic waste dumping; and strengthening the human rights dimension of cooperation in peace and security (Council of the EU 2014).

As mentioned, Africa's standing on the EU's agenda received a big boost-up since the dawn of the century. The changed contexts in both the continents and abroad have had a big role in that. On the African side is, of course, the creation of the AU together with its socioeconomic programme NEPAD, across the Mediterranean. The EU's grows from a union of 15 to 25 to 27 to 28 and counting, and broadly speaking the world has changed too, since the emergence of new post 9/11 international global challenges, which together with an accelerating of the globalisation have pointed out at an increasingly interdependent world. This is seen as the broad rationale for the intensified cooperation between the EU and Africa (Council of the EU 2007). On the road to the agreement of a Joint Strategy both parties have attempted to develop political strategies and policy documents aimed at providing guidance to their cooperation. They did create a momentum upon which to forge this new EU–Africa cooperation. The JAES at the beginning was seen to have brought the Africa–EU relationship at new highs strategically as well as politically.

We believe that this summit will be remembered as a moment of recognition of maturity and transformation in our continent to continent dialogue, opening new paths and opportunities for our common future. (AU Chairman Kufuor cited in Bonsu 2007)

One of the important features of this partnership is the fact that it is based on a shared consensus on values, common interests as well as common strategic objectives. Principles, such as the unity of Africa, interdependence, ownership and joint responsibility as well as respect for human rights, democratic principles, the rule of law and the right to development, lay at the foundation of this partnership. The JAES indicates the willingness for a strengthened Africa–EU political partnership through stronger institutional ties and treating Africa as one ensuring a strong and sustainable continent-to-continent interaction with the AU and EU at centre. Promotion of peace, security, democratic governance, fundamental freedoms, gender equality, sustainable development and regional/continental integration in Africa continue to remain at the forefront of objectives pursued. A further common objective that lies at the very heart of the European project is effective multilateralism and in line with recent developments and conceptualisation of participation and role of civil society JAES furthers the promotion of a broad-based people-centred partnership by facilitating civil society and private sector participations. The JAES was thus seen as a wide-ranging strategy considered as the 'capstone doctrine of EU–Africa relations' (Pirozzi 2010, p. 28), which takes stock of the fifty years of cooperation originated with the Rome Treaties. The JAES and its first Action Plan for 2008–2010, continued with the second Action Plan 2011–2013, identified eight priorities for cooperation, with peace and security featuring prominently. At the Brussels Summit in 2014 the European and African leaders issued the Road Map for 2014–2017 which by taking into account the changed context agreed on five priority goals and again the peace and security features prominently.

The strategic objective, as defined in the latest Roadmap 2014–2017 is 'to ensure a peaceful, safe, secure environment, contributing to human security and reducing fragility, foster political stability and effective governance, and to enable sustainable and inclusive growth' (Council of the EU 2014, p. 2). This is translated in a necessity for a strengthened dialogue and institutional cooperation which addresses both the African and EU security challenges, ensuring so the facilitation of a better coordination of efforts within the international arena, with a special reference to the UN Security Council. The main objective for the first priority action is to 'reach common positions and implement common approaches on challenges to peace and security in Africa, Europe and globally', which is translated in common understanding of root causes to conflict, strengthened cooperation, improved coordination all of which should increase the influence of EU and Africa within the international and global fora. Such enhanced coordination is foreseen to take place predominantly between the AU Peace and Security Council and EU Political and Security Committee. Secondly, the EU has committed, by taking into account the emergent AU's APSA, to support its operationalisation and its various components, especially CESW, Panel of the Wise and the ASF. This is translated in training exercises, exchanges and logistics, capacity building of African forces including civilian and police components. A newly added objective in the Roadmap 2014–2017 is he focus on strengthening coordination between the EU and AU as well as with regional organisations such as RECs in planning and conduct of conflict prevention and peace support activities in accordance with the UN. Another objective is the addressing of root causes of conflict and cross-cutting issues of common concern such as terrorism transnational organised crime including trafficking in human beings, drug and arms as well as illegal trade of wildlife. Maritime security, illegal fishing and toxic waste dumping are the issues addressed through the next JAES P&S objective. Another objective focuses on the strengthening of the human rights dimension in peace and security from conflict prevention, crisis management and post-conflict processes but also efforts in improving good governance and support in SSR. It addresses also the necessity to end sexual violence and protection of civilians in conflicts and ensuring the full participation and representation of women in peace and security processes. Lastly, support the establishment of a predictable and sustainable funding mechanism for African-led PSOs. This will be achieved by building on the experience of the African Peace Facility (APF) and the Additional Voluntary Contributions (AVCs) of EU MS as well as through the strengthening of mobilisation of African and international resources. These main issues are the points of departure for the work carried out within the partnership and contain clearly specified objectives, expected outcomes and planned initiatives. These priority actions of JAES P&S point at a remarkable similarity with the priorities set within the EU Strategy for Africa (ESA) adopted by the EU in 2005. JAES P&S takes advantage of a number of key mechanisms, such as the African Peace Facility (APF),[1] the EU concept for Strengthening African Capabilities for the Prevention, Management and Resolution of Conflicts,[2] the EU Delegation to the AU[3] and the Special Adviser for African Peace-Keeping Capabilities.[4] The first two mechanisms were established prior to JAES P&S and the last two ones at about the same time.

WHY ENGAGE IN AFRICA?

The EU is seen as the 'natural partner' for Africa. There are several reasons for it. Firstly, due to their geographical proximity which accounts for the long history on the relationship between the two continents which spans many centuries, a relationship not always harmonious as indicated by the colonialist legacy of the past. Despite this legacy, former colonial powers such as France, Belgium, UK and Portugal have maintained close ties with their former colonies. Secondly, the European trade and investment have continuously remained of particular importance to Africa—over 50% of global ODA is provided by EU and its MS and between 2004–2010, despite the financial crisis it increased by 6% which in absolute numbers counted for 62% of the ODA global increase. Despite the increase the EU and its MS were not able to reach the intermediary commitment goal of 0.56% of GNI by the end of 2010 and

[1]APF was created in 2003 upon a request by African leaders. It is funded through the EDF: €440 million for the period 2004–2007; €300 million for 2008–2010 and for 2013 alone €232 million were contracted. In 2007 it received additional funding through the voluntary contributions of EU MS. African countries also contribute, i.e. South Africa. APF is at the centre of JAES P&S priority action three. Its aims were twofold: support African led PSOs and capacity building for APSA including RECs. For instance, to African PSOs: €300 million to AMIS; €15.5 million to AMISOM; €23.4 million to FOMUC/CAR; €5 million to AMISEC; while in 2013.

[2]Initiated through an agreement between France and the UK in 2005–2006, and adopted by the EU in May 2006, was intended as the framework for implementing ESA, with the focus of supporting the establishment of AU APSA, including the creation of ASF, This focus has been transferred to JAES P&S.

[3]The EU Council established the position of an EU delegation exclusively dedicated to the AU. The position is a double-hatted, meaning it represents both the Council as the EU Special representative (EUSR) and the Commission as the Head of its Delegation.

[4]Established by the European Council in February 2008, with the aim of providing with decisive resources in order to implement the JAES P&S, 'coordinating all related activities' within the Council Secretariat.

given the still dragging crisis it seems unrealistic that it will reach the UN target of 0.7% by the end of 2015. Thirdly, the increased concerns about security.[5] And fourthly, the continent's abundance in natural resources, is an important factor as well, especially energy. EU is looking for other sources to secure supply and Africa is an alternative to the volatile Middle East and to her disadvantageous dependence on Russia (Götz 2015; Malek 2013; de Jong et al. 2013).

Another subjective factor may be seen on the EU's perception of being about to 'miss the boat', since Africa has been placed at the centre of foreign policies of old and new powers. Undoubtedly, the engagement of US in Africa and the establishment of AFRICOM, as well as the huge amounts on investment flowing to Africa from the emerging powers especially from China, do point out at this direction. Thus, the scramble between major players, such as the USA, China, India, etc., for access to the African market, has pointed to the importance perceived by the EU to continue to remain the biggest partner in Africa: out of this positions the EU can ensure her influence on the continent (Elowson 2009, p. 59).

Some would argue more directly that the EU action, concerning the strategic partnership with Africa, was exclusively pushed due to an imperative not to 'miss the boat'. For instance: 'The planned EU–Africa Summit [Lisbon 2007] is one example. This high-level meeting between the two continents had been put on the back burner for the past seven years. And then out of the blue, the EU made it a pressing issue. Without such a summit, the EU feared that it may lose its foothold in Africa. [...] Africa has now become the continent to be won over' (Karlen 2007). Not surprisingly, the same rhetoric was used by African journalists during the Lisbon Summit: '[The summit] took place at a time when there is growing Chinese investment and influence and a recognition that the continent is no longer 'Europe's private hunting grounds'' (Bonsu 2007). Others, though, would argue that the new contexts 'did not prompt this development but gave it new impetus' (Berger and Wissenbach 2007, p. 4).

---

[5] This factor will be handled at greater length on the following section of this same chapter 'Conceptualisation of Security & Securitisation of External Borders'.

CONCEPTUALISATION OF SECURITY & SECURITISATION OF EXTERNAL BORDERS

EU's internal development process has also to be taken into account when considering the reasons for the new found eagerness to engage Africa. The deepening of integration has brought EU MS together to coordinate their standpoints, including aspirations for a greater role within the international arena. The subsequent development concerning CFSP/ESDP raised questions on how to deal with arising issues from e.g. Africa. In the 1990s and at the dawn of the new century the centre-stage was occupied by issues concerning security, be it in terms of wars and conflicts in even the EU's very own backyard but also in Africa or in terms of new threats and their transnational nature such as terrorism. The EU had to, first and foremost, identify what her security interests as well as threats were, and what instruments it had to develop in order to deal with them. Therefore, in analysing the JAES P&S, of utmost importance is the inclusion within the discourse of the conceptualisation of security and how this is related to the African realities and sensitivities. The EU had to provide answers to questions such as what are her values and goals, what security instruments are used to protect them, as well as what is the security threat to the EU. The answer to such questions came not easily. The EU traditionally has not been conceived of as an international security object—it does not have a collective defence in the traditional sense—nor had it been analysed as a subject pursuing an active security policy because 'security policy' was competence of the EU member states (or to be taken care of in other organizations such as the NATO). Therefore, the EU had mostly been viewed as an outcome or reflection of the considerations of other players, rather than an actor in itself. This lack of own international security identity was seen as being addressed by one of the main strategic documents of the EU's security policy: the European Security Strategy (ESS). The ESS acknowledged that Europe has security interests beyond its immediate neighbourhood, which in some geographical areas, especially Africa, are negatively affected by conflicts, poverty and poor governance and require an active engagement. This marked what has been called 'the end of territorial defence' (Gärtner 2003, pp. 135–147) for the EU. Its objectives are in a narrower sense of course the protection of the EU citizens and the protection of EU as space but they do also include the protection of universal values wherever they are threatened in the world (Whitman 2002).

So seen, threats to the EU security are best defined as those who threaten the core values of the EU (such as those defined within the EU Charter of Fundamental Rights), as well as the international law, meaning that the EU addressed no specific external security space (Sundelius 2001). This rationale has made imperative the development of a foreign policy which requires an active engagement within the international security arena, making so crucial the development of a capacity which outlines a common focus on the promotion of peace in 'distant places' (ESS 2003, pp. 7–9). The ESS has put forward an activist agenda by stating that 'the first line of defence will often be abroad' and by emphasising that the EU is ready to 'shape events' and that the EU wants '[...] international organisations, regimes and treaties to be effective in confronting threats to international peace and security'.

The EU also recognises that the twenty-first century security picture has fundamentally changed: 'the post-Cold War environment is one of increasingly open borders in which the internal and external aspects of security are indissolubly linked' (ESS 2003, p. 2) and 'the crises within and beyond our borders are affecting directly our citizens' lives [...] we will invest in African peace and development as an investment in our security and prosperity' (EEAS EUGS 2016). Thus, the divide between external security, such as wars, international order and internal security matters such as terrorism, public order, and organised crime, has become to be considered largely inexistent, pointing so to the emergence of a security continuum (Gnesotto 2004). In terms of EU policies this resulted with a growing assimilation of Justice and Home Affairs (JHA) and EU external affairs, as indicated by the fact that addressing the instability of the African continent advanced as one of the major security concerns for EU MS. The JAES P&S, at the request of EU MS aims to address these issues, since they feel to experience repercussions in terms of drugs and arms trafficking, illegal immigration, transnational organised crime, illicit trade in natural resources and terrorism (Pirozzi 2010, p. 28).

In summarizing, there appear to be three major motives that seem to 'function in a conceptual and practical symbiosis and are mutually inseparable' which help shed light on EU's conceptualisation and approach to security: morality, legality and self-interest (Glasius and Kaldor 2005, pp. 62–82). The EU is seen as being morally committed to helping those who are lacking, or threatened to their, basic security. The legal motive as shaped within the international law, concerns the fact that the

EU is obliged to secure HS for all people. It seems that such approach was fuelled by the rationale that Europeans cannot be safe as long as others live in insecurity, for 'external insecurity' will ultimately affect Europe. EU's conceptualization of security provides a ground for agreement with the African counterpart, for they too see security not only in traditional terms but also in terms of HS.

SECURITY DEVELOPMENT NEXUS

The EU, especially since the Goteborg Programme in 2001,[6] has developed into a key actor in shaping and defining the agenda about issues concerning the security-development nexus. The EU has increasingly sought to influence the debate on this matter at an international as well as national level. For instance, it has provided a platform for launching discussions in the making of a 'Human Security Doctrine for Europe', and in these terms, the EC has proposed that the HS concept should be at the basis of bridging development and security policies. Internationally seen the HS is disputed, but at the EU level, the HS is sought with the aim to ensure that EU security policies do take into account the HS needs (Bueger and Vennesson 2009) in concerned countries, regions and continents such as Africa. The EU, by such 'multi-functional approach' promotes a holistic approach, through which it aims to position itself as a major actor on the international arena. The reasoning behind this is that the EU, inasmuch an international actor offering a multi-dimensional approach to security issues, can claim the status of an international power (Bretherton and Vogler 2006; Soeterdorp 1999). EU's added value as a multi-institutional and/or hybrid structure is likely to provide all types of crisis management tools—from humanitarian to civilian to military—within one unique framework (Bagayoko and Gibert 2007, p. 9). Due to the complexity and multiplicity of problems faced—poverty, conflicts, wars, and humanitarian catastrophes—the African continent fits perfectly within this EU approach. Such debate is also welcomed by Africa/AU since it too it looks to tackle security comprehensively. African perceptions of security threats include poverty, pandemic diseases such as HIV/AIDS and

---

[6]The Göteborg Programme concerns issues of conflict prevention with a focus on especially long-term commitments.

malaria, food insecurity, child soldiers, bad governance etc. (Beebe 2010, p. 96; Thomas 2001, pp. 59–75). At the EU, the security-development nexus is seen as to embrace two dimensions, the one concerning the politico-legal facet mentioned above, and the other, the implementation through instruments that comprehensively tackle the security and long term development agendas. This second dimension is fully included within the instruments funding JAES P&S such as the EDF, the African Peace Facility (APF), the Development Cooperation Instrument (DCI) and the Instrument for Stability (IfS) (Strzaska and Moeller 2008, p. 3; Elowson 2009, p. 20).[7] Although, it has to be said that, the fact that APF funds are sourced from the EDF has raised some restrictions on the type of support to be provided. APF funds are earmarked for personnel and logistical needs and cannot be used for direct military assistance. Such has, of course, created complications for the AU to effectively employ APF funds in supporting peacekeeping operations.

Coming back to the EU and African conceptualisations of the security-development nexus, both actors seem to share most of the common ground of what security for each of them is. From the official statements remarked at the Lisbon summit, it becomes clear that the JAES, its P&S partnership and especially its Action Plan/Roadmap aim at doing exactly this.

THE AFRICAN CONTINENT AS A TEST CASE FOR EU'S PEACE AND SECURITY CAPACITIES

Once the EU knew where it stood, there was an urge to try the ideas in practice. […] Africa is the opportunity – an ideal incubator, some argue – to develop greater EU coherence in foreign policy making and to further improve the external relations' capacity. Africa is also an arena in which the EU can fulfil its commitments under the 2003 Joint EU-UN Declaration

---

[7] The APF established in 2003, has come to be a major financing source to African Peace and Security Operations (PSOs) as well as to capacity building projects for APSA. Established in 2007, If S is an instrument that focuses on crisis management and peacebuilding concerning both short- and long-term interventions, and is envisioned as a complement especially to EDF and APF, in either to kick-start an initiative or when both EDF and PAF have temporarily run out. The budget for urgent interventions in Africa for 2007–2008 amounted to €64 million. DCI Thematic Budget Lines for Africa concern i.e. funds that enhance the collaboration between non-state actors and local authorities.

on Crisis Management, and where the battle groups concept could start to be implemented. (Elowson 2009, p. 59)

The dawn of the new century evidenced a growing desire on the EU's part to become increasingly involved in the resolution of Africa's security problems. It started with the launching of Operation Artemis from June to September 2003 in DRC,[8] which is seen as a founding act in the mobilisation of the second pillar instruments in Africa (Faria 2004). Operation Artemis opened the way to a new form of cooperation between the EU and the UN.

EU's engagement in Africa's conflict management and resolution have a deeper rationale which aimed at providing legitimacy, from an internal as well as external perspective, to the new EU military structures. On the one side, the EU had an interest in showing that its military structures—the Military Committee (EUMC) and Military Staff (EUMS)—were able to plan military operations autonomously (without resort to e.g. NATO means and instruments) and on the other hand, this newly founded niche can bestow to the EU with increasing international credibility. Engagement in Africa would test the decision-making procedures at the politico-military level—the Political and Security Committee (PSC) and the EU Military Committee (EUMC).[9] The initial relative success of CSPD missions in Africa served to consolidate the EU's legitimacy in peace and security in Africa but also at the international level.

Most importantly though, EU 'experimentations' in Darfur evidencing another crucial EU feature, that of being able to implement at an operational level its partnership with the AU. This exercising pointed at the EU's preference to work multilaterally, to enhance the capacity of African structures indicating the importance it places on the principle of

---

[8] Operation Artemis was launched on 12 June 2003, with the aim to prevent a humanitarian catastrophe in Ituri, in the North East of DRC, as a result of violent fighting between the Hema and Lendu ethnic groups. The operation was explicitly mandated by the UN's Security Council (Resolution 1484) in order to maintain the security in the camps hosting the internally displaced, secure the airport in Bunia and protect civilians, UN staff and humanitarian agencies in the region. It was intended as a bridging mission till the mandate of the United Nations Mission in the DRC (MONUC) was reinforced and its strength increased.

[9] It has, though, to be said that the outcomes of these relationships are dependent upon the political will of EU MS.

African ownership and at the same time building up the legitimacy of future EU–AU cooperation within peace and security sector.

MULTILATERALISM AND JAES P&S

[Regional] cooperation is a fundamental rationale for the EU's own peace and development in the 21st century. This is why we will promote and support cooperative regional orders worldwide [...] The EU will intensify its support for and cooperation with regional and sub-regional organisations in Africa. (EUGS 2016)

We want international organisations, [...] to be effective in confronting threats to international peace and security, and must therefore be ready to act when their rules are broken. [...] the African Union make[s] an important contribution [...]. (ESS 2003, p. 9)

As a result of the intensifying of regionalism processes, EU has been eager to assert itself as an important international actor by establishing communication channels and closely cooperating with regional and continental organisations such as the AU. Such cooperation is seen in terms of 'contributing to order in world politics' (van Veen 2006), inasmuch EU is perceived as a model for successfully tackling peace and security matters at the regional/continental level. Furthermore, EU's 'distinct nature' and her preference for cooperation rather than confrontation provide a significant goodwill basis for an enhanced dialogue with other international actors. The already mentioned EU strategies (ESS & EUGS) stress the need to work with international partners, including Africa. For instance, such stance has its origins in May 2001 when the Council adopted a Common Position Concerning Conflict prevention, Management and Resolution in Africa. It is with this common position that an essential feature of EU's security strategy in Africa was made apparent, namely that of an increased multilateralism aimed at intensifying EU's partnership with African regional organisations and the UN on the matter and at the same time an increased EU contribution in strengthening their capabilities. This Common Position was adapted to the changing times in 2004 and in 2005 and 2007. In the later, the imperative for greater coordination between EU MS bilateral actions was highlighted with special reference for the support of AU and African SROs. This last one also supports the notion of 'African Solutions to African Problems' that has been advanced by AU and NEPAD, by pointing out that ultimately the Africans maintain primary responsibility for the prevention, management and resolution of conflicts in Africa, and that the central actors are the AU and African SROs.

The JAES P&S partnership is obviously 'not an isolated occurrence on the EU Africa sky'. Its objectives have taken stock, continued on, have been formed, strengthened and complemented by several Africa–EU contacts and EU policies, which have increasingly expanded since 2000. In anyway, the creation of AU, undoubtedly, provided the EU with a platform for a more systemic engagement in Africa and the emergence of APSA with even clearer channels for dialogue. EU, through the JAES P&S, took advantage of these opportunities and put the AU/SROs at the centre of the partnership.

> The EU has a privileged relationship with the AU which is at the heart of the [JAES]. As a regional organisation itself the EU has experience of institution building, a history of integration and an inclusive approach to partnership. African states can benefit from working together through regional organisations, and the EU is best-placed to assist in this process. (House of Lords 2005–2006, p. 13)

Europeanisation of EU Member States' Africa Peace & Security Policies

Traditionally seen most of the EU's MS that do not drag a colonial past, have not vested in Africa any significant political or economic interest. For instance, Germany has long been adamant about the necessity to limit peace and security interventions within the enlarged European space and been against to the idea of any EU involvement in the management of Africa's conflicts. The other way round, France as one of former colonial powers in the continent, hasn't been keen to the idea of an EU involvement into Africa security matters, for it preferred a unilateralist policy, especially within the francophone Africa. Such behaviour prompted deterrence, toward France's Africa policy, on the part of other EU MS, especially Germany, who did not want to see themselves and EU acquiring a neo-colonial image in Africa (Bagayoko and Gibert 2007).

It has, though, to be said that France, particularly since the dawn of the new century, has been gradually and increasingly reducing its direct presence in Africa. It has become hesitant to act unilaterally as it is sustained by the rhetoric of a former French Foreign Minister who is quoted to have said that France would no longer be 'the gendarme of Africa' (House of Lords 2005–2006, p. 65). These developments bear witness to a sea change on France's behaviour: it has increasingly acquired a multilateral feature. The reason to it is that the inclusion of France within the EU framework allows France to remain involved in Africa—perceived by France as a crucial quality to ensuring its position on the international arena—but with the bonus of an image void/or reduced of a paternalist or neo-colonial trait. Such Europeanisation of France's Africa policy allows France also to share the costs of interventions. Thus, France acts in, what it sees as, an appropriate behaviour by Europeanising its Africa policy, for such is instrumental to her international image as well as cost efficient within this specific type of situation.

Very much like France, UK, another traditional actor in Africa, has not been keen to Europeanise it Africa policies, at least initially.[10] The UK given the specific situation in early 2000s, perceived their Africa polices as solidly efficient, and thus, saw it as appropriate not to Europeanise them. 2005, which was declared the 'year of Africa', Africa was placed at the centre stage of the G8 Summit at Gleneagles. 2005 is also the year when the EU MS agreed the EU Africa Strategy. UK showed a sea change to its attitude concerning the Europeanisation of its Africa policy: 'The European Union now covers most of Europe, including all those states with particular interests in Africa; it is the obvious means by which European countries should cooperate to deliver aid to Africa effectively and ensure coherent policies in areas such as peacekeeping [...]' (House of Lords 2005–2006, p. 14).

The British, also, insisted on the necessity of coordinating these activities at an international level, most obviously with USA, Canada etc. Germany also prefers a multilateral approach and promotes a closer cooperation among EU and NATO.

Due to the importance Africa has gained as it relates to EU security, as evaluated at the beginning of this chapter, many other EU MS, such as Sweden, the Netherlands, Belgium, Portugal, etc., have increasingly

---

[10]UK, since 2001, has considerably invested in developing African peacekeeping capabilities in former colonies via the British Peace Support Teams, which became part of an ambitious interdepartmental programme: the Africa Conflict prevention Pool (ACPP). The departments involved are that for International Development (DfID), the Foreign and Commonwealth Office (FCO) and the Ministry of Defence (MoD).

stepped up their involvement, via EU, within the African security concerns. At least initially, the EU MS seem to have developed a genuine interest in reinforcing African capabilities allowing this last one to erect an autonomous structure able to tackle security matters in own space, thus ultimately, avoiding an increase in costs on the side of EU.

INTER-INSTITUTIONAL & INTER-PILLAR COORDINATION: FROM A PRE- AND POST-LISBON TREATY POINT OF VIEW

JAES P&S, as well as each and every new policy paper concerning EU's security in Africa, stresses the importance for inter-institutional, and in a pre-Lisbon context also, inter-pillar coordination. The very success of the European approach to African conflict prevention, management and resolution relies heavily on the aptitude of the EU to overcome rivalry among its institutions. The competition is fuelled by the different interests and desire of relevant institutions to play the 'lead role' on the issues of peace and security. The literature offers us with concepts such as bureaucratic politics/behaviour that consists of power struggles among rival agencies (Allison 1971, p. 167). Accordingly, agencies concerned will resist any change that may diminish their role as a leading agency. Career officials will seek to maximise power, budget and mandate, all of which will ensure the organisational health of their own agencies. '[Organisational health is] defined in terms of bodies assigned and monies appropriated (Allison 1969, p. 700) [ensuring that the agency will continue to] maintain influence, fulfilling its mission, and securing the necessary capabilities (Allison and Zelikow 1999, pp. 301–302). This rationale warrants that career officials are prone to believe that the health of their organisation is vital (Allison and Zelikow 1999, pp. 301–302)'. Thus, in attempting to maximise tasks to be delegated to own organisation, the resultant, within the governance structure composed of these rivalling agencies, will be turf wars. JAES P&S in a pre-Lisbon context required inter-agency coordination, especially among Directorate General for Development and relations with ACP States (DG DEV) and Directorate General for External Relations (DG RELEX), who have 'the overall responsibility for policy steering, guidance and coordination' (Commission 2008, p. 2) and which are also involved with the rest partnerships of JAES. JAES P&S also required cooperation with the General Secretariat of the Council. It was envisioned that these three institutions/agencies should ensure coherence and overall coordination for JAES P&S.

Within the EC the rival agencies were most obviously its Directorate General, particularly those with a mandate focused on Africa. The most powerful agencies in this sense were DG RELEX and most obviously the DG DEV, this last one often tending to see Africa as its 'exclusive territory' (Dimier 2003). The discourse on the security-development nexus provided DG DEV with an approach that allowed it to defend their privileged geographic area of intervention and investing in a functional field which had not been traditionally theirs. Undoubtedly, that the 'organisational health' has received a distinct boom in terms of personnel and budget. The allocation of APF under the responsibility of DG DEV, decidedly, points at this direction. Thus, DG DEV acted with the aim of enhancing organisational health which ensured that it 'maintains influence, fulfilling its mission, and securing the necessary capabilities'.

DG RELEX played a pivotal role in conflict prevention through its Crisis Management and Conflict Prevention Unit, which was also 'in charge of coordinating and mainstreaming the Commission's conflict prevention and management activities [as well as it] provided the necessary link between the Commission's institutions and their Council counterparts' (Bagayoko and Gibert 2007, pp. 13–14). The fact that a Crisis Management and Conflict Prevention Unit's member was at the same time the Commission's representative within the Council's Political and Security Committee (PSC) as well as within the Committee for civilian aspects of crisis management (CIVCOM), was a very good omen concerning coordination efforts needed for the JAES P&S. Nevertheless, the EC was far from being a unified actor within the JAES P&S. As a matter of fact, EC was plagued by coordination problems among its DGs as a result of unclear divisions of labour caused from the securitisation and intertwining of different fields within conflict prevention, management and resolution. For instance, DG DEV and DG Trade were required to take into account the assessment reports/watch-lists on the root causes of conflict delivered by DG RELEX through its specific Country/Regional Strategy Papers (CSPs), but they did 'often pursue different, or even contradictory objectives' (Bagayoko and Gibert 2007, p. 15).

A further point of contention concerning coordination problems within the EC was provided through EU MS forwarding their national interests, and they too often are contradictory and pursue different objectives and using EU institutions as medium to forward own national interests.

Moving to the second pillar, the General Secretariat of the Council (GSC) together with its directorates general constituted another important actor among the EU actors for JAES P&S. DGE, which was in charge of external, political and military affairs, is of relevance here. DGE was divided into geographic and functional directorates. As of 2007 and prior to the Africa–EU Summit in Lisbon, the responsibility to coordinate the management of African security matters was hardly fought, especially among two DGE's directorates the DGE VIII and DGE IX. DG VIII, who oversaw defence matters, was animated to get involved in a turf war with DGE IX, out of a calculation that being endowed with the task of coordinating the management of African security matters would increase her legitimacy vis-à-vis other DGE directorates, implying an expanded mandate, higher budgets and, arguably, increased number of personnel. The DGE IX, on the other side, oversaw the civilian aspects of crisis management which included the following instruments: a Police Unit, relevant to SSR projects; a Policy Planning and Early Warning Unit (Policy Unit) responsible for strategic and geopolitical analyses at the service of HR CFSP; and the Situation Centre (SITCEN). The DGE IX saw itself as better positioned to coordinate the management of African security issues within JAES P&S, since it also nurtured closer relationships with the EC, especially DG DEV. A losing out to DGE VIII would have meant for the DGE IX a tough setback for its organisational health.

The cross-pillar rivalries provided further reason to worry concerning JAES P&S. The establishment of APF, the most important funding instrument for JAES P&S, is an interesting example which highlights such claim. The Commission, with the establishment of APF in 2004, reached an important victory against the Council, inasmuch APF is an instrument which funds African-owned peacekeeping operations, in a time when CFSP/ESDP and by extension peacekeeping missions, are a prerogative of the Council. The debate about the source of APF funding is revealing on the inter-pillar struggle. There were four possible alternatives. Firstly, it was the consideration to allocate the new funds from the then current EDF. Such would have had the consequence that despite the fact that EDF is not part of the Community budget, nevertheless, EDF and accordingly APF funds have been managed by the Commission/DG DEV. This would have meant that the Commission/ DG DEV's organisational health—defined at least partially, in terms of monies appropriated—would have had a great boost and accounted for assuring EC/DG DEV's influence, fulfilling its mission, and foremost, securing the necessary capabilities. The second option saw the CFSP budget as the source of APF, which would have implied a reduction of EC/DG DEV's influence. The Council would have savoured a Pyrrhic victory since: '[…] keeping APF funding within the EDF [would] avoid diverting resources away from the under-funded CFSP, and ensure that the EU remains fully involved in the process, thereby maintaining a coherent approach between the different European institutions and the EU Member States. [… Also] the CFSP budget is too small to support the minimum level of funding required for an effective APF […]' (House of Lords 2005–2006, p. 74). This option would have had only one winner, the European Parliament (EP), who as part of its competence in the CFSP budget would have had a say on the use of the APF funds. The third option contemplated was the creation of a new multi-annual EDF-like fund to be managed either through EDF procedure (EC/DG DEV) or wholly managed by EU MS. The fourth option would have seen the control of funds according to their purpose, i.e. funds used for AU capability-building would have been managed by EC, while the small support for AU PSOs would have been controlled by the EP. After the provisional period of APF ended, it was decided to maintain the procedures already used, meaning the choice fell on the first option portrayed above. Nevertheless, the heated inter-pillar turf war did not recede. Contention focused on two main subjects, firstly, on the EDF funds being used for security purposes; and secondly, the different conceptualisation of the notion of 'effective ownership' or 'African ownership'. The first was actually mirrored from the international dispute concerning the use of development monies for security purposes. Within the European context, for DG ECHO (European Commission Humanitarian Office), humanitarian assistance is apolitical, neutral and impartial. DG ECHO disputes the definition by the Petersberg tasks which claim humanitarian assistance as eventually an important part of CSDP missions. DG ECHO argues that such reasoning would contribute towards a politicisation of aid further blurring the difference between military and humanitarian actors. Accordingly, there was a frosty relationship among DG ECHO and the Council's DG VIII. The second concerns the idea of 'African solutions to African problems' meaning that the responsibility for EU's financial, technical assistance and training initiatives earmarked for supporting African capabilities in peace and security matters (conflict prevention, management and resolution), relies by the African partners. The Commission preferred to use APF funds to support AU, given the achievement it has booked especially with the creation of the AU's Peace and Security Council, while EU MS and GSC would predominantly or exclusively want to earmark these funds for supporting African SROs, especially ECOWAS which actually had the operational experience (Nivet 2006). As the very JAES P&S shows, the Commission had the upper hand.

The above gave concern and made room for strengthening inter-pillar inter-institutional coherence, cooperation, and coordination focused on Africa's peace and security issues. Still in a pre-Lisbon context this was addressed as follows: Since June 2007 an ad hoc group was established charged to draft and adopt the JAES and its Action Plan. Being an ad hoc instrument, the Council was on the looking for a more permanent provision. Two alternatives seemed at the time to crystallise. The first concerned the creation of a Brussels-based, cross-pillar working group vested with the responsibility to manage JAES. Such working group would cover geographically sub-Saharan and North African countries, and thematically the pan-African issues, and the preparation of Africa–EU Ministerial meetings and Summits. The second alternative saw the revision of the mandate and working modalities for the Africa Working Group (COAFR) already existing as well as the first option but with a reduced mandate, namely covering pan-African issues for both SSA and Northern Africa which would so reflect the new vision of treating Africa as one. This second option was adopted which accounted for a strengthening and expanding of the COAFR mandate (europeafrica.net).

With the entry into force of the Lisbon Treaty, the institutional setting of the EU changed as did the ones involved in the management and coordination of the JAES P&S. While there were initially great expectations that the Lisbon Treaty has taken care of all the bureaucratic bickering analysed above, very soon an awareness settled that these new institutional arrangements seem to have sourced further confusion of roles and responsibilities.

With the European External Action Services (EEAS) still taking shape, the division of roles has been confounding. The first EU High Representative (EU HR) removed key pre-Lisbon GSC figures who were involved with the implementation of JAES P&S. This action had the rather unfortunate consequence that established focal points, who provided the contact with African parties, disappeared. The bi-annual Joint

Task Force, which brings together representatives of the EC, EEAS, AU Commission, Member states and experts, has since its inception 'not really been owned' by the African party (Helly et al. 2014, p. 10).

Turning to the internal struggles within the EU, with a focus on the role of the EU MS, the Lisbon Treaty provided for the EU President and the HR to be as the main actors in terms of foreign policy matters. The MS feel that they have no longer a saying, or at least not as strong as it used to be. This has led to the situation were MS are increasingly taking a back seat in the implementation of the JAES P&S and expect that EEAS lead the process. A commendable behaviour, at least theoretically, in practice it has been a further obstacle. For instance, the biannual Africa EU Ministerial Troika meetings, which in a pre-Lisbon context were planned by the EU MS holding the rotating presidency, have been interrupted. Such has disenchanted the African parties, because they felt that these troika meeting were what effectively furthered the JAES P&S implementation. EEAS has tried to organise subsequent meetings, but it seems to have been less successful in garnering the needed attention from the EU MS and the African part.

The inter-agency coordination between the EEAS and the EC has not been favoured as well. One of the main obstacles for EEAS to effectively plan and implement policies and in particular JAES P&S, is the different budget cycles. APF as the main and most important financial instrument to the JAES P&S, falling under the management of DG DEVCO and being allotted within the EDF, is budgeted every 7 years. The EEAS, as per the nature of the different crises, has to act in more ad hoc way. This creates less possibilities for the EEAS to coordinate. At an organisational level, DG DEVCO decided to reshuffle its own departments at the directorial level in such a manner that they would correspond to those at EEAS. It has obviously marked a step in the right direction.

This fragmented EU coordination in matters of JAES P&S has caused some unwanted consequences. For instance, EU MS are seeking bilateral agendas and communication channels with Africa. At the EU level, and particularly with regard to EEAS, this bypassing accounts for the limited flow of information between the singular EU MS and EU-level structures.

On the African side, the AUC seems to not be putting enough earnestness on the management of the Joint Partnership. The management is carried out through the Economic Department of the AUC, despite repeated requests by the EU to embed it at the top level of AUC

(Helly et al. 2014, p. 13). Another challenge, at least initially, has been the 'unawareness' of some African states and some Regional Economic Communities/Regional Mechanisms (RECs/RMs) about the JAES P&S and its implementations (Elowson 2009, p. 8).

Voices have increasingly been heard for a clear JAES P&S vision and others who argue for a revision of the EU–AU partnership. The JAES was conceived as a framework providing a continent-to-continent approach and putting an end to the segmented EU policies with regard to Africa. The implementation of JAES P&S has unfortunately not been taken as the framework where political dialogue between the EU and Africa takes place. Other frameworks such as the European Neighbourhood Policy (ENP) have insinuated themselves as the more adequate choice for political dialogue between the two continents. With the different and still current challenges (Eurozone/financial crisis, inadequate response to Arab Spring and turf-wars), the EU seems to have lost some of its lustre and the African parties view it as having failed to be a credible dialogue partner.

Nevertheless, the relevance of the JAES P&S, as underpinned by various crises, is still a given thing. The difficulties in reaching unity and convergence of views as in case of the 2011 Libyan crisis that clearly showed that European states especially UK and France largely ignored the efforts on the part of the AU, have contributed to the budding of some much needed lessons learned. For instance, consecutive crises in Mali in 2012 and Central African Republic in 2013 indicated a collaborative modus operandi between the EU (rapid intervention) and African support in the absence of capacities for African-led and African-owned PSOs (Helly and Rocca 2013). Dialogue takes place quite often and at all level, such as between the EU delegation to the AU and concerned AU institutions and offices, most notably the AUC's Peace and Security Department, but also through International Contact Groups, or between the EU's Political and Security Committee (EU PSC) and AU's Peace and Security Council (AU PSC). Intra-body cooperation with AU and RECs/RMs has developed positively, but is has also raised questions on the primacy and subsidiarity among them (Helly and Rocca 2013, p. 17). The newly acquiring of peace and security mandates on the part of RECs/RMs, but also better RECs/RMs performance in executing said new mandates has created turf wars between them and the AU.

Many involved within JAES feel that the EU had been far too ambitious and has put unrealistic expectations (Elowson 2009, p. 55), which may further contribute towards an EU being perceived as an actor with a, already familiar term, 'capability–expectations gap' problem. JAES emphasises an EU and AU relationship among equals, which is in stark contrast to the recurrent underfunding and understaffing of AU (Mangala 2014). The EU has more resources and capacities, and may 'push too much [...] and put too much pressure on the African partners by overdoing things, such as preparing ready 'lists of things to do'. However, due to its ownership of the process, the African side controls the pace' (Elowson 2009, p. 55). The combination of unrealistic expectations with the African way of doing things may give rise to frustrations.

Concluding Remarks

By concluding, it can be said that the geographical proximity, the long history, the high trade and investment volume as well as the natural resources' abundance of Africa make the EU the 'natural partner' to Africa. The renewed interest that Africa gained especially post 9/11 and the perceived scramble for its resources between traditional and emerging powers just provided an impetus for relating with Africa at a strategic level. In particular, the rationale behind JEAS P&S is to be found at the way EU frames/conceptualises her own security, which goes beyond the spatial area of EU as well as its citizens to include the world citizens who are lacking, or being threatened to their basic HS needs. Further the EU's added value as a multi-institutional and/or hybrid structure that is likely to provide all types of crisis management tools—from humanitarian to civilian to military—within one unique framework, accounted for her being viewed by the AU officials as a 'preferential partner'.

Due to the complexity and multiplicity of problems faced—poverty, conflicts, wars, and humanitarian catastrophes—the African continent fits perfectly within this EU approach. The EU takes into account the changed African continent, and puts the AU/APSA at the centre of the JAES P&S. Also the fact that the EU sees a close relationship between security and development, and that it implements policies accordingly, make it a preferred AU partner. The privileged relationship it has forged with the AU, as well as it being taken as a model regional organisation point out at the benefits that Africa may seize by working together.

One can argue that the EU MS common position concerning the JAES P&S, has to be seen under the prism offered from the 'logic of appropriateness' concept. By fulfilling the obligations, as required by the practices and expectations of the community they are members— i.e. EU's preference for multilateral cooperation, or moving away from paternalistic, neo-colonial behaviour—, they did what they saw as appropriate—common position concerning JAES P&S—given the specific situation they were in—as defined by the security threats and opportunities in Africa. The euro-crisis and the Arab Spring have shifted the focus of EU priorities, at least as expressed by a majority of EU MSS, inwardly, and the EEAS has badly suffered for that.

By taking into consideration that 'roles of actors are determined both by an actor's own conceptions about appropriate behaviour and by the expectations, or role prescriptions, of other actors', then the EU's approach to foreign policy which is based on civilian/normative means and structural stabilisation processes, has found broad acceptance at the AU level. The broad acceptance is also sourced by the fact that the EU is seen by Africa as a model of achieving peace through integration and her insistence for African ownership as it is evidenced by the APF process. In these terms, JAES P&S' priority actions, concerning respectively enhanced dialogue between AU–EU, support for the operationalisation of the APSA structure and financing, dwell in already fertile grounds.

In taking a look on the inter-pillar/inter-institutional coordination challenges the overall picture gets smudged. EU is plagued by turf wars and the Lisbon Treaty while being accredited for solving some of them, has in turn contributed additional ones.

At an intercontinental level there have been some bumps but also reinforced cooperation at the institutional and political level, which highlight the increased interaction between the AU and EU PSC. A concrete example is their joint mission to Mali, tackling so concrete situations and enlarging so the scope of said collaboration as well. Further, the research results point out that while the standing up of JAES P&S did take into consideration the necessary strategic steps, the implementation of JAES P&S even after some adjustments still faces considerable operational challenges.

References

Allen, D., and M. Smith. 2002. External Policy Developments. *Journal of Common Market Studies*, Annual Review of the European Union 2001/2002. 40: 97–115.

Allison, G. 1969. Conceptual Models and the Cuban Missile Crisis. *American Political Science Review* 63 (3 September): 689–718.

Allison, G. 1971. *Essence of Decision: Explaining the Cuban Missile Crisis*, 1st ed. Boston: Little Brown.

Allison, G., and P. Zelikow. 1999. *Essence of Decision: Explaining the Cuban Missile Crisis*. New York, NY: Longman.

Bagayoko, N., and M.V. Gibert. 2007. The European Union in Africa: The Linkage between Security, Governance and Development—From an Institutional Perspective. IDS Working Paper 284.

Beebe, S. 2010. Solutions Not Yet Sought: A Human Security Paradigm for Twenty-First-Century Africa. In *US Strategy in Africa: AFRICOM, Terrorism and Security Challenges*, ed. J.D. Francis. Oxon, NY: Routledge.

Berger, B., and U. Wissenbach. 2007. EU–China–Africa Trilateral Development Cooperation: Common Challenges and New Directions. DIE-GDI Discussion Paper 21/2007, Bonn, German Development Institute.

Boer, M., and J., Monar. 2002. 11 September and the Challenge of Global Terrorism to EU as a Security Actor. *Journal of Common Market Studies*, Annual Review of the European Union 2001/2002 40: 11–28.

Bonsu, K.O. 2007. EU–Africa Pledged New Strategic Partnership. *Ghana Web*. Available at: http://www.ghanaweb.com/GhanaHomePage/NewsArchive/artikel.php?ID=135637. Last accessed on 27 June 2017.

Bretherton, C., and J. Vogler (eds.). 2006. *The European Union as a Global Actor*, 2nd ed. Oxon: Routledge.

Bueger, C., and P. Vennesson. 2009. *Security, Development and the EU's Development Policy*. Firenze: European University Institute.

Cardoso, F.J., W. Kühne, and J.B. Honwana. 2000. *Reflection Paper: Priorities in EU Development Cooperation in Africa: Beyond 2000*. Brussels: Council of Ministers.

Council of the European Union. 2003. *European Security Strategy (ESS) A Secure Europe in a Better World: European Security Strategy*. Brussels. Available at: https://www.consilium.europa.eu/uedocs/cmsUpload/78367.pdf. Last accessed on 27 June 2017.

Council of the European Union. 2007. *The Africa–EU Strategic Partnership: A Joint Africa–EU Strategy*. Brussels. Available at: http://www.consilium. europa.eu/uedocs/cms_data/docs/pressdata/en/er/97496.pdf; The Joint Official Website of the JAESP available at: http://www.africa-eu-partnership. org/. Both last accessed on 27 June 2017.

Council of the European Union. 2014. *Fourth EU–Africa Summit Road Map 2014–2017*. Brussels. Available at: http://www.consilium.europa. eu/en/press/press-releases/2014/04/pdf/fourth-EU-Africa-Summit-ROADMAP-2014-2017/. Last accessed on 27 June 2017.

de Jong, S., J. Woulters, and S. Sterky. 2013. The EU in Multilateral Security Governance: The Case of Russian-Ukrainian Gas Dispute. In *The EU and Multilateral Security Governance* (Routledge Advances in European Politics), ed. S. Lucarelli, L. van Langenhove, and J. Woulters. Oxon: Routledge.

Dimier, V. 2003. *Institutional Change Within a Multinational Organisation: Life and Death of DG DEV (European Commission) 1958–2002.* Edinburgh: European Consortium for Political Research.

EEAS. 2016. *Shared Vision, Common Action: A Stronger Europe—A Global Strategy for the European Union's Foreign and Security Policy.* Brussels: EEAS.

Elowson, C. 2009. *The Joint Africa–EU Strategy: A Study of the Peace and Security Partnership.* Stockholm: Swedish Defence Research Agency/FOI.

European Commission. 2008. Commission Staff Working Document: Commission Contributions to the Implementation of the EU–Africa Action Plan (2008–2010). Brussels.

Faria, F. 2004. La Gestion des Crises en Afrique Subsaharienne: Le Rôle de l'Union Européenne. ISS Occasional Paper 55.

Gärtner, H. 2003. European Security: The End of Territorial Defence. *Brown Journal of World Affairs* 9 (2): 135–147.

Glasius, M., and M. Kaldor. 2005. Individuals First: A Human Security Strategy for the European Union. *Internationale Politik und Gesellschaft* 1: 62–82.

Gnesotto, N. (ed.). 2004. *EU Security and Defence Policy: The First Five Years (1999–2004).* Paris: Institute for Security Studies.

Götz, E. 2015. It's Geopolitics, Stupid: Explaining Russia's Ukraine Policy. *Global Affairs* 1 (1): 3–10.

Hadfield, A. 2007. Janus Advances: An Analysis of EC Development Policy And the 2005 Amended Cotonou Partnership Agreement. *European Foreign Affairs Review* 12: 39–66.

Helly, D., and C. Rocca. 2013. The Mali Crisis and Africa–Europe Relations. *ECDPM Briefing Note 52.* Available at: http://ecdpm.org/fr/publications/la-crise-au-mali-et-les-relations-afrique-europe/. Last accessed on 27 June 2017.

Helly, D., E.A. Bekele, S. El Fassi, and G. Galeazzi. 2014. *The Implementation of the Joint Africa Europe Strategy: Rebuilding Confidence and Commitments, ECDPM Study Commissioned by DG for External Policies of the Union for the European Parliament.* Available at: http://ecdpm.org/publications/implementation-joint-africa-europe-strategy-rebuilding-confidence-commitments/. Last accessed on 27 June 2017.

House of Lords. 2005–2006. *The EU and Africa: Towards a Strategic Partnership, 34th Report of Session 2005–06,* vol. I. London: House of Lords.

Karlen, M.-T. 2007. New Donors: China's Africa Policy as a Prime Example. Development Policy Briefing 02/07, Swiss Agency for Cooperation and Development.

Malek, M. 2013. The EU as a 'Target' of Russia's 'Energy Foreign Policy'. In *The EU: A Global Actor? Global Leadership*, ed. S.B. Gareis, G. Hauser, and F. Kernic. Berlin/Oplade: Barbara Budrich Verlag.

Mangala, J. 2014. Africa and the US AFRICOM. In *Handbook of Africa's International Relations*, ed. T. Murithi. Oxon, NY: Routledge.

Nivet, B. 2006. Security by Proxy? The EU and (Sub)Regional Organisations: The Case of ECOWAS. ISS Occasional Papers No. 63.

Pirozzi, N. (ed.). 2010. *Ensuring Peace and Security in Africa: Implementing a New Africa—EU Partnership*. Rome: IAI.

SN 106/4/00 REV 4. *Africa–Europe Summit under the Aegis of the OAU and the EU, Cairo, 3–4 April 2000 'Cairo Declaration'*. Available at: http://europa.eu/rapid/press-release_PRES-00-901_en.htm. Last accessed 27 June 2017.

Soeterdorp, P. 1999. *Foreign Policy in the European Union*. New York, NY: Longman.

Strzaska, A., and J. Moeller. 2008. *The African Peace Facility*. European Commission DG DEV & DG AIDCO. Brussels. Available at: http://europafrica.files.wordpress.com/2008/05/african-peace-facility.ppt. Last accessed on 27 June 2017.

Sundelius, B. 2001. The Seeds of a Functional Security Paradigm for the European Union. Paper presented at the Second Pan-European Conference on EU Politics of the ECPR Standing Group on European Union Politics (note 37).

Thomas, C. 2001. Global Governance, Development and Human Security: Exploring the Links. *Third World Quarterly* 22 (2): 159–175.

van Veen, E. 2006. Order in World Politics: An Inquiry into the Concept, Change, and the EU's Contribution. UNU-CRIS Occasional Papers, 02006/17.

Whitman, R.G. 2002. The Fall, and Rise, of Civilian Power Europe? Paper presented at the Conference on the European Union in International Affairs, National Europe Centre, Australian National University, 3–4 July. Available at: https://openresearch-repository.anu.edu.au/handle/1885/41589/. Last accessed on 27 June 2017.

Boko Haram and Identity Reconstruction in Lake Chad Basin Region

Blessing Onyinyechi Uwakwe and Buhari Shehu Miapyen

INTRODUCTION

The twenty-first century international conflict landscape at the onset revealed unique conflict trends from the preceding centuries. The decreasing sovereignty and dwindling influences of state actors on the world political arena, and the growth and expansion of non-state actors at both the domestic and international levels presented a new outlook to the conflicts of the twenty-first century—particularly to the problems of extremism, radicalization, and terrorism. This increasingly new multi-lateral and plural interactions emerged on a global scale with numerous challenges, despite the advantages it offered for pluralism,

B. O. Uwakwe
Department of Conflict Studies, University of Humanistic Studies,
Utrecht, The Netherlands
e-mail: blessinggabriel37@yahoo.com

B. S. Miapyen (✉)
Department of International Relations, Eastern Mediterranean University,
Famagusta, Cyprus
e-mail: buharisf@gmail.com

© The Author(s) 2018   141
P. Frankowski and A. Gruszczak (eds.),
Cross-Disciplinary Perspectives on Regional and Global Security,
https://doi.org/10.1007/978-3-319-75280-8_7

multi-culturalism, greater involvement of stakeholders and the wider window for participation to variety of actors on the world stage.

Ethno-political, religious and primordial factors supporting persistent violent upheavals became one of the initial challenges that manifested at the domestic level. Conflicts that assumed such characteristics were presumed by most major political players and experts to be domestically centred, with lesser or even without implications for regional and international security concerns. This is evident by the nature and response strategy; non-interventionist, to such countries by the international community, and in which case, often justified by the respect for state sovereignty (Pieterse 1997).[1] Equally, the recommendation by powerful developed western states of the nexus between Democratization and Improved Human Development Indices (HDI) as remedies to the wide arrays of violent scenarios based on informed knowledge about domestic conflicts created more challenges in finding strategic and sustainable interventions. The alarming 9/11 attack appeared to have changed perspectives and even strategies of major international political players about the characteristics of domestic violent conflicts. Conflicts earlier perceived as mere domestic upheavals and non-threatening are now considered legitimate regional and international threats.

In 2009, Boko Haram emerged in the North-eastern part of Nigeria, initially as an impulsive reaction to the extra judicial killings perpetrated by the Nigerian security forces to avenge the death of Mohammed Yusuf, the leader of the Boko Haram organization. The dynamics of the group indicate divergent events. What appeared as an ephemeral response by the group at the early days of its public violence, turned out to be a sustained tactical terror campaign shaped along the ideological orientation of radical Salafi Jihad. As a norm with African political institutions, the Nigerian government viewed Boko Haram as a local militant group with neither national nor regional implications. The involvement of Boko Haram in the other Lake Chad Basin states of Chad, Cameroun, and Niger later revealed the trans-border tenacity and capability of the organization for expansion. Its strategic transition process from a local militant group to a trans-border terror group revealed new dimensions to the

---

[1] The humanitarian intervention situations in Bosnia, Rwanda and Somalia are good examples. See Pieterse (1997).

underlying objectives of the group. A terror organization entrenched in the radical Jihadist ideology—an organization that tacitly but tenaciously engaged in the state politics at the early stage of the campaign as a larger strategy for the attraction and consolidation of legitimate local support. The conflict dynamics is indicative that, the involvement in local politics was a means of establishing local support and international connections to raise resources for implementing pre-conceived goal for the establishment of a caliphate.

However, so much discussion about Boko Haram is out there in media, policy, and academic domain since 2009. The review of prevailing literature, observation of policy discourses and media reports link the conflict roots to material lack; suggesting materialist ontology as basic, independent and a causal factor. Arguably, historical (precolonial), economic, political and social factors are rife as the main drive for not just the violent conflicts but also terrorism and insurgency in the northern region (Ajayi 2012; Loimeier 2012; Thomson 2012). Valarie Thomson emphasized, it is disingenuous to limit the analysis of the causes of Boko Haram to specific-domino factors. Such misrepresentations can obstruct the ability to offer constructive policy recommendations likely to counteract the group's ill objectives. She further noted, Boko Haram can be unpredictable as 'other events may likely motivate the group to channel its focus on neighbouring states (Thomson 2012), just as the case with the group's current trans-border activities. This present article is in consensus with Thomson's position, and rejects the specific-domino factors limiting knowledge on various other casual and motivating factors.

This chapter attempts to support analysis on the motivations of the Boko Haram insurgency movement. Preceding debates offer significant insights on the group, however, ideological and cultural motives supersede; to which other reasons support. The tactical transitional process and dynamic expansion of the movement from a local militant group to a trans-border or regional terror organization is arguably some strategies for a reconstruction of the identity of the citizens. The extreme violence provides the stage for identity reconstruction process. Understanding terrorism and insurgency in the Lake Chad Basin through ideological and cultural lens can reduce the misconceptions that abounds and promote further efforts for credible solutions to the violent malaise that have overtaken the region.

Understanding Identity and Interest Formation in Lake Chad Basin Under Terrorism and Insurgency: The Constructivist Perspective

Today, most researchers on social problems are concerned with how the world or a particular phenomenon exists. Instead of explaining the world or phenomenon as it is, it is most often explained, as they ought to be.[2] This explains the reason most researchers lay emphasis on specific approaches to understanding the world as much as the social problems emanating from the world. Boko Haram is widely seen as part of the global Jihadi network, as partly demonstrated by the group's pledge of allegiance to the Islamic State of Iraq and the Levant (ISIL), and the recent change of identity to Islamic State of West Africa (ISWA) (Voll 2015). Looking at the group from a narrow perspective in analysis could distort efforts for comprehensive knowledge of the group motivations (Loimeiers 2012).[3] Such perspectives have pervaded Boko Haram discourses and have tremendously influenced public commentators, policy makers, journalists, and wide array of stakeholders. News reports, stories, and analysis framed in today's social and mainstream media portray these analyses of the group's motivations and possible causes for its rise. Constructivist theoretical ideals could enhance adequate knowledge and illuminate the narrative pathways in the search for better comprehension of the underlying causes and motivations for Boko Haram insurgency as instrument in service of radical and extreme groups, locally and regionally.

Observing the group's reasons for rise and expansion, from Nigeria to neighbouring Cameroun, Chad and Niger from the constructivist's lens, is to unbundle the ideological and cultural components of the movement more so the regional security implications. There exists glaring inadequacy of one reason to explain all social problems. Constructivist theory bolsters and strengthens social science epistemology and it is relevant in understanding the process of identity and interest formation. Hence, some elements of the theory hinges on the primacy of ideology

---

[2] It is important to indicate our appreciation of the theoretical propositions (constructivist theory), which we adopted as framework of analysis, however, due to the scope of the article, our intention is not to deeply discuss the theory.

[3] See Loimeier's (2012) comprehensive analysis on the true character of Boko Haram.

and culture, described as social structures over other materialist considerations, as material resources find meaning only within those social contexts in which they are embedded (Wendt 1992). In essence, the social
structures help facilitate understanding, on why someone would forfeit
all material motivations in pursuit of an ideology, which are often rooted
firmly within specific cultural, social and ideological contexts, to commit
suicide, maim or kill others. Perliger and Pedahzur (2016, p. 297), argue
that, "ideologies are breeding grounds for radicalization".[4]

Considering Perliger and Pedahzur's notion, an understanding of the
regional security in the Lake Chad region is significant. There is need
to understand the process of the emergence of the active regional actors
and the securitized threats. Region in this context imply the sub-system
of security relations among set of states geographically contiguous to
one another (Buzan 1991). The countries of Nigeria, Niger, Chad, and
Cameroon have presented these characteristics by their geographical
contiguity. Traditionally, state actors are the primary security providers,
considering that the regional actions and any regional agency of sort are
sub-ordinate to sovereign states in such region (Hynes 2015). Realism
assists security studies with such preliminary focus, putting greater
emphasis on military security and states as the main referent objects to
which the breach of its security are often seen as a threat to states and
impliedly, regional security. Arguably, these states cause insecurity nation-
ally, regionally and globally. Central to the goal of human security
attempts to compel states to become sensitive and committed in preserving and enhancing the security of individual persons. The call to diversify
the referent objects to include human person and the nature of security
threats to environmental, social, and economic factors are imperative
(Buzan et al. 1998).

The regional security architecture in the Lake Chad Basin is comprehensible from these referent actors and the nature of threats that pervades
the region. Wendt (1992) provides a clear framework to understand the
underlying social structures that breed the threats and define the identity
and interest of the actors and how these interest and identity explain the
violent behaviour and the dynamics of the conflict situation. Contrary to
the neorealist argument that anarchy breeds self-help and power politics
exercised by states, the anarchic nature of international system or lack of

---

[4]See Perliger and Pedahzur (2016, p. 297) on totalistic ideologies and the impacts on
radicalization.

overarching governance including the regional government is precisely a by-product of the power politics and the self-help approach states employ in regional actions. Lack of central authority in the region has no meaning besides the practice that instantiate on the structure of identity and interest in the region. Identity and interest are therefore, the creation of the social structures that underlie the region (Wendt 1992). This is important in understanding identity-motivated conflicts as a form of new wars rather than conventional. Identity motivated conflicts are "messy and blur" the boundary between domestic and international—because it involves groups and states, local and international actors. Conventional conflict theories in which the Lake Chad regional states adopts their securitization approach are incapable of contending the news war championed by Boko Haram (Kaldor 1999 cited in Pilbeam 2015).

Factually, the nature of the security threat under consideration in the Lake Chad is a form of new war shaped by identities and interests in the region. The identities manifest as the state actors; Nigeria, Niger, Chad, and Cameroon considered as allies in the conflict and perceiving Boko Haram and its activities as an enemy or threat that must be neutralised and resolved. Boko Haram sees these state actors as apostates and agents of evil to be neutralised and resolved. The states' interest is the restoration of peace and security in the region while Boko Haram's interest rests in the propagation of an 'ideology' and elimination of western influence in all ramifications. The identities and interests of the actors are shaped by the underlying values around which each of their identities emerged. The identity and interest of state actors shaped by the Westphalia sovereign state values to an extent informs their behaviours. Although these regional state actors imbibe liberal democracy and capitalist socio-economic values even as they vary in some ways, yet, they maintain similarities in wide arrays of issues, including their intersubjective perception of what constitute security threats in the region. This identity and interest shapes the regional states' responses to the Boko Haram regional threats collectively identified as radical Islamism. Radicalism to any ideology is a dialectical process that pushes an individual or group gradually towards a commitment to violence over time (McCormick 2003). The radicalisation of these adherents could take various pathways to which are influenced by diverse reasons (Borum 2011).

The social groups' identity, to which Boko Haram is a case, is shaped by the Salafi Jihadist ideology, which underlies it. That identity and interest resonates with other Jihadi groups around the world, precisely because of the underlying social values around which such struggle is shaped. Extreme organisations like Boko Haram in other regions of the world explore communities to seek for adherents. They explore vulnerable neighbourhoods (neighbourhoods with adherents that their ideology finds appeal) where information on incentives for participation in such groups are availed. These neighbourhoods are mostly those with entrenched ideologies that share sense of cultural alienation or threat from outside sphere on the one hand and those who share similar cultural values, beliefs, and aspirations and consider other actors, for instance, in the region as threat to the survival of their group identity (Perliger and Pedahzur 2016). Wendt (1987) will argue that, state agents (Nigeria, Niger, Chad and Cameroon) and individual and group agents (Boko Haram) with both perceiving each other as enemies because of the conflicting social structures that caused the identities and interest of the actors in the region, making possible the behavioural response in the region. The state sought to neutralise and destroy Boko Haram. On the other hand, Boko Haram directs substantial violence to civilian population and occasionally wage battle on state strategic assets as part of attempts to whittle down and resolve the threats posed by the Westphalia state system in the region.

Arguably, power and interest are constructed social realities. Social structures, which underlie the society, create identity and interest. Identity manifests as state, individual, or group agencies, with each having its perception of the other as either a friend or a foe within the regional system. The underlying social structures with the state or human agencies determine social action (Wendt 1987). Social actions put through practice create inter-subjective meaning that defines what material resources mean. The meaning of material resources is comprehensible only through these discursive practices and the social context in which they are embedded (Wendt 1992). This is the extent and context within which, the meaning of material resources differs to the various identities. This is why material resources mean differently to both Boko Haram and state actors and its employment either as a value to hold or object to dispense as valueless.

Boko Haram's Rise and Expansion in the Lake Chad Basin

Today, the discourse of terrorism and insurgency has formed part of international relations reality with millions of people around the world constantly affected either directly as victims or indirectly from the impact of terrorism. Although the discourses about terrorism has no territorial boundary no matter how remotely the activities may appear, however, few challenging questions remains: Is terrorism or insurgency a spontaneous reaction to poverty (economic), government policies (political) and inequality/inequity (social) in the society? Is this phenomenon a carefully thought out ideas or existing ideology, well designed to accomplish pre-conceived goals? Scholarly debates and policy dialogues vary and differ considerably, especially on causes of terrorism and insurgency more so the motivations of Boko Haram violent involvement in the Lake Chad Basin. The current contribution to this debate stems from the prevailing polemical perceptions that characterised existing literature on this subject, with an aspiration to articulate a perspective, perhaps on what accounts for the rise and spread of Boko Haram's in the Lake Chad Basin Region.

Economic Factors

To begin an examination of these varying perspectives, Hansen and Musa argue that, Boko Haram was created about a decade ago based on "spontaneous explosion of rage and desperation" (Hansen and Musa 2013, p. 291). However, poverty, inequality and injustice in another view, constitute the triggers and motivations for violent conflicts perpetrated by boko haram so the organization continues to feed on the condition (Kwanashie 2013). As a counterpoise, poverty seem not to actually cause the violent conflicts, rather, they predisposed poor people to terrorist exploitation. While it exposes such social category, it is important to note that, poor people are not terrorists (Christopher Smith, Global Health and Human Rights Representative). The clarifications thereto, have improved our vision about the role of poverty either as precursor or as drive to terrorist or insurgent violence. Boko Haram as an epitome and manifestation of Islamism is a specific reaction to modern social and economic conditions, most especially, the rapid change in the demography of urbanization, the disarticulation of local economies like craft, the rising unemployment, and the glaring absence of basic norms to guide good conduct in the society (Black 2011, p. 306 cited in Adamu 2013). In addition, the rising level of frustration and poverty among youthful population in Nigeria and the neighbouring Chad, Cameroun and Niger republics is worthy of note. Regardless of the way, we perceive them; these challenges create a fertile ground for the activities of Boko Haram and its expansion (Ayegba 2015). Poverty and unemployment is inextricably connected to terrorism among youthful population on a global scale (Ucha 2015, p. 51; Onimade cited in Ayegba 2015). The unemployment exacerbates and deepens conditions that lead to increased militancy, violent crimes, kidnapping and several other bad behaviours amongst youths in Nigeria. Unemployment creates the dialectic of poverty and insecurity. In this line of argument therefore, unemployment leads to poverty and insecurity to which Boko Haram typifies the case.

Arguably, Boko haram's anger was directed initially at corrupt Muslim political class in the Northeast, who they perceive as collaborators and apostates. Similarly, distaste with democracy was the major militating force for adoption of violence by the group. Democracy is perceives as a system creating a tiny parasitic class that rides on the back of dominated majority who wallow in abject penury. In their conclusion, the tiny few (the dominated political class) are continuously and corruptly siphoning the collective patrimony (Hansen and Musa 2013). This perspective suggests that, material explanations will help the understanding of the problem. This article finds these reasons porous. Arguably, the operators of these terrorist and insurgent organizations as much as some of their ideologues may not necessarily suffer any form of material want. These terrorists' members (operators) are not necessarily poor or wretched as most analysis indicates. The lead operators (rational prospectors) expend or spend the poor followership as they do to battle riffles, suicide belts, bullets, and other war paraphernalia. It is indisputable that the poor followership has no opinion or any interest, less the organization fights to redeem, unless in the context of the ideology and underlying culture to which the terrorist and insurgent struggle is embedded.

The veracity of the "poverty theory" as a yardstick for terrorism and insurgency remain unconvincing (Akinola 2015). If poverty does underlie the struggle, what are the costs of war grade riffles, the logistics expended on various operations conducted by these groups and what are the costs of planning, including intelligence gathering and prosecution of the heavy violent encounters with government forces? These questions should deepen analysis of Boko Haram activities beyond the poverty cursor. When examined closely, the character of the violent struggle and the interest of the organization resonate with the bourgeoning appetite of the northern political and religious elites, who best thrive on the poverty, ignorance and vulnerabilities of their immediate communities (Maiangwa et al. 2012). This then leaves us with more zeal to probe further, to establish the fundamental cause of this social malaise.

The Political Debates

Interestingly, not most scholars share this socio-economic paradigm approach to the understanding of the Boko Haram phenomenon in the Lake Chad Basin. The emergence of radical Islamic groups like Boko Haram and their counterparts around the world is to certain extent a specific reaction to the United States of America's foreign policy options (Patel 2007). The rise of Boko Haram has been expansively analysed through political and economic lens. These parallel factors provoked Boko Haram campaign and violent activities in the Lake Chad Basin Region (Comolli 2015, p. 208). The political facets of insurgency are significant. New recruits to the fold of Boko Haram learn deliberately in camps, the politico-religious messages of the struggle as part of the wider strategic ambition and militant orientation (Sandig 2015). To the militant ideologues, "Sharia" (Islamic Jurisprudence) presents a credible and incorruptible alternative to the failing secular order. As a political gesture to appeal to the northern political audience, northern governors, in the years 2000s, pledged allegiance to Sharia (ibid.).

Preceding analysis gives credence to political reasons as the precursor for terrorism and insurgency in the Lake Chad Basin. It portrays Boko Haram as an organization with specific political objectives, seeking to destroy existing democratic political order. If the goal of the organization is to destroy the incumbent secular order, what order is the organization contemplating to guide human engagements? The struggle never contemplates political void or vacuum. Boko Haram seeks to position instead a robust Islamic jurisprudence of the Salafi Wahhabist ideology. Largely, this is the dimension the political component of the struggle takes precedence (Fafowora 2013). Equally, the numerous messages propagated by the Boko Haram exposed an organization, who have repeatedly stressed the solution to the plight of northern Muslims in Nigeria can only be addressed by a radical break with secular tradition and modern political order (Sandig 2015). A closer look at Boko Haram's antics revealed an organization committed to inflicting fears on Nigerians, and particularly, discouraging those living within the range of the areas of their influence from enrolment into western education.

Often, the group reiterate their abhorrence to western influence, as it socializes people against the will of God, they claim. Hence, radical revival through jihad is necessary to establish a new social order based on the principles of Sharia. In essence, Boko Haram is diametrically opposed to western education (Aghedo and Osumah 2012; Ishaya 2011 cited in Aghedo and Osumah 2015).

It is very clear from the methodological approaches and the ensuing analysis, that existing discussions about the group is hinge on materialist ontology. If poverty (economy), government policy (politics) and inequality (social) can explain the causes of terrorism and insurgency, what explanation can support situations where members of terror groups are willing kill self or others. How then can the dead utilize the material benefits in which the socio-economic settings of the struggle? The underlying social structures that influence the material perception through discursive practice by perpetrators will provide answers. Against this inadequacy, this article emerged with the constructivists approach to explain this social phenomenon, and to link the cause of the rise of Boko Haram to the underlying social, ideological, and cultural structures in the region as embedded, which supports it. This work contends that, the economic and political factors nurture and sustain the violence but the cause of the terrorism and insurgency in the region are- social, ideological, and cultural factors rooted in Salafi Jihadism. It is crucial to note, terrorism and insurgency violence are not the ends in themselves but just means to an end.

The Ideological Underpin

Let us begin with this argument by Voll that, based on recent social media engagement of Boko Haram, it is kidnapping, bank robbery time enjoyed the support and encouragement of Al-Qaeda, the Al-Qaeda in the Maghreb (AQIM) and the Islamic State of Iraq and Syria (ISIS) (Voll 2015). The active engagement of the group on social media shows a group who seeks to impress the terror organizations and other passive persons who belief tenaciously in the radical Salafi ideological approach to the spread of Islam. Such approach we consider as basically, their "Public", in the sense, that terrorism and insurgency resonate with this "public reason".

This article views terrorist and insurgency as grounded in the ideological and cultural preferences of the ideologues and managers of the organisations. They are inseparable with their immediate social and ideological environments and the geographical settings in which the terrorists and insurgent militants are rooted. The rationality, justification, and great rewards both spiritual and temporal that awaits adherence are carefully thought-out approaches towards the accomplishment of some pre-conceived goals and supported by the prevailing social structures. Terrorism and insurgency are constructed social realities within the Salafi Radical ideology. Such constructed social realities have justifications, embedded in socio-economic and spiritual rewards. Boko Haram builds its radicalism on this tradition, have carefully imbibed the ideology, planned its activities with organised and robust terrorist and insurgent infrastructures to support these activities, to establish a caliphate for the reconstruction of the identity of the citizens of the new caliphate along the Salafi ideological orientation.

A War Judiciously Planned

Between 2000 and 2009, well over twelve states in Northern Nigeria have declared Sharia as part of their state's political and legal jurisprudence. Most scholars and political commentators argued that such Sharia is for poor people, given that most of the prominent political and economic elites were not subjecting themselves to the Sharia, this added credence to the notion that, it was a Political Sharia (Akinola 2015). Boko Haram organisation was part of Borno political arrangement, particularly in the days of implementing the Political Sharia. Boko Haram members were overtly part of Borno and Yobe political life. The group assisted Governor Modu sheriff of Borno state in the 2003 elections campaign where they intimidated and threatened the political opponents of the Governor. As compensation and recognition to the group after the 2003 election victory, Mohammed Yusuf, the leader of the group enjoyed appointment into the government as a member of the Borno state Sharia Board whilst his close ally, Alhaji Buji Foi was appointed the Commissioner for Religious Affairs (Akinola 2015; Harnischfeger 2014).

The involvement of Boko Haram in secular politics is arguably part of the scheme and design of the organisation to understand secular politics. To use acquired knowledge to attain their pre-meditated goal of abolishing the modern Nigerian state. The expansion to the contiguous neighbours in the Lake Chad basin is a product the conflict dynamics. It is suggestive that, the organisation utilized almost a decade long opportunity of their political participation to build primary popular support and sympathy at the grass root level, establish connections within and outside the country and perhaps, resources. The implications of the involvement of the organisation in Borno secular politics meant, virtually all travellers for annual Hajj (Saudi Arabia) and lesser Hajj (Um'Rah) was influenced by the organization. Authenticating radicalized travellers who could easily abscond and access terrorists training infrastructures that abounds in the Middle East were all implications to that effect. Especially, given that the organisation's patrons and ideologues influenced this critical ministry for some years. To this, we argue cannot be a coincidence but part of the larger scheme of the organisation to utilise legitimate state structures for their ideological struggle.

Boko Haram War: Reactionary Response to State Violence Verses Planned Violence for Identity Reconstruction

Views vary considerably on the war waged by the Boko Haram. The resistance and later activities of the group perceived in many quarters as reactionary. Predominant position locates the actions of the group as a response or reaction to poverty, political motives, and social inequality. A validation of almost a decade unending war engaged by the sect, framed as a "spontaneous explosion of rage and desperation" (Hansen and Musa 2013, p. 291). Some scholars argue that, it is much more that, there exist evidence of deliberate planning, the sect sponsored students abroad surreptitiously for medical training (Madunagu et al. 2009, p. 2 cited in Adesoji 2010). In Borno, Yobe and parts of Adamawa states, the sect allegedly floated and operated a functional cooperative finance scheme (Hansen and Musa 2013). Perhaps, such acts depict expression of generous magnanimity towards the poor and the less privileged in the face of apparent state failure on their responsibility to the populace. It is tactical ploy to prey on the less privileged group for the radicalization agenda.

Interestingly, there was huge interest for the group to raise funds. Rich members of the group; Buji Foi (a former commissioner for Religious Affairs in Borno State), Kadiru Atiku (a former lecturer) and Bunu Wakil (a prominent contractor in Borno State) played significant roles in mobilizing funds and resources. Besides these influential individuals, over 280,000 members spread across Northern Nigeria, Niger,

Chad and Sudan were recruited (Lawal 2009, p. 35 cited in Onuoha 2012). Each member pays a daily sum of 100 Naira each, besides the donations and patronage enjoyed from politicians, government officials, and other organizations. The arrest of Bunu Wakil and 91 others was revealing. This is part of the group's source of domestic resource and financial mobilization strategy (Idris 2011 cited in Onuoha 2012).

Likewise, Mohammed Damagun, standing trial before an Abuja Federal High Court, accused of link with terror groups and accused of being the foreign funds and resources raiser for the sect further lend credence and evidence to the planned character of the group. Damagun is accused of having in his possession about, 300,000 US Dollars traced to him and it was believed to be given to him by Al-Qaeda meant for Boko Haram (Suleiman 2007, p. 24; Onuoha 2010a, p. 56 in Onuoha 2012). Apart from these much publicised sources, the sect is believed to have benefited tremendously from proceeds of crime committed by AQIM, kidnapping, bank robbery and car hijacking (Barrett 2012, p. 723; Davies 2012; Walker 2012; Waldek and Jayasekara 2011 cited in Elden 2014, p. 416). The economic repositioning is troubling for any serious government but it meant nothing too serious to the erstwhile regime. The sect understood the strategic significance of political planning and organization, hence, took great advantage and time. Politically, the critical evolutionary dynamics of the group as from 2003 to 2009 highlights the process of mass recruitment of members using open preaching as a cover. By 2010, the sect commenced active terrorism and by 2013, they transformed to insurgent guerrillas. Finally, territorial acquisition and expansion commenced 2015 (Perouse de Montclos 2016).

Interestingly, the group, on its own had severally put up many claims, one of which was alluding to it having sent its members for training in Afghanistan, Lebanon, Pakistan, Iraq and Mauritania (Adesoji 2010, p. 101). Many may consider these claims as spurious and possibly a strategic blunder. Evidently, such claims may be too good to be true; volunteering too much strategic and operational information could be misleading, but again, preceding trends suggest that, the sect's announcement of an intended plan or action is not strange. It is possible they could make much more risky claims with the most pompous audacity than this. From whichever angle one views the strategic and operational plans, it is here evident that, the sect has proven links with outside fundamentalist groups (Alli 2009, p. 1; Oyebile and Lawal 2009, p. 69; Saboyede 2009, p. 14; Clayton 2010 in Adesoji 2010, p. 101). From all indications, Adesoji argued that, Boko Haram had been around under different names for the past 15 years, before its public recognition as a terror and insurgent sect (Adesoji 2010). Based on the preponderance of facts, Boko haram battle could not be reactionary rather an ideologically driven war- carefully thought-out and planned in the Lake Chad Basin Region.

The Patterns of the War and the Goals of the Struggle

The attack launched by the Nigerian Security Forces at Dutsen Tashi in late July 2009, revealed surprising discoveries. The police found and confiscated high war grade weapons and several materials for improvised explosive devices (IEDs) for bomb-making (Adesoji 2010). The group's alliance with AQIM has further improved their skills in making IEDs, using suicide attackers and effective use of social media (Voll 2015). The dynamics of the violent encounters with state actors in the Lake Chad Basin Region had evolved along certain strategic and tactical trends. From July, all the territory won by the group were marked for keeps (Aghedo 2015). The insurgent war is not haphazard in manner rather, organised with central command, reminiscent of modern national military formations.

The revolutionary command structure of the group is very discipline and orderly with recognizable hierarchical features known to everyone in their struggle. At the top of the hierarchy command, is the "Amir Ul-Aam" (the commander of the faithful). Below him, are the two "Na'ib Amir Ul-Aam" (1&2) (the Deputy Commanders of the faithful). These are the top officers at the helm of affairs of the command. At the state level, there exist the "Amir" (State Commander) and the local "Amir", coordinating the local government areas. The lower rungs of the socio-political hierarchy are members who constitute the reserved army of insurgents organised into the militant army and sharia police. While the sharia police enforce local order given by the command in the held territories, the army are the militant insurgents charged with the responsibility of protecting the territorial gains, ward- off threats to the held territories and expand the region of control.[5] From all indication, the group seem more organized than what people see from afar.

[5] See, Da'wah Coordination Council of Nigeria, 2012 in Onuoha (2012).

All forms of reprisals and provocations by belligerents are not reasons or the causes of the violent behaviours of the sect nor the retaliations or revenge mission's reaction by the group; such only exacerbate and intensify the violence. The target of the sect is the creation of a religious society through reconstruction of existing diverse social identities to reflect the ideals and social reality constructed by the sect and their ideologues.

The (Re)Creation of the "Caliphate"

This is quite a difficult narrative discourse considering the satisfactory criteria for such declarations in the Islamic world. For most periods of the violent encounters, observers have speculated possible connections with outside jihadi network. Earlier in 2009, Boko Haram declared support for Al-Qaeda and vowed to carry out its activities in Nigeria until the country is islamised according to divine injunction.[6] This was contained as a press release, issued by Abu Qaqa (Perouse de Montclos 2016). Until present, the group has put up several claims including the religious justification of violence and mayhem on civilian noncombatants. Such assertions depict a group with intent to establish an extreme Salafi style state in Nigeria, with ties to global Jihad (Voll 2015). While the globe was engrossed with the audacity of the group's violent activities, the Islamic State released a statement accepting Boko Haram as its province in West Africa. A further indication of the group's possible links with Al-Qaeda and AQIM (ibid.). On the 25 February 2015, Abubakar Shekau took oath of loyalty to the leader of Islamic State and recognized as Islamic State West African Province (ISWAP) (ibid.). Shekau swore: "we announce our allegiance to the Caliph of Muslims… and will hear and obey him in difficulty and prosperity" (Nathaniel 2015). At this stage, the group had made significant territorial gains in the Lake Chad Basin Region, especially, between Nigeria and Cameroun borders (ibid.). Before all the exchanges of loyalty, allegiance and declarations took place, the group was already operating and conducting its activities like "a state within a state", with cabinet members and a very strong religious police as they maintained a very large homestead (Walker 2012, p. 3 cited in Elden 2014, p. 421).

[6] See, *Vanguard* News Paper, 14 August 2009.

Despite occasional denouncement of the group's activities by the few prominent Muslim clerics and personalities, the group continued to enjoy great inspiration and cited extensively the Islamic scholarship of Al-Maghili on jihad, which permit Muslims to wage war against its oppressors (Non-Muslim rulers). This part of the scholarship urged that whoever (Muslim) is killed in the process of the Holy war, is the best of Martyr, whereas, the oppressors (non-Muslims) killed in the struggle are the worst of the slain men (Voll 2015). This is perhaps the ideological and cultural basis around which the group construct their social reality and about which all the violence perpetrated are justified. The violent acts are means to the ends, and therefore, to interpret the group's terror acts in the lake Chad Basin as ends in themselves and approaching the challenges as ephemeral reactions to poverty, government policies, or social inequality could be misleading.

The group had fought severally with the state security forces in attempts for territorial gains and expansion. They lost and won in different instances. The war for the practical establishment of the declared aspiration (Caliphate) is the drive toward the attainment of the ends; reconstructing the social identity of the inhabitants. The battle for Gwoza signified the starting point of tangibly manifesting this aspiration of a caliphate in the lake Chad Basin region. On the 6 of August 2014, the group beseeched the city of Gwoza massively, as heavy gun shots kept sounding like music orchestra. In this huge pandemonium, the Emir (paramount ruling Monarch) and large civilian population fled to the Mandara mountains (*Syndi Gate Media* 2014). Although the State Armed Forces responded but the battle for Gwoza raged on. The state could make no gains in spite of the eighteen days' heavy bombardments, artillery firing, and ground troop combat with the insurgents.

The failure of the state's armed forces to secure outright defeat, restore law and order, and bring back the fleeing civilians was a boost to the morale of the group. On 24 of August 2014, the group announced victory over government troops and proclaimed the formation of "Islamic Caliphate", in parts of Lake Chad basin areas with the headquarters in Gwoza. The message was circulated through a 52 minutes' video clip, containing the under quoted prefatory declaration that, "*Oh people*, I am Abubakar Shekau here standing, the leader of Jama'atu Ahlissunnah Lidda'Awati Wal Jihad in Nigeria. We do not believe in the name Nigeria. We are in Islamic Caliphate. We have nothing to do with Nigeria" (ibid.). The victory over Gwoza embolden the sect and their leader, Abubakar Shekau, who proclaimed himself the great Imam and Commander of the faithful, proceeded to proclaimed Gwoza, the headquarters of the Caliphate (Perouse de Montclos 2016). Meanwhile, the group took over the Palace of the Emir of Gwoza, transformed the Palace Court to the Supreme Court of the Caliphate (*Syndi Gate Media* 2014). In Gwoza, as a norm for any controlled territory by the group, a black flag with Arabic inscription hoisted, signifying that, such area is within the control of the Islamic caliphate in the Lake Chad Basin (ibid.).

Gwoza is a border town between Nigeria and the Cameroun republic. It has a population of 276,312 people, by the 2006 Nigerian population figures. Other towns, villages and communities include but not limited to; Damboa, Bama, Konduga, Mafa, Dikwa, Benisheik, Mainok, Baga, parts of Maiduguri Metropolis, Jere, Gomboru, Gulami, Marte, Abatam, Iziye and Madagali. This is apart from the over 200 neighbouring villages and communities proximate to Gwoza, which were the worst affected by the violent militant campaign (*Syndi Gate Media* 2014). The areas of Sambisa Forest, Mandara Mountains and parts of not less than 15 other local government areas spread across Borno, Yobe and Adamawa States, especially, along the border communities of lake Chad Basin countries are under the control of the Boko Haram (Aghedo 2015).

The battle for Mubi, the second largest town in Adamawa State, is also significant in the Caliphate agenda. About 151,000 people according to the 2006 population head count in Nigeria inhabit the town. Despite the demographic significance, it fell to the insurgent group in October 2014. Following the group's control of Mubi, the town's name changed to "*Madinatul Islam*" (meaning the city of Islam). Like Gwoza, the Emir Palace in Mubi became the administrative control location of the group. The insurgents rendered few minor services such as traffic control while assuring the trapped residence to remain calm (ibid.). Although the group gained several control of territories, the notorious Sambisa forest remains the insurgent's warehouse and provided the needed strategic cover to the insurgent battalions reserved for the anticipated battles with the Lake Chad Basin States and perhaps their allies like African Union Multinational Task Force and the rest of the western world who feel concerned. In this forest, the 270 abducted Chibok pupils were alleged to being kept hidden in three separate camps with other hostages. The effective control of the forest area by the group forced the villages hitherto living within and around the area to relocate to neighbouring countries (Ladan 2014). The group did not just gained control of some towns in northeast Nigeria but also exerted effective control of the border areas of Borno State along Chad, Cameroun, and Niger Republics. Reports indicated the group to have adopted extreme measures of repression and control in trying to create and maintain a religiously identified new political order in the areas within their control. For instance, women are subjugated in these areas and have little role, except that they are servants or slaves (Voll 2015).

As regard the "Caliphate" agenda, we may not out rightly take side in this article. The prevailing narratives speak volume about the intention and manifestation of a "new Caliphate" in lake Chad Basin Areas. Arguably, it is not problematical to emphasize that the new Caliphate is confronted with constant reprisals, recapture, and outright defeats by the combined efforts of security forces from the affected countries in the Region. The Caliphate is waning and their control dwindling as they constantly suffer loses of the "conquered territories". Hence, this is the tool or means and not yet the ends.

IDENTITY RECONSTRUCTION PROJECT

Arguably, Boko Haram remains the first religious group in Nigeria to carry out ideological hybridization integrating the theologico-Judicial resources of the global Jihadi-Salafism with modification of cultural and historical framings of religious revival in Northern Nigeria (Voll 2015). The Sunni Islam has provided general guideline for religious reformers who advocate for moral reconstruction in their societies. Within such framework, Ibn Taymiyya receives recognition for his contribution to this Wahhabist tradition. The agenda of Boko Haram is set towards the path of moral reconstruction in Nigeria, and by implication in the Lake Chad Basin region so they seek an end to modern secular culture for an exclusive society based on the literalist interpretation of Islam (ibid.). The major ideologues of the group have their modern inspiration and knowledge from the Salafi ideology of Abu Mohammed Al-Maqdisi (a Palestinian-Jordanian). The same Islamic Cleric mentored Abu Mus'ab Al-Zaqawi (the leader of Al-Qaeda in Iraq) (Perouse de Montclos 2016).

Abubakar Shekau, the leader of Boko Haram declared that Christianity is Paganism. He is therefore under divine instruction of "Allah" to coerce everyone to embrace Islam (Shea 2014, p. 41). If religion is a form of social identity to which it is, moderate Muslims of all climes, Christians and all other social identities other than the Salafi wahabist tradition are offensive and hostile to the Jihadi project. The Jihadi project captured in a statement made by the group, reiterated commitment against any system of government besides the one recognized by Islam. Hence, the group abhors all orthodoxy, traditional, democracy, socialism, and capitalist system of government. They would neither allow the Federal Republic of Nigerian Constitution to replace the laws already enshrined in the holy Qur'an nor allow any western education to replace Islamic teachings (Agbiboa 2013, p. 4). The Boko Haram group feels a sense of moral obligation to deconstruct any social identity that does not resonate with strictly interpreting the Sharia. Interestingly, such moral obligation does not detest the weaponization of civilian facility but promote it. Indiscriminate human carnage, rape and material destructions are not only used as weapons (weaponization of civilian facility), but violent territorial conquest is permitted by such ideology for Sharia consolidation, which even violates the constitution of the Federal Republic of Nigeria (Idowu 2013 cited in Elden 2014). The group seeks not only such territorial control and the laws over the territory, but also the control of the people within such space (Peters 2014 cited in Elden 2014).

With this background, identity reconstruction of the people and social identities in parts of Lake Chad basin region remain the cause and sustaining motivation of Boko Haram violent involvement in the region. Apparently, the territories captured need to be peopled, hence the kidnappings, mass abductions of people into the controlled areas for the identity reconstruction project. This is evident in the kidnapping of the over 276 Chibok girls, which according to the Federal Government of Nigeria are about 85% Christians. A video clip released by the group and monitored revealed all the girls been coerced to Islam; therefore, their identities have been re defined by violent reconstruction. They are to such end designated for sale as slaves or given in marriage to Muslims (Shea 2014, p. 42). Since the commencement of the Boko Haram insurgent campaign, the group has taken hostage of over 2000 people. These include the over 276 Chibok girls, 218 Katarko villagers captured and the raid in Damasak which the group took over 500 hostages (Oyewole 2015). Arguably, the remaining 15% could be moderate Muslims. Since secular education is sinful to the radical group, assumedly, none of their adherent could have been in secular school as at the time of the Chibok girls' school kidnapping.

CONCLUSION

This article attempts to contribute to the debate on the theoretical dilemma of the cause of the rise of Boko Haram in the Lake Chad Basin region. Scholars have written extensively on the causes and motivations of the terror activities of Boko Haram in the Lake Chad region. Similar with previous research outputs, this article has engaged and participated in the ongoing debate on Boko Haram discourse. From most of the preceding works reviewed, scholars project Boko Haram's cause of rise and motivation from the materialist framework. Our contribution to this debate took an exception from the materialist ontology. We approach the discourse rather from a constructivist perspective, whereas, the materialist ontology limits the causes to poverty, economic reasons, political factors and social inequality as the root causes of violent scenarios in the Lake Chad basin region. These materialistic factors proffered rather nourish, drive, and sustain the circle of internecine violence in the region. This article argues that Boko Haram in the Lake Chad Basin region aims precisely at reconstructing the social identity of the people. The social, ideological, and cultural undertones, expressed in the enthusiasm for martyrdom, deepen our comprehension on the commitment of the group rather than the material motives.

REFERENCES

Adamu, A.U. 2013. Insurgency in Nigeria: The Northern Nigerian Experience. In *Complex Emergency in Nigeria*, ed. O. Obafemi and H. Galadimas. Kuru, Nigeria: National Institute for Policy and Strategic Studies.

Adesoji, A. 2010. The Boko Haram Uprising and Islamic Revival in Nigeria. *African Spectrum* 45 (2): 95–108. Institute of African Affairs, GIGA, Hamburg-Germany. www.jstor.org/stable. Accessed 30 Aug 2016.

Agbiboa, D.E. 2013. Why Boko Haram Exists: The Relative Deprivation Perspective. *African Conflict & Peacebuilding Review* 3 (1): 144–157.

Aghedo, I. 2015. Nigeria's Boko Haram; From Guerrilla Strategy to Conventional Warfare? *The Round Table* 104 (4): 515–516.

Aghedo, I., and O. Osumah. 2015. Insurgency in Nigeria: A Comparative Study of Niger Delta and Boko Haram Uprisings. *Journal of African and Asian Studies* 50 (2). www.jas.sagepab.com. Accessed 22 Aug 2016.

Ajayi, A.I. 2012. 'Boko Haram' and Terrorism in Nigeria: Exploratory and Explanatory Notes. *Global Advanced Research Journal of History, Political Science and International Relations* 1 (5): 103–107.

Akinola, O. 2015. Boko Haram Insurgency in Nigeria: Between Islamic, Fundamentalism, Politics and Poverty. http://www.tandfonline.com. Accessed 22 Aug 2016.

Ayegba, U.S. 2015. Unemployment and Poverty as Sources and Consequences of Insecurity in Nigeria: The Boko Haram Insurgency Revisited. *African Journal of Political Science and International Relations.* http://www.academicjournal.org/AJPSIR. Accessed 23 Aug 2016.

Borum, R. 2011. Radicalization into Violent Extremism: A Review of Social Science Theories. *Journal of Strategic Security* 4 (4): 7–36. http://scholrcommons.usf.edu/Jess/vol4/iss4/2.

Buzan, B. 1991. *People, State and Fear, An Agenda for International Security Studies in Post-Cold-War Era,* 2nd ed., 186–229. Colchester: ECRP Press.

Buzan, B., O. Waever, and J. deWilde. 1998. *A New Framework for Analysis Boulder.* Boulder: Lynne Rienner.

Comolli, V. 2015. *Boko Haram: Nigeria's Islamist Insurgency,* 208. London: Hurst.

Elden, S. 2014. The Geopolitics of Boko Haram and Nigeria's War on Terror. *The Geographical Journal* 180 (4): 414–425.

Fafowora, O. 2013. Understanding Insurgencies in Nigeria: Nature, Types, Dynamics and the Way out; A Key Note Address. In *Complex Emergency in Nigeria,* ed. O. Obafemi and H. Galadiman. Kuru, Nigeria: National Institute for Policy and Strategic Studies.

Hansen, W.W., and U.A. Musa. 2013. Fanon the Wretched and Boko Haram. *Journal of African and Asian Studies.* www.jas.sagepub.com. Accessed 29 July 2016.

Harnischfeger, J. 2014. Boko Haram and Its Muslim Critics: Observation from Yobe State. In *Boko Haram: Islamism, Politics, Security and the State in Nigeria,* ed. Marc-Antoine Pérouse de Montclos, Leiden.

Hynes, J. 2015. Religion and International Conflict. In *International Security Studies; Theory and Practice,* ed. P. Hough et al. New York: Routledge.

Kaldor, M. 1999. *New and Old Wars; Organised Violence in the Global Era* in Pilbeam, B. 2015. New Wars, Globalization and Failed States. In *International Security Studies; Theory and Practice,* ed. P. Hough et al. New York: Routledge.

Kwanashie, M. 2013. Diagnostic Review of Insurgency in Nigeria, Sources, Causes and Remedies: The Economic Dimension. In *Complex Emergency in Nigeria,* ed. O. Obafemi and H. Galadiman. Kuru, Nigeria: National Institute for Policy and Strategic Studies.

Ladan, S.I. 2014. Forest and Forest Reserves as Security Threats in Northern Nigeria. *European Scientific Journal* 10 (35): 120–142.

Loimeier, R. 2012. Boko Haram: The Development of a Militant Religious Movement in Nigeria. *African Spectrum* 47 (2/3): 137–155.

Maiangwa, B., et al. 2012. Baptism by Fire: Boko Haram and the Region of Terror in Nigeria. *Africa Today* 59 (2): 41–57.

McCormick, G.H. 2003. *Terrorist Decision Making* in Borum, R. 2011. Radicalization into Violent Extremism: A Review of Social Science Theories. *Journal of Strategic Security* 4 (4): 15.

Nathaniel, A. 2015. The Islamic State, Boko Haram and the Evolution of international Jihad. Washington Post, Web Blog, Post-blogss, WP, Company LLC.

Onuoha, F.C. 2012. The Audacity of Boko Haram: Background, Analysis and Emerging Trend. *Security Journal* 52 (2): 134–151. www.palgrave.journals.com/sj/.

Oyewole, S. 2015. Boko Haram: Insurgency and the War Against Terrorism in the Lake Chad Basin. *Strategic Analysis*. 39 (4): 428–432. http://dx.doi.org/10.1080/09700161.2015.1047227.

Patel, I.A. 2007. The Scale for Defining Islamic Political Radicalism; A European Perspective. In *Complex Emergency in Nigeria*, ed. O. Obafemi and H. Galadiman. Kuru, Nigeria: National Institute for Policy and Strategic Studies.

Perliger, A., and A. Pedahzur. 2016. Counter Cultures, Group Dynamics and Religious Terrorism. *Political Studies* 64 (2): 297–314.

Perouse de Montclos, M. 2016. A Sectarian Jihad in Nigeria: The Case of Boko Haram. *Small Wars and Insurgencies*. www.tandfonline.com.

Pieterse, J.N. 1997. Sociology of Humanitarian Intervention: Bosnia, Rwanda and Somalia Compared. *International Political Science Review* 18 (1): 71–93.

Pilbeam, B. 2015. New Wars, Globalization and Failed States. In *International Security Studies; Theory and Practice*, ed. P. Hough et al. New York: Routledge.

Sandig, S. 2015. Framing Protest and Insurgency: Boko Haram and MASSOB in Nigeria. *Civil War*. www.tandfonline.com. Accessed 22 Aug 2016.

Shea, N. 2014. *Barberism 2014: On Religious Cleansing by Islamist*, World Affairs Institute.

Syndi Gate Media. 2014. Boko Haram—How "New Caliphate" Emerged. www.allafrica.com.

Thomson, V. 2012. Boko Haram and Islamic Fundamentalism in Nigeria. *Global Security Studies* 3 (3): 46–60.

Voll, J.O. 2015. *Boko Haram: Religion and Violence in the 21st Century*. Washington, DC: Georget University. www.mdpi.com/journal/religions, African Research Bulletin, Political, Social, and Cultural Series, vol. 52, no. 1.

Wendt, A. 1987. The Agent-Structure Problem in International Relations Theory. *MIT Press, International Organization* 41 (3): 335–370.

Wendt, A. 1992. Anarchy Is What States Make of the Social Construction of Power Politics. *MIT Press, International Organization* 46 (2): 391–425.

Peacekeeping in the African Union: Gender, Women and the Battle Against Sexual Exploitation and Abuse

Sabrina White

INTRODUCTION

The institutional actors involved in United Nations Peace Operations (Unpos) primarily perform a security role in their efforts to move a conflict-torn country towards an environment of lasting peace. However, their arrival is also associated with gendered sexually exploitative conditions which negatively impact the local civilian population, and which can have far reaching consequences. The scale of sexual exploitation and abuse (SEA) committed by Peacekeeping Personnel during the 1990s in Cambodia and Bosnia and in the early 2000s in the Democratic Republic of the Congo (DRC) spread shock waves throughout the United Nations (UN) as it found itself embroiled in a scandal threatening the impartiality, effectiveness and trust and confidence in peace operations. The links between SEA and human trafficking, organised

S. White (✉)
Regent's University London, London, UK
e-mail: WhiteSa@REGENTS.AC.UK

© The Author(s) 2018
P. Frankowski and A. Gruszczak (eds.),
Cross-Disciplinary Perspectives on Regional and Global Security,
https://doi.org/10.1007/978-3-319-75280-8_8

165

crime, economic insecurity, gendered-power dynamics and other factors have detrimental effects on the security and development of post-conflict countries, and ultimately of long-term peace.

The public unveiling of SEA coincided approximately with the adoption of Security Council Resolution 1325 (SCR 1325) in 2000, which formally recognised the link between the security of women and the security of states. Insecurity in post-conflict societies is gendered, and women and girls are disproportionately negatively affected (Pettman 1996; Tickner 1992; Enloe 2002). Women's insecurity post-conflict is compounded by obstacles to political acknowledgement, physical insecurity, sexual violence, exploitation and abuse, access to economic security among other intersectional factors (Ni Aolain et al. 2011, p. 68). Since SCR 1325, there have been several additional resolutions[1] expanding on the securitisation of women, or what is now called the WPS Agenda, all of which also address issues relevant to addressing UNPOs and SEA; however, it was not until 2003 that the issue was specifically addressed, prompted by a resolution passed by the General Assembly.[2] Despite an increase in research and political attention, SEA in UNPOs has not been reduced, suggesting that policies and/or their implementation fall short.

Article 1(1) of the UN Charter states that a key purpose of the UN is "to maintain international peace and security, and to that end: to take effective collective measures for the prevention and removal of threats to the peace." The Charter also articulates the need for cooperation in economic, social, cultural and humanitarian issues and the promotion of respect for human rights (Article 1, 2–4). The UN Security Council (SC) is tasked with the primary responsibility to maintain international peace and security, and while not officially stated in the charter, deployment of Peacekeeping or Peace Operations serves as an integral part of their remit as well as one of the most visible symbols of the UN's role in international peace and security (Thakur 2016, p. 41).

Since the end of the Cold War, multi-dimensional peacekeeping has evolved to address complex peace operations and facilitate a security

---

[1] Resolutions 1820 (2008), 1888 (2009), 1889 (2009), 1960 (2010), 2106 (2013), 2122 (2013), 2242 (2015) and (contestably) 2272 (2016). For an overview of the resolutions, please see Peace Women: http://www.peacewomen.org/resolutions-texts-and-translations.

[2] UN General Assembly 2003. *Investigation into Sexual Exploitation of Refugees by Aid Workers in West Africa.* A/RES/57/306.

situation conducive to making transformations which are necessary to ensure sustainable peace. The core functions of such operations are: to create a stable security environment, facilitate political processes, support establishment of institutions of governance, and provide a framework for other actors to perform their duties in a coordinated manner. Human rights serve as a cornerstone of the normative framework for UNPOs, and UN peacekeeping personnel are expected to act in accordance with international human rights law (United Nations 2008, p. 23); when peacekeeping personnel are accused of or commit crimes, it is exclusively the responsibility of the troop-contributing country (TCC), not the UN, to exercise criminal jurisdiction. As accountability and strength of judicial institutions varies widely internationally, accountability is often a source of discontent in addressing crimes committed by peacekeeping personnel.

Despite their significant shortcomings, there is a positive correlation between fewer civil wars, less armed conflicts and increased UN missions in the post-Cold War Period (Dobbins et al. 2001). Peacekeeping missions excel in securing borders in fragile states, preventing the spread of conflict (Fortna 2008; Howard 2008; Beardsley 2011) and have left behind societies that are more stable and secure, especially where they have worked to influence the behaviour of local actors to pursue transformative goals (Whalan 2013, p. 3; Sandler 2017, p. 19). However, the security of women in all of these successes has been a critical point.

SEXUAL EXPLOITATION AND ABUSE IN UNPOS

The UN defines sexual exploitation as "any actual or attempted abuse of a position of vulnerability, differential power, or trust, for sexual purposes, including, but not limited to, profiting monetarily, socially or politically from the sexual exploitation of another" and sexual abuse as "the actual or threatened physical intrusion of a sexual nature, whether by force or under unequal or coercive conditions" (UN Secretariat 2003).

The geographical spread of alleged abuse is not isolated to one set of countries or region where UNPOs are active, although most missions are in the African continent, suggesting that there are inherent issues in peacekeeping operations themselves, and possibly in the institution of the military, which fail to prevent impunity for these crimes. In 2016, there were 145 allegations of SEA involving 311 civilian victims, of whom

309 were women and girls in 2017 (UN General Assembly 2017, para. 8). Of the fifteen current peacekeeping operations, eight are located in Africa, and a 2016 review found that 68% of allegations of SEA took place in the missions in Central African Republic (MINUSCA) and Democratic Republic of the Congo (MONUSCO), which both involve African Union and UN leadership and support (United Nations 2017).

Prosecution for crimes of SEA committed by peacekeeping personnel has been sporadic and woefully inadequate (OIOS 2015), resulting in those countries who often contribute the least troops to call for improved accountability and 'naming and shaming' of relevant TCCs. Thus lies a political dilemma in improving accountability: if certain states are singled out, then they may be hesitant to contribute as many troops. The UN already struggles to secure sufficient personnel from states, and a reduction in political will to contribute could impact the success and sustainability of operations (Sheeran et al. 2014, p. 5).

This chapter broadly examines the meaning of the WPS Agenda in relation to securitization of women/gender equality in addressing SEA in peacekeeping operations, with a special focus on the role and practice of the African Union, its member states and civil-society organisations under the auspices of the UN. The core *idea* to review centres on the conceptualization of securitization of women/gender equality and its relationship to the pursuit of peace. It will also explore how active players use WPS to pursue interests in how they define borders of security and political spaces. The *institutions* related to policy development and implementation of WPS SEA policies in peacekeeping will be critically analysed, revealing inconsistencies and gaps in political will. Lastly the *interactions* between various actors in the policy-making and implementation process and the various *instruments* used to develop, adopt and implement the policies will be discussed. The broader purpose of the chapter is to examine the status of the WPS agenda in addressing SEA in peacekeeping in the context of the African Union, the perceived place of securitization of women/gender equality, and to link it to broadly to the future legitimacy of Peace Operations in the maintenance of international peace and security.

SECURITISATION OF WOMEN

The security-development nexus in pursuit of the liberal peace is in part exemplified through the human security paradigm, which considersnon-traditionalapproachestosecurity,orapproachesnotprimarilyfocused on state security; instead, it focuses on the root causes of insecurities by addressing individual human needs and sees the stalling or unravelling of development progress as a threat to international security, stability and sustainability (UN Trust Fund for Human Security 2009; Duffield 2014). The concept is normative, and according to the UN, in line with the principles and standards of universal human rights. Popularised in the 1990s, the concept and was formally introduced in the 1994 Human Development Report and is embedded in the international approach to the Millennium Development Goals and the Sustainable Development Goals. In 2012, the UN General Assembly (GA) clarified the definition of human security as including a people-centred approach which links peace, development and universal human rights, and emphasises the right to live a life free from fear, want and with equal opportunity to enjoy their rights. It is not meant to replace State security, nor violate sovereignty, but focuses on national ownership, recognising the diverse needs and circumstances of each individual state, supported in part by the international community (UN General Assembly 2012, p. 3a–h).

While approaches to human security agree on the place of the individual as the centre of security policy and analysis, there are differences in terms of which threats should be prioritised or if human security should be prioritised in practice. Newman (2010, pp. 79–81) condenses the differing approaches into four areas of priority: (1) all threats to human integrity which threaten the life chances of most people; (2) the human consequences of armed conflict, repressive governments and state failure; (3) non-traditional issues, such as disease, drugs, terrorism, small arms and light weapons (SALWs) in order to attract more resources to tackle these problems; and (4) theoretical perspectives which explore the sources of insecurity, such as gender, gender relations and patriarchal institutions. The human security approach was advocated by feminist, post-colonial and post-modern scholars, as well as security scholars in the Aberystwyth, Copenhagen and Frankfurt Schools (Hendricks 2015, p. 366).

Feminist engagements with security studies have long criticised the absence of gender as a relevant point of analysis and the gender bias present in the core concepts within security studies. Human Security provided an additional platform for international discussions on women, gender, and security where advocates pushed for more expansive understandings of security, moving beyond the narrow state-centric notions to a paradigm which reveals the "gender and gendering play in security, showing how post-conflict security priorities accord with masculine conceptions of safety" (Ni Aolain et al. 2011, p. 61; Sjoberg 2009, pp. 196–197). Securitisation of women emerged both from cognitive ideas about the experiences of women in conflict and the impact of insecurity of women on peace as well as normative ideas about women gender role, especially the association of women as victims in need of protection and as agents of peace.

There are also questions surrounding the political rather than humanitarian agenda of states in adopting a human security perspective (Buzan 2008, p. 7). For example, the proliferation and support of women's organizations who focused on social issues in some parts of Africa from the 1960s to the 1990s saw a depoliticization of women's rights and more of a political motivation in gaining favour from the public and the international community (Basu 2016a, p. 40). Regardless, the approach required institutions, including security institutions, to reconceptualise and reform security theory and practice.

Until the 1990s the experiences of women in conflict where rarely discussed in international policy-making, creating a void of silence in addressing security concerns from a more multi-dimensional perspective. State and non-state actors, civil society activists, scholars and others played a significant role in getting women on the security agenda, most notably at the 1995 Beijing World Conference on Women, which saw the adoption of the Beijing Declaration and Platform for Action. These efforts saw an expanded the space for security frameworks to see and prioritise women and gender not only as a human rights issue, but as a security issue which is fundamentally linked to international peace and security, and thus compatible with pursuit of a liberal peace. In 1998 the Commission on the Status of Women (CSW) and a series of NGO networks, including the NGO Working Group on Women Peace and Security and the Peace Women project of the Women's International League for Peace and Freedom (WILPF) focused on the theme in pursuit of a relevant Security Council Resolution (Basu 2016b).

In 2000, the UN Security Council has passed landmark resolution 1325 on women in on WPS, which highlights the role of women in prevention and resolution of conflicts, peace processes, peacekeeping, humanitarian response, post-conflict reconstruction and emphasises the importance of their equal involvement and representation in conflict and post-conflict processes. It also recognised two main ideas: (1) that the UN should prioritise the equal participation of women in promotion of peace and security and (2) that the international community recognises the burdens faced by women, especially physical and sexual violence, and must work to protect them. This securitization of women through resolution 1325 led to the development of the UN's two principal gender equality policies, which hinge on Gender Balance and Gender Mainstreaming (Cohn 2013, p. 222). Gender balance indicates a need to have more equal representation of people in the councils of human and societal decision-making. Formally defined by the UN Economic and Social Council in 1997, gender mainstreaming is essentially a strategy for achieving gender equality which involves incorporating gender perspectives into all activities.

Amid increased attention to and desire to understand the securitisation of women since the adoption of SCR 1325, there have been eight additional resolutions[3] expanding on the securitisation of women, or what is known as the WPS Agenda, which have primarily focused on the issues of conflict related sexual violence (CRSV) and increased participation of women in all areas of peace processes, but have also included provisions to address the issue of SEA committed by UN personnel in peace operations. There has been a relatively wide diffusion of efforts to implement gender mainstreaming across states, suggesting its normative status.[4] Gender justice is now "broadly recognized as an international norm that is part of the requirements for legitimate statehood" (True and Mintrom 2001, p. 40). Despite its gains in drawing attention women's security issues to the international arena, the application and understand of WPS has been subjected to extensive scholarly criticisms which primarily highlight the fundamental mismatch between WPS and the strategy of gender mainstreaming (Huehnast et al. 2011, pp. 2–4). Ultimately, the predominant barrier lies with how gender is understood, in terms of changing normative thinking about gender at the conceptual and operational levels as well as in generating reliable data and gender-sensitive analysis in international peace and security issues.

---

[3] Resolutions 1820 (2008), 1888 (2009), 1889 (2009), 1960 (2010), 2106 (2013), 2122 (2013), and 2242 (2015) and (contestably) 2272 (2016). For an overview of the resolutions, please see Peace Women: http://www.peacewomen.org/resolutions-texts-and-translations.

[4] For example, as of May 2017, 66 states have also adopted National Action Plans (NAPs) to demonstrate their strategies for implementation of the WPS Agenda (Peace Women).

The UN has evolved and reacted in its approach to gender and security, as it found itself forced to act to mitigate the long-term consequences of what is already a challenging task: ensuring that the UN, and especially UN peacekeepers, have some semblance of legitimacy and trust in the countries in which they are deployed as well as in the eyes of the wider international community. It has primarily relied on SC resolutions, Security Sector Reform and institutional updates[5] in its pursuit of WPS and tackling SEA in POs; it has also conducted a significant series of reviews since 2015 on peace operations, peacebuilding architecture and special measures for protection from SEA. However, despite the outrage, despite the media attention, despite the policy and practice adjustments, training manuals and strategies, SEA by those involved in UN POs continues (OIOS 2015).

The current UN policy takes a zero-tolerance approach to SEA and forbids "sexual relations with prostitutes and with any persons under 18, and strong discourage relations with beneficiaries of assistance" (UN 2015). The UN strategy addresses SEA through prevention, enforcement of codes of conduct and remedial action, and this is done through training, awareness raising, investigations, disciplinary measures and assistance to victims, which is very much along the traditional lines of responding to SEA through prevention, protection and prosecution. However, the UN falls short in all three of these areas, both in relation to implementation of the standards to UN staff as well as in relation to the overall policies in place on the ground, which also apply to NGOs and other foreign actors in theory.

McGill (2014, p. 20) argues that the current Department of Peacekeeping Operations (DPKO) zero tolerance policy is problematic and insufficient because it regards "virtually all sexual encounters between peacekeepers and locals as per se exploitative and therefore inherently harmful to the participant". Gira Grant (2014, p. 131) points out that in a system where prostitution is criminalised, sex work is still regulated, but in a much riskier way. The criminal and legal system, including police forces, serve as the regulatory force. An environment

---

[5] Including the 2003 Bulletin on SEA: Zero Tolerance Policy; 2005 Zeid Report (updated 2015): DPKO Conduct and Discipline Unit/Teams; 2013 General Recommendation 30 (CEDAW Women in conflict and post conflict); 2014–2018 DPKO/DFS Gender Strategy; 2015 SG Report on Special Measures for Protection from SEA; 2015 Global Leaders Meeting on Gender Equality and Empowerment.

in which power relations between men and women, foreign nationals and locals is conducive to SEA inevitably stresses gender inequalities in the post-conflict community. These environments pose very real security threats, as the growth of illicit industries, especially industries which involve slavery, is inhibitive to human security and post conflict reconstruction.

The May 2015 Evaluation Report released by the Office of Internal Oversight Services (OIOS) reveals a plethora of inadequacies in relation to the UN response to SEA by UN and related Personnel in Peacekeeping Operations. The report revealed that there seemed to be a lack of understanding relating to the command responsibilities as they pertain to preventing and addressing SEA, and that there was not sufficient will delegation and understanding of responsibilities for effective measures against SEA to be appropriately taken.

Security officials tend to not address the issue unless "commercialised sex appears to have become a threat to male soldiers' health and discipline" (Enloe 2002, p. 27). While seeking to advance their socioeconomic and political situations without sufficient access to resources, the likelihood of women falling victim to human traffickers dramatically increases. Socio-economic difficulties allow for traffickers to exploit the market demand and women's need to find jobs (Nikolic-Ristanovic 2003). Additionally, a common route to the sex industry for women is through rape, compounded by prevailing attitudes of stigmatisation towards the victims (Kelly 2010).

The most recent resolution, Resolution 2272 (2016) on SEA by UN Peacekeepers, calls for background checks on personnel, naming and shaming of TCCs who do no investigate prosecutions, the removal and replacement of personnel involved in allegations, until they are appropriately investigated, as well as the repatriation of entire units where there is found to be widespread allegations. While the resolution progresses in addressing some of the reasons for enduring impunity, assumption that the problem is solved through punishment and inclusion still misses sight of the fundamental underlying causes of SEA.

Several resolutions have reacted to gender and security concerns, and have built on existing research, especially regarding gender in UNPOs, and have acknowledge the risks of the legitimacy of the operations because of cases of SEA by UN Peacekeepers. However, despite the advancement of the WPS Agenda, SEA primarily against women and children by UN personnel in UN Peace Operations continues.

THE INSTITUTION OF THE MILITARY

The WPS Agenda has prioritised, rather unintentionally and to the criticism of feminist scholars and advocacy groups, the masculinist institution of the military. The institution of the military is an expression of masculine culture which systematically 'others' women in ways that not only materially, but symbolically undermine their access to agency and security (Higate and Henry 2004, p. 494). For example, increased demand for a variety of goods and services, which accompany the mostly male international staff that arrive with the mission, results in increased economic opportunities for the host country (Jennings 2014). These so called "peacekeeping economies" usually serve as a much-needed boost to the economy of a country emerging from conflict; however, these economies also typically create an increase in cases of transactional sex. Women and children may also engage in "survival sex" in exchange for food and protection from people (usually men) with more resources (True 2012, p. 137). Godec's (2010, pp. 245–246) Kosovo study found that military personnel increased the demand for sexual services, and post-intervention militarization facilitated an environment where criminal networks could thrive, economic disruption resulted in increased number of vulnerable women and girls, and a fundamental failure of UNMIK to address the situation has allowed the industry to thrive. Peacekeeping economies are particularly worrisome because they tend to live beyond the formal post-peacekeeping process, and they have an impact in shaping structural gendered economic and social power relations long into the future (141). Peacekeeping economies "interact with, and inevitably shape, the societies in which they operate" (Jennings 2014).

The existing research indicates that the institution *is* a part of the problem, not the solution, as peacekeeping economies facilitate the development of *new* structures which contribute to the subordination of women. True (2012) indicates that since the militarised model of peacekeeping and peacebuilding is dominant, gender mainstreaming does not seem to address post-conflict cultures of impunity, which are conducive for violence against women, as well as parallel economies which may foster corruption and criminality.

The UN and the Security Council

Although external actors were a key driver of WPS, the Security Council's motivations have been described as characterised by a need for more direction in responding to new substantive issues and possibly more support for its increased intervention in areas traditionally outside its mandate. Luck (2006, p. 131) points to the former dilemma, and the Council's need to develop normative standards and a clear scope for engagement in increasingly hazy and evolving areas which have created anxiety about its legitimacy, such as humanitarian issues, intervention and terrorism. Otto (2010, pp. 242, 253) describes the latter, especially relating the expansion of the SC's mandate that followed the end of the Cold War and which accompany the 'war on terror' and climate change which have affected its symbolic capital. For example, the war on terror in Afghanistan and intervention in Iraq negatively impacted the symbolic capital of the Council. The Security Council itself would not have passed Resolution 1325 if it weren't strategically in their interests, indicating that the inclusion of the WPS Agenda could be seen as a concession to gain positive favour rather than in line with the goals of feminism (Basu 2016b, pp. 261, 264; Otto 2010, p. 261). Nonetheless, despite the multiple motivations for WPS, it has opened political space for discussion and action on women's and gender issues.

The WPS agenda relies on some normative notion of the universal human rights agenda, as do its provisions for addressing SEA in UNPOs. The UN thus has a clear interest in progressing to address the abuse, so as not to undermine its previous work to develop and expand international human rights and security instruments. Grady (2010) argues that UN impartiality, which is a core principle of peacekeeping, is threatened by the abuse, which can have political implications which further financial and propaganda benefits for warring parties. The abuse undermines the core principles of their deployment by betraying the trust of the people they are meant to protect. The UN is motivated to act to address SEA, or as some scholars would say they have more of a tendency to 'react' after media exposure and public outcry (Westendorf and Searle 2017, p. 382) in order to maintain some semblance of legitimacy and confidence in its Peace Operations.

While the concept of gender is often understood as relating to women's issues, many member states have identified gender as an area of international concern and national interest. It has featured in the foreign policies of many countries and gender mainstreaming in UNPOs has also led to explicit articulations of foreign policy positions by donor and host countries (Basu 2016b, pp. 265–267). States individually may have an interest in ensuring the legitimacy of peacekeeping, and especially of their contributions to peacekeeping. The state could be motivated to expand its military competencies, as participation in peacekeeping positively improves state militaries and civilian control of the military (Desch 1999; Sotomayor 2007).

States may find their motivations to address the WPS agenda in order to fulfil their normative commitment to human rights, to appease active national and international women's organisations (Klot 2015), as well as to be seen to react to the perverse (such SEA of young children) in order to fulfil their position as the masculinist-hero state. The 'hero state', and especially the democratic state, who is willing to contribute soldiers and/or resources to risk their lives to protect the innocent and work towards peace may receive international favour characterised as politically and/or economically motivated (Lebovic 2004). Young (2003) describes the role of viewing war and security through a gender lens can reveal different logics of gendered meanings that further illuminate other possible sources of interest, such as maintenance of the security state which prioritises the masculine protector and suppresses other groups, such as women and children. For example, the policy response of the Bush administration after the 9/11 attacks, emphasised the 'logic of masculinist protection' and subsequently garnered support for restrictions on liberty and dissent at home (Young 2003, p. 3). Additionally, Ní Aoláin (2016) sees the extra attention given to sexual violence under WPS, and especially relating to the War on Terror, as a justification for actions that may have otherwise been subject to further debate, such as restrictions on personal freedoms.

THE AFRICAN UNION (AU)

The predecessor of the AU, the (OAU)[6] was heavily criticised for its failure to act to address human rights issues, despite its few moderate successes in responding to African conflicts in the late 1990s and

---

[6]Dissolved in 2001.

early 2000s (DRC, Ethiopia and Eritrea). The OAU prioritised non-interference in domestic affairs, a common thread after the colonial legacy of detrimental interference, but they also feared backlash from member states in pressing their human rights records, which resulted in poor political will to move forward in promoting and increasing respect for human rights (Sarkin 2009, pp. 16–17).

The issue of foundationalism in human rights sparks the enduring debates between the universalist and relativist notions of an international human rights agenda. Of relevance to linking the human-rights based human security and securitisation of women is the presence of anti-colonial human rights narratives which contest the universalist approach. During the 1970s and 1980s, as former colonies exercised their independence, many also presented a radical position on sovereignty and non-intervention which was designed to challenge western hegemony. The Organisation for African Unity (OAU), for example, was one of these staunch critics of attempts to impose the historical continuum of the western-formulated human rights corpus in Africa. These arguments have also been expanded by Mutua (2001), who describes this view as reinforcing colonial narratives which separate states into relational categories of superiors (western saviours) and subordinates (non-western savages and victims).

Feminism in Africa has also been a contentious point in the human rights and security-development agendas. Hendricks (2015, p. 368) also highlights the narratives of gender equality which essentialise non-Western women as victims and non-Western men as perpetrators of violence. These discourses also tap into criticisms made by intersectional feminists, who point to the monolithic representation of women from the developing world as victims of their culture. This singularity emphasises perspectives which place culture at centre of the 'problem' of achieving human rights, thus restricting potential for transformative change. As Tamale (2008, p. 157) states, "in other words, if in Africa culture is synonymous to women, and the concepts of 'rights' and 'culture' continue to be viewed as being at odds, it means that African women would have to first strip themselves of culture before enjoying their rights".

However, its creation of a regional human rights regime based on adoption of the 1981 African Charter on Human and Peoples' Rights represents a reaction to the UN-declared universality, which aims to challenge western hegemonic domination and escape the grip of its former colonial masters. The Charter has been criticised for its series of clauses which weaken the protections by allowing states to create laws to bypass many of the core rights. Additionally, the African Commission on Human and People's Rights (formed 1986) has been heavily criticised for its poor visibility, delays in review complaints from individuals and NGOs, poor follow-up, non-binding decisions and 'sporadic' compliance by parties, while the African Court (adopted 1998, in force 2004) has been slow to start (adopted 1998, in force 2004, first ruling in 2013), among other issues (Donnelly 2013, pp. 176–177). Despite the criticisms, it does lay a foundation for building a stronger human rights corpus in the region which could expand its international influence.

The AU emerged to replace the OAU in order to better tend to African needs outside the direct decisions of the UN Security Council. The AU and its fifty-five member states aspire to have a position as the key African peace and security organisation which delivers African solutions to African problems. The ideas of pan-Africanism champion a united Africa who is more able to advocate for its interests in international spheres of influence as well as recover from its historical colonial legacy (Møller 2009, p. 5). The AU signifies a normative shift in security and human rights in Africa, which saw a reversal of the OAU's position, and determined to prioritise the duty to protect from gross violations of human rights over the principle of non-interference (Sarkin 2009, p. 17).

Africans are involved in peacekeeping operations in African conflicts; it thus seems reasonable to suggest that securing the future of POs and the AU's involvement in such operations motivates an interest to address the SEA. Participation in POs is an important part of the interests of the AU, and African countries are among the top contributors to peacekeeping operations. Deployment of peacekeepers from the poorest countries, and missions which are frequently partly financed by the EU and US, is "a means of gaining compensation for their poorly trained troops" (Tardy 2013), as the salaries afforded to peacekeeping troops is often significantly higher than expected salaries in the world's least-developed countries. Beswick (2010) found that Rwanda was motivated to contribute peacekeepers to the African Union Mission in Sudan (AMIS), it successor the African-Union Assistance Mission in Darfur (UNAMID) partially to help cement a stronger domestic position as well as continuing or emerging relationships with key bilateral donors.

AU countries have benefited from capacity building, experience and lessons learned from peacekeeping missions, although they have suffered from heavy reliance on a few key countries (including South Africa and Nigeria) and insufficient foreign assistance in access to necessary resources. Williams and Boutellis (2014, p. 257) point to the relationship between the UN and the AU as "a turbulent international normative context characterized by legitimacy struggles over" who should take the lead in making decisions regarding responses to peace and security crises in Africa. Sandler (2017, p. 13) found that public outcry, rather than donor-specific interests motivated UN member states actions in UN missions on sub-Saharan Africa and that investment interests and nearness to the conflict region play a role in a country financially supporting non-UN peacekeeping missions (Sandler 2017, p. 14). Despite these gaps, the AU and its sub-regional organisations have met relative success in facilitating relative peace in countries where the international community reacted slowly, such as Burundi, Liberia, Sierra Leone and Sudan (except Darfur) (Møller 2009, pp. 15–16). While the AU has been supported through intense capacity building, especially since the early 2000s, the organisation has not yet met its desired full potential (Brett 2013, p. iii).

Additionally, amidst the power politics of the often-delayed reform of the UN Security Council, those regional powers with ambitions of regional leadership and middle power status internationally have vested interests in cooperation on issues relating to international peace and security. There is a powerful desire for states to become non-permanent members of the Security Council, as it represents a symbolic legitimacy or resource that can serve as a tool in power-politics with other states (Hurd 2008, p. 131). There are issues of regional hegemony in the African Union, illuminated by multiple Security Council reform debates Nigeria and South Africa both seek to serve as this hegemon who would take the lead in the AU. However, Kuziemko and Werker (2006) found a positive correlation between non-permanent status and increased foreign aid during a rotating-member's seat on the council, suggesting that seeking membership has additional economic and political payoffs outside of the elevated decision-making status that comes with Security Council membership. It is also worth noting that human rights have become a sort of currency of political legitimacy, in so far that "full political legitimacy is increasingly judged by and expressed in terms of human rights" (Donnelly 2013, p. 55). Thus, the African Union may be motivated to in part to pursue the WPS agenda vigorously in order to be seen to adhere broadly to the human rights corpus in order to increase its political legitimacy as well as to counter neo-colonial narratives.

AU and Gender Policies

The AU and its predecessor have interacted and engaged with civil society in peace and security and post-conflict reconstruction issues in developing policy instruments. For example, the OAU and the United Nations Economic Commission for Africa (UNECA) created the grass-roots oriented peace mechanism of the African Women's Committee on Peace and Development (AWCPD), later becoming the African Union Women's Committee (AUWC), who in collaboration with the Foundation for Community Development (FCD) in 2003 advocated for legal protection of women's rights in Africa, gender mainstreaming and empowerment of women. This collaboration lead to the contribution to implementation of Resolution 1325 through the establishment of the 2005 Maputo Protocol on Women's Rights in Africa (Diop 2010, p. 175) and eventually saw the introduction of a 50% quota for women AU commissioners (Ceesay-Ebo 2010, p. 194).

African women's movements have a long and varied history, from roots in pre-colonialism and nationalist movements to modern-day advocacy, they are not a new phenomenon. These movements have also notably drawn from local cultural norms, such as threatened naked protests to ridicule and shame male authorities, as was used in the 1950s and more recently in Liberia's peace process—reference definitely missing here. Independence saw a resurgence in these groups, while post-independence to the 1990s saw a rise in elitist and depoliticised women's organisations which saw states controlling women's mobilization through politics. Some groups focused on charity work while others demanded stricter morality for women. However, from the 1990s onward, and especially following the UN 3rd World Conference on Women in Nairobi in 1985, women's organisations saw a resurgence and energy which expanded spaces for feminist engagement. By the start of this conference most African countries had already adopted national machineries for coordination of gender policy, and increasingly looked to women's organizations to set the agenda on women's issues (Tripp 2016; Klot 2015).

The African Union has a much higher success rate in political representation of women than most developed countries. While colonialism saw a reduction in women's power and status in Africa, women currently occupy 24% of parliamentary and ministerial seats in sub-Saharan Africa, and Rwanda has the highest female representation in the world at 61% in government (Anite 2017). While political representation alone does not 'fix' the problems associated with gender inequality, African countries have adopted national machineries to coordinate gender policy (Basu 2016a). The AU itself leads in setting a normative agenda for gender equality in the region, and actively advocates for gender mainstreaming and implementation of SCR1325. It has developed a series of gender equality and empowerment of women strategies, such as: the Protocol to the African Charter on Human and Peoples' Right on the Rights of Women (2003), the Solemn Declaration of Gender Equality in Africa (2004), the Framework for Post Conflict Reconstruction and Development (2006), a Gender Policy (2009), and the Policy Framework for Security Sector Reform (2011).

The African Peace and Security Architecture (APSA), formed by the Peace and Security Council Protocol in 2002, represents a move towards normative and institutional transformation in its pursuit of improved capacity and professionalisation of the AU in addressing peace and security issues in a more holistic manner. It also has principle components relating to human rights, and specifically women and gender in Peace Operations, and provides mechanisms for greater collaboration with stakeholders (Engel and Porto 2014). This ambitious approach, while applauded is subject to many of the same worries in AU operations, especially of durability in the face of inadequate resources for operationalisation and the continuation of violent conflicts on the continent (Engel and Porto 2009, 2014).

The 2004 AU Solemn Declaration on Gender Equality in Africa (SDGEA) provides provisions for more involvement of women in peace operations, peace processes and reconstruction and contains a component to address SEA, and sexual and gender-based violence. The 2009 Gender Policy (AUGP) and Action Plan, reiterates its previous gender commitments, and cites that pursuit of Africa's development agenda needs an enabling, stable and peaceful environment for women in which they are able to enhance their roles. It also expands the remit for engagement with relevant sub-national actors, encourages the creation of regional consultative platforms, expands training on gender securitization for peacekeeping forces, and saw the appointment of the Special Representative on WPS who will interact with AU-UN partnerships on WPS issues (St-Pierre 2010, pp. 6–8).

These initiatives have led to expanded resources and attention to gender issues, including the implementation of gender quotas in elections

(Hendricks 2015, p. 365; Paxton and Hughes 2015, pp. 381–383). However, the political gains for women in Africa are not solely due to the magic wand of the AU, but heavily result from pressure applied by women's organisations and activists. Despite this flurry of activity, AU personnel continue to be implicated in SEA in Peace Operations, including abuse of children, in missions in Somalia, Uganda, Burundi and other countries. Impunity continues the thrive as the AU faces continued challenges to maintenance of the rule of law and pressuring TCCs to act in prosecuting the abuses (Human Rights Watch 2014, 2016).

CONCLUSION

While the UN has interacted with various actors to address the issue, and has developed institutional mechanisms to begin approaching the problem of SEA, there is still a long way to go. It is generally agreed by scholars and practitioners that there is much to learn, understand, evaluate and implement in relation to 1325, securitisation of women and gender mainstreaming. The gap between rhetoric and reality is quite vast. (Ní Aoláin et al. 2011, p. 134). The rhetoric is also part of the problem, as stereotypical gendered language prevails in UN documents, and the subject has a tendency to be viewed as a non-political task (Puechguirbal 2010). It is poorly understood, and institutions seem to, at times, have a lack of interest in seriously pursuing it.

The African Union has additional hurdles to jump through to tackle the abuses, but it does seem that its continued engagement with NGOs and civil-society organisations offers opportunities for the development of meaningful instruments based on these interactions, but the issue of making these instruments a reality is another matter. The AU, with support, will still need to grapple with its insecurities, resource-needs, diversity of actors and interest groups, governance and other capacity issues in its aims of playing a leading role in addressing security and conflict on the continent before significant gains will be made in addressing SEA in Peace Operations. As stated by Brett (2013, p. ii) "It is relevant that the AU and the sub-regional organisations are faced with the challenge of responding to crises on the continent at the same time as they are developing the capacity to do so". Where capacity does not only represent available resources and know-how, but also political and social will to drive change, there are certainly more hurdles to overcome in pursuing greater legitimacy of AU POs. The AU may possess the capacity to create relevant and democratically-driven instruments to address the topic, but without the resources to drive operationalisation and in the face of numerous obstacles relating to war and conflict on the continent, these initiatives risk amounting to a motivated driver in a petrol-less car.

Nevertheless, True and Mintrom (2001, p. 51) found that openness to new ideas and voices among decision-makers in the international community leads to advocacy from sub-national actors who are then able to diffuse ideas quickly to innovate policies; the AU has in part demonstrated a capacity to engage. Where this openness coincides with engagement with human security, there is a greater chance that more attention and resources will be provided to address non-traditional security challenges (Newman 2010, p. 81). Feminist actors, who far from represent a unitary vision, struggle to organise themselves around a specific goal or set of goals, as there is a risk that once the short-term objectives are reached or the political motivation wanes, the organisation around these goals weakens (Caglar et al. 2013, p. 4). Feminist organisations have encountered innumerable hurdles in navigating through and influencing multilevel governance (Haussman et al. 2010, p. 49), and the adoption of the WPS agenda the leadership of the WILPF, who has taken a lead role in the NGO Working Group on WPS, represents an 'alliance of gender legitimacy' between the Security Council and international women's peace advocates (Otto 2010, p. 240). However, while this alliance motivated increased feminist activity on gender and security issues, it has also experienced its own political struggles as differences emerged in deciphering the meaning and implementation of Resolution 1325 (Otto 2010, p. 263).

Securitisation of women is predominantly associated with empowerment of women and gender equality, and AU initiatives seem to pursue these same grounds. However, despite attempts from the international community to incorporate a gender perspective, the securitisation of women has somewhat reinforced unequal gender relations in many areas. The approach to SEA in POs is subject to many of the same scholarly criticisms as the frame of the WPS Agenda: that gender equals women; that gender mainstreaming is somewhat meaningless in the absence of a clear understanding and application of the concept of gender; that a heteronormative approach will continue; that gender equality is achieved through adding any women to the equation, or giving them a seat in the room, regardless of their capacity for agency or their relative position of privilege; that women are essentialised as victims in need of protection or natural agents of peace; and that the root causes of gender inequality are not yet normatively acceptable for higher level decision making levels. The response also suffers from the belief that masculinities are not worth mentioning as part of the problem, nor militarisation as the dominant security narrative. Ní Aoláin et al. (2011, p. 19), have questioned the success of relevant international norms in their ability to address gendered aspects of post-conflict processes, and have especially highlighted that action is insufficient in unless "gender is integrated into all aspects and levels" of the state emerging from conflict. Additionally, as stated by Westendorf and Searle (2017) the treatment of SEA as homogenous obscures how the behaviour of the exploiter is understood, as well as the different forms it takes, causes and behaviours involved; and, that SEA policy has been "developed in isolation" from the WPS Agenda, thus undermining its overall effectiveness. Simić (2010) argues that measures directed at countering the abuse focus too narrowly on diverting responsibility to women through gender balance and equality initiatives, rather than on holding TCC's accountable for prosecuting troops. In order to progress in this area, regardless of political motivations, complex international systems need to engage more closely with feminist critiques of policies and their implementation in order to tackle the underlying causes of the abuses in order to better secure the legitimacy of international peace operations. If the goal is to reduce conflict and ensure sustainable peace, these points cannot be subject to compromise.

References

Anite, E. 2017. It's Tough for Women to Get to the Top in African Politics—But we're Blazing a Trail. *The Guardian*, June 12. https://www.theguardian.com/global-development/2017/jun/12/african-politics-blazing-a-trail-african-women-leaders-network-evelyn-anite. Accessed 12 June 2017.

Basu, A. 2016a. *Women's Movements in the Global Era: The Power of Local Feminisms*. UK: Hachette.

Basu, S. 2016b. Gender as National Interest at the UN Security Council. *International Affairs* 92 (2): 255–273.

Beardsley, K. 2011. Peacekeeping and the Contagion of Armed Conflict. *The Journal of Politics* 73 (4): 1051–1064.

Beswick, D. 2010. Peacekeeping, Regime Security and 'African Solutions to African Problems': Exploring Motivations for Rwanda's Involvement in Darfur. *Third World Quarterly* 31 (5): 739–754.

Brett, J. 2013. *The Inter-relationship between the African Peace and Security Architecture, the Global Peace and Security Architecture and Regional Initiatives.* Report prepared for the Danish Embassy in Addis Ababa 24th October.

Buzan, B. 2008. *People, States & Fear: An Agenda for International Security Studies in the Post-Cold War Era.* Colchester: ECPR Press.

Caglar, G., E. Prügl, and S. Zwingel (eds.). 2013. *Feminist Strategies in International Governance*, vol. 70. London and New York: Routledge.

Ceesay-Ebo, A. 2010. The Gender Dimensions of the ECOWAS Peace and Security Architecture: A Regional Perspective on UNSCR 1325. In *Women, Peace and Security: Translating Policy into Practice*, ed. F. Olonisakin, K. Barnes, and E. Ikpe, 184–198. London: Routledge.

Cohn, C. 2013. *Women and Wars.* Malden, MA: Polity Press.

Desch, M. 1999. *Civilian Control of the Military: The Changing Security Environment.* Baltimore, MD: Johns Hopkins University Press.

Diop, B. 2010. The African Union and Implementation of UNSCR 1325. In *Women, Peace and Security: Translating Policy into Practice*, ed. F. Olonisakin, K. Barnes, and E. Ikpe, 173–183. London: Routledge.

Dobbins, J., S. Jones, K. Crane, A. Rathmell, and B. Steele. 2001. *The UN's Role in Nation-Building: From the Congo to Iraq.* Santa Monica: Rand Corporation.

Donnelly, J. 2013. *Universal Human Rights in Theory and Practice.* Ithaca and London: Cornell University Press.

Duffield, M. 2014. *Global Governance and the New Wars: The Merging of Development and Security.* London: Zed Books.

Engel, U., and J.G. Porto. 2009. The African Union's New Peace and Security Architecture: Toward an Evolving Security Regime? *African Security* 2 (2–3): 82–96.

Engel, U., and J.G. Porto. 2014. Imagining, Implementing, and Integrating the African Peace and Security Architecture: The African Union's Challenges. *African Security* 7(3): 135–146.

Enloe, C. 2002. Demilitarization—Or More of the Same? Feminist Questions to Ask in the Postwar Moment. In *The Postwar Moment: Militaries, Masculinities and International Peacekeeping*, ed. Cynthia Cockburn and Dubravka Zarkov. London: Lawrence and Wishart.

Fortna, V.P. 2008. *Does Peacekeeping Work? Shaping Belligerents' Choices after Civil War.* Princeton, NJ: Princeton University Press.

Gira Grant, M. 2014. *Playing the Whore: The Work of Sex Work.* London: Verso.

Godec, S.T. 2010. Between Rhetoric and Reality: Exploring the Impact of Military Humanitarian Intervention upon Sexual Violence–Post-conflict Sex Trafficking in Kosovo. *International Review of the Red Cross* 92 (877): 235–258.

Grady, K. 2010. Sexual Exploitation and Abuse by UN Peacekeepers: A Threat to Impartiality. *International Peacekeeping* 17 (2): 215–228.

Haussman, M., M. Sawer, and J. Vickers (eds.). 2010. *Federalism, Feminism and Multilevel Governance*, vol. 17. Farnham: Ashgate.

Hendricks, C. 2015. Women, Peace and Security in Africa: Conceptual and Implementation Challenges and Shifts. *African Security Review* 24 (4): 364–375.

Higate, P., and M. Henry. 2004. Engendering (In)security in Peace Support Operations. *Security Dialogue* 35 (4): 481–498.

Howard, L.M. 2008. *UN Peacekeeping in Civil Wars*. Cambridge: Cambridge University Press.

Huehnast, K., C. de Jong Oudraay, and H.M. Hernes (eds.). 2011. *Women & War: Power and Protection in the 21st Century*. Washington: United States Institute of Peace.

Human Rights Watch. 2014. *The Power These Men Have Over us: Sexual Exploitation and Abuse by African Union Forces in Somalia*. https://www.hrw.org/report/2014/09/08/power-these-men-have-over-us/sexual-exploitation-and-abuse-african-union-forces. Accessed 1 July 2017.

Human Rights Watch. 2016. *UN: Stop Sexual Abuse by Peacekeepers*, 4 March. https://www.hrw.org/news/2016/03/04/un-stop-sexual-abuse-peacekeepers. Accessed 3 May 2017.

Hurd, I. 2008. *After Anarchy: Legitimacy and Power in the United Nations Security Council*. Princeton: Princeton University Press.

Jennings, K.M. 2014. Service, Sex and Security: Gendered Peacekeeping Economies in Liberia in the Democratic Republic of the Congo. *Security Dialogue* 45 (4): 1–18.

Kelly, J. 2010. *Rape in War: Motives of Militia in DRC* (Special Report). United Stated Institute of Peace.

Klot, J.F. 2015. UN Security Council Resolution 1325: A Feminist Transformative Agenda? In *The Oxford Handbook of Transnational Feminist Movements*, ed. R. Baksh and W. Harcourt. New York: Oxford University Press.

Kuziemko, I., and E. Werker. 2006. How much is a Seat on the Security Council Worth? Foreign Aid and Bribery at the United Nations. *Journal of Political Economy* 114 (5): 905–930.

Lebovic, James H. 2004. Uniting for Peace? Democracies and United Nations Peace Operations after the Cold War. *Journal of Conflict Resolution* 48 (6): 910–936.

Luck, Edward C. 2006. *The UN Security Council: Practice and Promise*. London: Routledge.

McGill, Jena. 2014. Survival Sex in Peacekeeping Economies: Re-reading the Zero Tolerance Approach to Sexual Exploitation and Sexual Abuse in United Nations Peace Support Operations. *Journal of International Peacekeeping* 18: 1–44.

Møller, B. 2009. The African Union as a Security Actor: African Solutions to African Problems? Working Paper 57, Regional and Global Axes of Conflict. *Crisis States Working Papers Series No 2*, LSE Destin Development Studies Institute.

Mutua, M. 2001. Savages, Victims, and Saviours: The Metaphor of Human Rights. *Harvard International Law Journal* 42 (1): 201–245.

Newman, E. 2010. Critical Human Security Studies. *Review of International Studies* 36 (1): 77–94.

Ní Aoláin, F. 2016. The 'War on Terror' and Extremism: Assessing the Relevance of the Women Peace and Security Agenda. *International Affairs* 92 (2): 275–291.

Ní Aoláin, F., D.F. Haynes, and N. Cahn. 2011. *On the Frontlines: Gender, War, and the Post-conflict Process*. Oxford: Oxford University Press.

Nikolic-Ristanovic, V. 2003. Sex Trafficking: The Impact of War, Militarism and Globalization in Eastern Europe. *Michigan Feminist Studies* 17: 1–26.

OIOS. 2015. *Evaluation Report: Evaluation of the Enforcement and Remedial Assistance Efforts for Sexual Exploitation and Abuse by the United Nations and Related Personnel in Peacekeeping Operations*. Inspection and Evaluation Division.

Otto, D. 2010. The Security Council's Alliance of Gender Legitimacy: The Symbolic Capital of Resolution 1325. In *Fault Lines of International Legitimacy*, ed. H. Charlesworth and J. Coicaud. New York: Cambridge University Press.

Paxton, P., and M.M. Hughes. 2015. *Women, Politics, and Power: A Global Perspective*. Washington, DC: CQ Press.

Peace Women. *Member States, WILPF*. http://www.peacewomen.org/member-states. Accessed 30 June 2017.

Pettman, J.J. 1996. *Worlding Women: A Feminist International Politics*. London: Routledge.

Puechguirbal, N. 2010. Discourses on Gender, Patriarchy and Resolution 1325: A Textual Analysis of UN Documents. *International Peacekeeping* 17 (2): 172–187.

Sandler, T. 2017. International Peacekeeping Operations: Burden Sharing and Effectiveness. *Journal of Conflict Resolution* 61 (9): 1–23.

Sarkin, J. 2009. The Role of the United Nations, the African Union and Africa's Sub-regional Organizations in Dealing with Africa's Human Rights Problems: Connecting Humanitarian Intervention and the Responsibility to Protect. *Journal of African Law* 53 (1): 1–33.

Sheeran, S., L. Zegveld, M. Zawanenburg, E. Wilmshurst (chair). 2014. *Peacekeeping and Accountability*. International Law Programme, Meeting Summary 28 May. Chatham House, the Royal Institute of International Affairs.

Simić, O. 2010. Does the Presence of Women Really Matter? Towards Combating Male Sexual Violence in Peacekeeping Operations. *International Peacekeeping* 17 (2): 188–199.

Sjoberg, L. 2009. Introduction to Security Studies: Feminist Contributions. *Security Studies* 18 (2): 183–213.

Sotomayor, A.C. 2007. Unintended Consequences of Peace Operations for Troop-Contributing Countries in South America: The Cases of Argentina and Uruguay. In *Unintended Consequences of Peacekeeping Operations*, ed. R.C. Thakur, C. Aoi, and C. De Coning. United Nations University Press.

St-Pierre, K. 2010. Implementing the Women, Peace and Security Agenda in Peace Operations: Overview of Recent Efforts and Lessons Learned. *International Peacekeeping* 14 (4): 519.

Tamale, S. 2008. The Right to Culture and the Culture of Rights: A Critical Perspective on Women's Sexual Rights in Africa. *Feminist Legal Studies* 16 (1): 47–69.

Tardy, T. 2013. Funding Peace Operations: Better Value for EU Money. *European Union Institute for Security Studies*. http://www.iss.europa.eu/uploads/media/Brief_38_Funding_peace_operations.pdf. Accessed 28 April 2017.

Thakur, R. 2016. *The United Nations, Peace and Security: From Collective Security to the Responsibility to Protect*. Cambridge: Cambridge University Press. https://doi.org/10.1017/9781316819104.

Tickner, J.A. 1992. *Gender in International Relations: Feminist Perspectives on Achieving Global Security*. New York: Columbia University Press.

Tripp, A.M. 2016. Women's Movements in Africa. In *Women's Movements in the Global Era: The Power of Local Feminisms*, ed. A. Basu. UK: Hachette.

True, Jacqui 2012. Oxford Studies in Gender and International Relations. In *The Political Economy of Violence Against Women*. New York: Oxford University Press.

True, J., and M. Mintrom. 2001. Transnational Networks and Policy Diffusion: The Case of Gender Mainstreaming. *International Studies Quarterly* 45: 27–57.

UN General Assembly. 2012. *Follow-up to Paragraph 143 on Human Security of the 2005 World Summit Outcome*. GA/RES/66/290, 25 October.

UN General Assembly. 2017. *Special Measures for Protection from Sexual Exploitation and Abuse: A New Approach*. Report of the Secretary General, A/71/818, 28 February.

UN Trust Fund for Human Security. 2009. *Human Security in Theory and Practice: An Overview of the Human Security Concept and the United Nations Trust Fund for Human Security*. United Nations: Human Security United.

United Nations. 2008. United Nations Peacekeeping Operations, Principles and Guidelines. *Department of Peacekeeping Operations*. http://www.un.org/en/peacekeeping/documents/capstone_eng.pdf. Accessed 1 May 2017.

United Nations. 2015. *Conduct and Discipline: United Nations Peacekeeping.* http://www.un.org/en/peacekeeping/issues/cdu.shtml. Accessed 17 June 2015.

United Nations. 2017. *Peacekeeping Initiatives in Action, Addressing Sexual Exploitation and Abuse.* Conduct and Discipline, DPKO, March. https://conduct.unmissions.org/sites/default/files/factsheet_v._8_march_2017.pdf. Accessed 1 May 2017.

United Nations Secretariat. 2003. *Special Measures for Protection from Sexual Exploitation and Abuse.* Secretary-General's Bulletin, ST/SGB/2003/13, 9 October.

Westendforf, J.K., and L. Searle. 2017. Sexual Exploitation and Abuse in Peace Operations: Trends, Policy Responses and Future Directions. *International Affairs* 93 (2): 365–387.

Whalan, J. 2013. *How Peace Operations Work: Power, Legitimacy, and Effectiveness.* Oxford: Oxford University Press.

Williams, P.D., and A. Boutellis. 2014. Partnership Peacekeeping: Challenges and Opportunities in the United Nations–African Union Relationship. *African Affairs* 113 (451): 254–278.

Young, I. M. 2003. The Logic of Masculinist Protection: Reflections on the Current Security State. *Signs* 29 (1): 1–25.

Women's Participation in Peace Processes in East Africa—Selected Aspects

Anna Cichecka

INTRODUCTION

The United Nations indicate women to be one of the most vulnerable group during both war and conflict, as well as, civil strife (UN WOMEN 2016a). On the one hand, women's need for the promotion of equality, development and peace is often read as the objection of the victim (Iwilade 2011, p. 23), and on the other hand, as a result of political changes and the strengthening role of women, playing into conflict resolution and peace-building agenda. This process started with the international changes initiated by a series of Conferences on Women. After the Conference in Nairobi, in 1985, a new course of action for the advancement of women was devised, this outlined measures for achieving gender equality and for promoting women's participation in peace and development efforts. The increasing involvement of women in national, regional and international institutions and mechanisms has been aimed at preventing and managing conflicts through various activities.

A. Cichecka (✉)
University of Wroclaw, Wrocław, Poland
e-mail: anacichecka@gmail.com; anna.cichecka@uwr.edu.pl

© The Author(s) 2018
P. Frankowski and A. Gruszczak (eds.),
Cross-Disciplinary Perspectives on Regional and Global Security,
https://doi.org/10.1007/978-3-319-75280-8_9

The main aim of this paper is to examine the role of women in peace processes in the East Africa region. The paper refers to the role that women have played in shaping peace processes, considering the selected aspects of East Africa as a case study. The analysis will refer to social constructivism. The assumption is that the actors (women) may interact and affect the normative and the ideational structures, and shape the behavior of different entities (entities responsible for peace) (Wendt 1987, pp. 335–370). However, the author does not attempt to take a comprehensive explanation of the relations between actors and structures, or build assertions about the nature of cause and effect. It is not intended either to judge whether the women's participation in peace processes may be treated as an introduction to gender equality or sustainable peace (this is one of the most frequently asked questions in the field of such issues) (Nakaya 2003, pp. 459–476), but only to consider and understand this phenomenon.

Observing various levels of interdependence on this issue leads to several research questions, such as:

1. What kind of factors encourages women to engage in peace processes?
2. What roles do women play in peace processes?
3. What institutions are involved in the phenomenon of women's participation in peace processes?
4. What happens after the end of the conflict? Under what conditions do women's groups play a significant role at this stage?

The paper first gives an overview on both the historical and the legal background of the rising involvement of women in peace processes and investigates the ideas linked with it. In the second section the main interests and roles of women are specified and characterized. The third part traces institutions related to the phenomenon of women's participation in peace processes. Then, the situation after the end of conflicts is analyzed with particular attention on interactions between actors. The last part of the paper is devoted to a conclusion. The paper is based on the content analysis of both, writings and reports on: women's activity, conflicts and peace processes and negotiations, as well as, political and mass media discourse (including: BBC, CNN, Al Jazeera, All Africa).

THE IDEAS AND DETERMINANTS OF THE INVOLVEMENT
OF WOMEN

As has been mentioned above, two main factors are often indicated as the motives for women's involvement in peace processes. On the one hand, it is the objection of being the victim which leads to the need for the promotion of equality, development and peace. And on the other hand, it is said that it is a result of political changes and the empowerment of women, which is reflected in strengthening the role of them, participating in conflict resolution and peace-building agenda. Therefore, this part of the paper is intended to analyze, order and discuss the most crucial ideas and circumstances that have contributed to the involvement of women in peace talks within the East Africa region.

The first assumption is that **the nature of conflict** determines women's behavior and "pushes" them to organize themselves into groups, movements and so on, and to take an action on peace. In this approach women are seen as one of the most vulnerable group (**UN WOMEN 2012**), which simultaneously makes them the group among which peace is the most needed. It is stated that the nature of conflict is oppressive especially when it comes down to women. At this point rape is indicated as one of the cruelest weapons used against women during war. It is seen as obvious that in contrast to dutifully killing the enemy, a soldier is not supposed to rape a woman, but the fact is that rapes occur in war. Observers note that rape in war assumes the level of being a weapon because it serves a specific military purpose. It is a tool of demoralizing and intimidating the side of the victim which may be used to dishonor the body and pride. In most traditional African societies rape affects also the family in which the woman lives because it is viewed as a disgrace for all the members of the community. So, this violence against women has an added negative effect and in this manner raping the women of a defeated people or nation becomes a part of the effort to destroy them (Neill 2000, pp. 43–51).

Further consideration of the nature of war leads to the ideas of "victimization" and gendered aspects of conflicts. The first one is based on the statement that, as has been raised above, women's experience of conflict is different from that of men. Generally, it may be interpreted as a situation in which women are more vulnerable to being victims, which consequently makes them more accepting of compromises and less likely than men to believe that armed force is necessary or appropriate. It is suggested that the victimization of women pushes them to take an action against the aggression. The latter concept is closely linked to the victimization and it is based on the assertion that wars or conflicts are diversified in terms of gender, on both the planning as well as the levels at which they evolve. There are two key underlying hypotheses. The first one states that men are in the center of the conflict, which means that men are those who have the power to initiate and maintain conflict and it puts them into the "center." In this case women's position, as well as their opinion and expectations, are marginalized. It is explained that discrimination against women before war time is directly reflected in other forms of structural inequalities that are often at the heart of conflict. However, this hypothesis is true only under the assumption that women generally neither perform decisive functions during war, nor supply the army. The second hypothesis assumes that the different positions of men and women give them different experience during war. Then, women become victims while men are seen as oppressors (Iwilade 2011, pp. 24–26). As evidence of the gendered nature of conflict resource is often made to the genocide in Rwanda. It is noted that the elements of gender discrimination can be found in much of the Hutu extremist ideology used to promote the ethnic cleansing. In this propaganda Tutsi women were portraying as seductresses who would use their sexuality to trick and entrap Hutu men. Such discourse continued throughout the massacre with the systemic use of rape as a weapon (Hogg 2009, pp. 34–55).

The second assumption on the determinants of women's involvement in peace talks is that the **outside pressure** aimed at the empowerment of women has resulted in their bigger concern about peace agenda. This was started after the First World Conference on the Status of Women that was convened in Mexico City in 1975. This meeting was the idea of the United Nations which tried to remind the international community that discrimination against women continued to be a major problem in much of the world. After the conference, the General Assembly of the United Nations declared a Decade for Women (1976–1985) which launched a new vision of equality and created new approaches to promoting the role of women by opening a worldwide dialogue on gender equality. Furthermore, the Conference adopted a World Plan of Action, a document that offered guidelines for governments and the international community to follow for the next ten years (UN 2016a). However, the most important moments are considered to be the Third World Conference on Women in 1985, which took place in Nairobi and the Conference on Women in 1995, in Beijing. The Nairobi Conference not only set international standards for public sphere participants something which gave a new look at the capabilities of changes in the policy of equality for women's movements, but also resounded widely in Africa and stimulated local initiatives to take vibrant action. This meeting ended up with the adoption of the Nairobi Forward Looking Strategies. It revealed also that women movements have a significant voice in the process of shaping the policy of equality and after the conference the women's movements sector began to emerge more frequently on the global scene (Tripp et al. 2012, pp. 240–398). The conference in Beijing brought the Beijing Declaration and Platform for Action—other important documents on fighting discrimination (UN WOMEN 2016a).

In the early 1990s the role of United Nations in promoting women's rights increased significantly and a variety of international commitments equalizing the rights of women and men were developed. Among the most crucial from that time and later reference should be given to: the Convention of Elimination of all Forms of Discrimination against Women (CEDAW), the International Covenant on Economic, Social and Cultural Rights (ICESCR), the International Convention on the Rights of the Child (ICRC), the South African Development Community (SADC) Heads of States Declaration on Gender and Development (Ellis et al. 2007, pp. 2–5) and the Millennium Declaration and Development Goals (UN 2016b). Other relevant international commitments include: the Convention on the Political Rights of Women, the Cairo Declaration on Population and Development—ICPD, the Universal Declaration on Democracy, the United Nations Security Council (UN-SC) Resolution 1325 (2000) and the Resolution 1820 (2006) (UN 2016a). The Resolution 1325 was strictly devoted to strengthening the role of women in the maintenance of international peace and security. Such a discourse, aimed at supporting gender equality and developing the activity of women's movements is apparent until the present day. One may find these trends in the rhetoric of the U.S.—one of the biggest worldwide donors on non-governmental initiatives. The main patterns on this issue may be briefly described using the popular motto "when women succeed America succeeds". Simultaneously, directions determined by the UN and the U.S. are reflected in the activities of international entities, which eagerly seek to cooperation with NGOs working against the discrimination and developing peace agenda (U.S. Department of State 2016).

Outside pressure and international trends aimed at strengthening the policy of equality have been reflected on African soil. This may be found in analyzing the process of establishing the African Union (AU), which was supported by a variety of ideas on peace development and gender equality. It is worth mentioning the most significant among them, such as: the Conference on Women and Peace in Kampala (1993) and the Action Plan on Women Peace (1995); the African Women Committee on Peace and Development (1998); the Federation of African Women's Peace Networks (1994). Consequently, the author assumes that all of these **local initiatives** may be treated as the third crucial factor that to some extent determined women's involvement in peace processes.

THE INTERESTS AND ROLES OF WOMEN

One of the most controversial statements about the interest of women in peace processes is that "the war brings an opportunity for women to take an action and finally become apparent" (Neill 2000, p. 43). On the other side, there is an approach in which the role of women during peace talks is ascended to the heights and becomes almost sacred by the assumption of the predestination of women to promote peace. The author suggests a further critical examination of both of these concepts due to the fact that both of them seem to be too simplified and unilateral.

When one takes into consideration mass media discourse on the role of women in peace talks then one may observe that the role of women is described as crucial, unique and irreplaceable (All Africa 2015; BBC News 2015; Al Jazeera 2014; CNN 2014). When it comes to East Africa, women's groups are perceived as significant elements in peace processes and peace negotiations. They are recognized as powerful and effective actors who give a different point of view and who are able to influence the warlords and leaders during conflicts. It is said that they indicate common aims, such as: equality for all, respect for human rights, and development for the society. And it has been pointed out that it works effectively during the peace talks and leads to compromises and to the end of conflicts, because women have played a "special role" in building the peace agenda. However, there is no empirical evidence to regard this statement as fully justified and that women should not be treated as inherently peace makers (Mili 2013, pp. 3–11). Thus, is there any reason to talk about the causal effect between women's engagement and the peace building process? The author suggests analyzing critically different concepts linked with the issue and subsequently to try and for-mulate more coherent conclusions.

The conviction as to women's predestination to build peace is linked with the concepts of the gendered aspects of conflict (which have been discussed above) and with "motherhood". In fact, it may be stated that to some extent the phenomenon of "motherhood" comes from the notion of the gendered nature of conflict. In the center of the "moth-erhood" idea is the assumption that women's preoccupation with main-taining family ties and protecting children tends to reflect itself on the negotiating table in pacifism and a human centered conception of secu-rity. As evidence different types of comparison are indicated. Thus, it is demonstrated that Liberia had a total of about fourteen peace talks between 1990 and 1997 and they all excluded women groups and they all failed. In contrast, negotiating tables in post-apartheid South Africa and in Burundi invited women's groups and both processes seem to have resulted in lasting peace (Iwilade 2011, p. 25). But is there a connec-tion between the success of peace talks and the presence of women? And, does the presence of women really mean that their role is predestinated to build peace?

According to this question, the author suggests a critical consider-ing as to why women take action during wars and if it really means that war may be treated as an opportunity for women to become apparent? Firstly, it should be noted that participation in a round of peace talks is a right not a privilege (Iwilade 2011, p. 31), which means that negotiat-ing peace agenda should take the point of view of different social groups and different genders seriously. This kind of diversification gives a more coherent overview on the basic needs of ordinary people, which is the first step to try to meet these needs. Simultaneously, it makes it possi-ble to avoid a situation in which the informal grassroots peace building initiatives are disregarded. This is perceived as a crucial point, because this exclusion of key social stakeholders like women groups, leads only to technically viable peace agenda not ones that are socially and culturally feasible (Iwilade 2011, p. 30). Going further, women are considered as one of the most vulnerable group during conflict. This vulnerability is evident not only when it comes to physical and moral aggression but also at economic level. Women are often left without men during war, from which should be understood that men are those who are mostly involved in the fighting and who die (obviously, women do fight and die as well but they are less involved in fighting when compared to men). It makes women entirely responsible for supporting the family, which is especially difficult for them as a group marginalized on the labor market (in pre-conflict era, during conflict and in the post-conflict reality). It means also that the nature of the **conflict changes the perception of gender role** and forcing women to earn money, something which is an extraneous idea in patriarchal societies in many parts of the East Africa region. All of these aspects may be perceived by women as very difficult to deal with. And in the author's opinion, as well as those of other observers (Iwilade 2011, pp. 24–30) of the issue, this is the reason which drives women to organize themselves into groups and to take action to change the situation and establish peace. In this manner, **war does not create the "opportunity" for women but forces them to change extremely tough living conditions**.

When one examines the demands put by women at the negotiating table one may observe that they are not simply about pacifism, equality for all, respect for human rights, and development for society, but mostly about equality for women. This does not mean of course that the empowerment of women is not important but it is not true that women's movements talk about "everybody"—they talk about themselves and about their particular role in building and maintaining peace (Irvine and Hays-Mitchell 2012, pp. 1–9). Therefore, in the author's opinion, the concept of predestination to develop peace agenda deriving from unique experience such as motherhood is simply a far-reaching simplification. In most sub-Saharan countries social structures may be described as patriarchal. This means that the role of man is more significant than women in various areas, such as: the social, economic and political spheres (Tripp et al. 2012). In this manner women have been structurally excluded from having power, starting at the household level and finishing at the official decisive point. Understanding these deep ingrained structural inequalities and discriminations gives a broader view on the issue of the role of women—before conflict, during conflict as well as in post conflict reality. War does not eliminate the previously known patterns of behavior in social structures, despite the fact that undoubtedly because of war, the boundaries between what is allowed and what is not becomes blurred. But if one assumes that behavioral patterns are shaped by actors and structures (Wendt 1987), one may notice that the main core of the social roles typical for women and men from times before the conflict remain the same in the post conflict era. Therefore, the author states that **the interests and roles of women played by them during peace processes** come from the social and cultural structures rather than from the moral authority of "motherhood".

The other side of the coin is that the concept of "motherhood" has become politicized. This glorification began in the 1970s, in Argentina with "Las Madres de la Plaza de Mayo" women's peace movements. The group received great attention on the part of feminist scholars and international society, which was maintained later in reference to women's peace initiatives in Israel, Liberia, Palestine, Guatemala and Nepal, and so on (Irvine and Hays-Mitchell 2012). Motherhood became a symbol and a key word, used constantly as a proof of "women's unique power," although there is no empirical evidence for connections between motherhood and peace building abilities. And although the concept of motherhood has various completely different meanings around the world it is treated besides the biological part as a combination of cultural and social determinants (Hooks 2000).

THE INSTITUTIONS INVOLVED IN THE PHENOMENON OF WOMEN'S PARTICIPATION IN PEACE PROCESSES

As the major institutions which influence women's participation in peace negotiations are deemed global/international organizations—such as the United Nations, the International Monetary Fund (IMF), the World Bank and the Commonwealth; regional—such as the AU, the United Nations Economic Commission for Africa (UNECA) and sub regional—such as the SADC, the West African Economic Community (ECOWAS) (Tripp et al. 2009, pp. 63–80). The turning point in relations between women's movements and these various organizations began at the beginning of 1990. The above-mentioned international institutions focused their work on the issues of peace, democratization, development as well as human rights and women empowerment. The pressure to implement specific strategies in this area has spread among regional and sub-regional entities and has directly or indirectly influenced local initiatives—by creating space for their development and by giving various forms of support (Ellis et al. 2007, pp. 2–5).

When it comes to institutions at local level one should be aware that besides formal organizations one may find also clan leaders, elders and religious leaders. Their position and importance provide the basis for highlighting them among others entities. Their role is particularly important in shaping post-conflict realities because their opposition may block social reforms. They are indicated as the strongest supporters of tradition, morality and customary law (Htun 2003, pp. 79–85)—the main factors that keep women under discrimination.

At the same time it should be noted that legal reforms in post-conflict countries prove that the resistance of local leaders is possible to break. Then, it is worth asking the question as to what factors influence the authorities that sometimes they agree to approve legal guarantees for women? The analysis of the subject literature allows one to formulate the statement that this attitude is determined by the experience of conflict or war. It is pointed out that this traumatic experience has contributed to redefining the meanings of such terms as "violence," "aggression," and "rape" and simultaneously has changed the perception of the issue of equality. In this manner empowerment begins to be seen as a necessary element for stabilizing the situation and building peace. Post-conflict societies are more sensitive to oppression, and therefore have a greater understanding of the prohibition of various forms of discrimination against women (Hogg 2009, pp. 35–43)—including domestic violence, which in many other African countries this remains unregulated.

Traumatic experience has often motivated the establishment of peace associations to opposite the violence. In this way, women in conflict countries have begun to be visible in the public and political spheres and ultimately to have played a significant role in both, stabilizing the situation and shaping post-conflict realities—as in Rwanda. However, one may also observe that the postulates advanced by them could be enforced through a universal social consensus which may be treated as being as equally important as external pressure and the permission for change amongst local authorities.

What Happens After the End of Conflict? Interactions Between Actors

The late 1990s of twentieth century brought to a close many conflicts in East Africa (Burundi—2004; Mozambique—1992; Rwanda—1994, Uganda—2007). At that time political and legislature changes also started to be implemented. After conflicts and wars new constitutions and new rules of governance were created and most of them included some provisions on equality between women and men (Tripp et al.

2012). It is stated that on the one side it was a result of outside pressure coming from such initiatives as: the Beijing Platform for Action, which called for increased participation of women in conflict resolution at the decision making level; from the UN-SC Resolution 1325, which recognized as crucial the role of women in the maintenance of international peace and security; or from the European Parliament resolution which encouraged women's participation in conflict resolution (Nakaya 2003). And on the other side, it was the outcome of the increasing power of women's organizations which have used the political experience gained in the peace talks and mobilized themselves to work for building the post-conflict reality. Therefore, this part of the paper is devoted to an analysis of the situation of women's peace movements after the end of conflicts. The analysis is aimed to answer the question as to what interactions appears and what happens with women's groups when the conflict comes to an end. It is based on a brief overview of the actions of women taken in the East Africa region.

Peace negotiation in Somali included about one hundred women but after this process women continued to be marginalized. Women's participation in the Somali peace talks was formalized at the Conference on National Reconciliation, in 1998. This meeting resulted in the establishment of the Transitional National Council which required that one woman must be included in each three representatives from the 18 regions. But this initiative failed quickly and the state started to fight again (as one of the possible reasons for the failure is often indicated the lack of clan's representation). It is assumed that the Somali women's movements emerged out of a humanitarian necessity during the prolonged war. Women provided shelters and medical care for soldiers, supplied clean water for communities, and restored destroyed schools. However the most significant is that they initiated inter-clan dialogue for peace. Somali women belong to their father's clan and to their husband's clan (while children belong to the husband's clan alone). Recognizing that clan engagement was crucial for building peace they have started dialogues between clans and pushed to form an umbrella organization to coordinate these talks. The subsequent National Reconciliation Conference held in 2000 was based on a clan-based formula and consisted of 4 main clans delegations, each including 20 women. As a result, the power-sharing arrangement was formulated and also the Transitional National Assembly (TNA) was created with 12% quotas for women. The women's groups engaged in peace talks were named the "Sixth Clan".

They were encouraged and promoted by the United Nations as a crucial element for building lasting peace in Somali. But they had no experience in either, decision making as well as the power-sharing processes and after a short time of their glory at the negotiating table they have stared to be marginalized again (Nakaya 2003, pp. 459–476).

In Burundi, women were made party to official peace talks and they have proposed issues that they wish to see in peace agreements, such as: quotas; a strengthening of women's rights; women's right to property, ownership and inheritance; the end of impunity for perpetrators of gender-based violence. It was indeed a voice for the promotion of women and not social equality but it has brought a gender perspective to the peace building (Nakaya 2003, pp. 461–474). Also Uganda was seen as a state with very advanced, articulate and organized women's peace movements. Women's groups headed the peace talks with the Lords' Resistance Army (LRA) between 1994 and 2004 and it is assumed that they had a great impact on the ending of the conflict in Northern Uganda. Women organizations, such as the Civil Society Women's Peace Coalition, participated during the peace talks in Juba (two women directly on the peace team) (Permanent Mission of Uganda to the United Nations 2008). However, after that period the situations of women started to be marginalized again in both, Burundi and Uganda. Moreover, present-day Uganda is identified as seriously oppressive to women with a weak representation of women's NGOs and strong governmental opposition to women's rights.

At first sight, it seems that the story of women's movements in Rwanda is different. Again, women's groups are recognized as crucial for building peace after the genocide but simultaneously it is pointed out that women maintained their high political position after the end of conflict (McCarthy 2011, p. 70), which makes them different from the women's groups which have been described above. As evidence the world's highest percentage of parliamentary representation for women—at 56%, is indicated. At the same time however, some observers state, that there is another side of the coin and that the engagement of women in the Rwandan political sphere has another explanation. Carey L. Hogg suggests, that one should take into consideration two opposing trends in Rwanda's post-conflict environment. The first one is that of the Rwandan Patriotic Front (RPF)—which heads the government, "has advocated for women greater political inclusion under the premise that women will 'better' the political climate" (Hogg 2009, p. 39) just by being a woman (what has clear connotations with the concept of "motherhood"). And the second one is that in exchange for support, RPF expects total separation from any form of political dissent or ethnic identification among women's representatives. As a result, women representation in the political sphere has been objectified and limited—or rather overwhelmed by the burden of taking action for the rehabilitation of the whole nation beyond ethnicity (Hogg 2009, pp. 34–55). Then, it may be stated that the situation of women in Rwanda is only superficially different from that of others in the East Africa region. In fact however, women's groups are not treated as equal with men.

Thus, how did it happen that **women's peace movements became marginalized after the end of negotiations and after the end of conflict?** The subject literature offers an explanation that it occurs due to the fact that the situation of women is discriminated against before and during conflict (Iwilade 2011, pp. 27–32). It means that the end of conflict does not simply bring solutions on social inequality. One should remember that the structure of states, in which war breaks out, are weak and probably full of social, economic and political problems which do not disappear when conflict comes to an end. Moreover, these structures are created and influenced by the authorities and those who have "the power" to govern, which means by those who could not avoid the outbreak of conflict. These political elites maintain their power even when conflict ends and want to hold high position in the post-conflict reality. It seems then that **although the conflict ends, the behavioral patterns and structures remain almost the same.** And even when women's peace movements had a great influence on the political situation at the negotiating table time is needed to change the structure for more equal and power-sharing ideas, which include women's participation.

Moreover, it is pointed out that the power of women after conflict has weakened because they do not have enough competences to hold high political positions. This is a result of the marginalization of women before conflict, which is linked with worse access to education and labor markets comparing to men. It is also suggested that not every woman who took a seat at the negotiation table comes as a representative of great social demands for peace or equality. Some of them are friends of prominent political elites and just seize the moment and grasp the opportunity for a political career and access to resources—in the same way as men. This is fostered by the undermining of gender roles which have been classified above as one of the outcomes of prolonged conflict.

Therefore, whether conflict is ended by a military victory or a negotiated settlement, the capacity of women to effectively engage in its aftermath is a major challenge. Even when women are invited to peace talks, they are often incapable of articulating their views in legalistic terms, which is a testimony of the generations of discrimination against them (Tripp et al. 2012).

CONCLUSION

On the basis of the research questions which have been raised in the introduction to this paper, the author has specified three main ideas that encourage women to play a role in peace talks at the negotiating table. They are: the nature of conflict, outside pressure and local initiatives. All of these elements influence each other and force women to some extent to take action for peace building and the ending of ongoing war or conflict. Women are recognized as one of the most vulnerable groups during conflict. They live under extremely difficult conditions which strengthen their need to change this plight for the better. Moreover, women's groups have the support of both international entities and donators, such as the United Nations and the U.S., as well as local initiatives on an African soil.

Women are a part of peace processes not because war is a kind of opportunity for them or because they are predestinated to build peace by the experience of motherhood. Therefore, their role and interest is not just "to be a woman" and wait for lasting peace. Women's movements give a gender perspective to the necessary changes in post-conflict reality and they are also the voice of a marginalized social group. Their roles come from pre-conflict social and cultural structures which are full of behavioral patterns remaining almost unchanged despite the outbreak of war. There are global, regional and sub regional institutions involved in the phenomenon of women's participation in peace processes which are able to encourage women to take an action by giving different kinds of support. On the other side one may also find local groups, such clans, elders and religious leaders who have the power to block social reforms.

This seems particularly important because when the structure of power is not changed during peace processes there is very limited room for women's groups in post-conflict reality. In most cases after the end of conflict the role of women is marginalized and they are not able to act within the political sphere and to influence the decision making process of the government. Moreover, the representation of women in the political sphere is weak, which generally means that the important activities of women's groups end when the conflict itself ends.

REFERENCES

Al Jazeera. 2014. Why Aren't More Women Participating in Peace Talks? http://stream.aljazeera.com/story/201408251449-0024097. Accessed 26 Feb 2016.

All Africa. 2015. Africa: Beyond Rhetoric—The Role of Women in Sustainable Peacebuilding. http://allafrica.com/stories/201505210486.html. Accessed 26 Feb 2016.

BBC News. 2015. Peace Process Training for Syrian Women. http://www.bbc.com/news/uk-scotland-34953758. Accessed 26 Feb 2016.

CNN. 2014. Building Peace in Africa? Give Power to Women. http://edition.cnn.com/2014/05/19/world/africa/building-peace-africa-give-power-women/. Accessed 26 Feb 2016.

Ellis, Amanda, et al. 2007. *Gender and Economic Growth in Tanzania. Creating Opportunities for Women.* Washington: World Bank.

Hogg, Charu L. 2009. Women's Political Representation in Post-conflict Rwanda: A Politics of Inclusion or Exclusion? *Journal of International Women's Studies* 11 (3): 34–55.

Hooks, Bell. 2000. *Feminist Theory: From Margin to Center.* Cambridge: South End Press.

Htun, Mala. 2003. *Sex and the State: Abortion, Divorce and the Family under Latin American Dictatorships and Democracies.* New York: Cambridge University Press.

Irvine, Jill A., and Maureen Hays-Mitchell. 2012. Gender and Political Transformation in Societies at War. *Journal of International Women's Studies* 13 (4): 1–9.

Iwilade, Akin. 2011. Women and Peace Talks in Africa. *Journal of International Women's Studies* 12 (1): 22–37.

McCarthy, Mary K. 2011. *Women's Participation in Peacebuilding: A Missing Piece of the Puzzle?* Pennsylvania: University of Pennsylvania.

Mili, Amel. 2013. Gender Standards v. Democratic Standards: Revisiting the Paradox. *Journal of International Women's Studies* 14 (2): 3–11.

Nakaya, Sumie. 2003. Women and Gender Equality in Peace Processes: From Women at the Negotiating Table to Postwar Structural Reform in Guatemala and Somalia. *Global Governance* 9: 459–476.

Neill, Kevin G. 2000. Duty, Honor, Rape: Sexual Assault against Women During War. *Journal of International Women's Studies* 2 (1): 43–51.

Permanent Mission of Uganda to the United Nations. 2008. *During the Open Security Council Debate on Women and Peace and Security.* New York.

Tripp, Aili M., et al. 2009. *African Women's Movements. Changing Political Landscapes.* New York: Cambridge University Press.

Tripp, Aili M., et al. 2012. *Afrykańskie ruchy kobiece w negocjacjach pokojowych.* Warszawa: PAH.

United Nations. 2016a. Gender. Challenges and Opportunities. http://tz.one. un.org/index.php/core-commitments/gender?showall=1&limitstart=. Accessed 21 Feb 2016.

United Nations. 2016b. We can End Poverty. Millennium Development Goals and Beyond. http://www.un.org/millenniumgoals/. Accessed 21 Feb 2016.

UN Women. 2016a. 12 Critical Areas. http://www.unwomen.org/en/news/in-focus/csw/feature-stories. Accessed 21 Feb 2016.

UN Women. 2016b. Facts and Figures: Peace and Security. http://www.unwomen.org/en/what-we-do/peace-and-security/facts-and-figures. Accessed 17 Feb 2016.

UN Women Report. 2012. *Addressing Conflict-Related Sexual Violence An Analytical Inventory of Peacekeeping Practice.*

U.S. Department of State. 2016. U.S.-Africa Leaders Summit: Investing in Women, Peace, and Prosperity. http://allcontentmp3videopdf.xyz/watch/OiY3whFHDM4/u-s-africa-leaders-summit-investing-in-women-peace-and. html. Accessed 21 Feb 2016.

Wendt, Alexander. 1987. The Agent-Structure Problem in International Relations. *International Organization* 41 (3): 335–370.

International River Basins as Regional Security Communities: The Okavango River Case

Douglas de Castro

INTRODUCTION

Over the years, we have been receiving bad news from Africa in terms of political crisis and its implications over society and environment. A wave of political independency started in the 70's in the continent,

Paper submitted to the *Interdisciplinary Approaches to Security in the Changing World Conference 2015*, Jagiellonian University, city of Krakow, Poland. My sincere thanks to CNPQ for funding my research; São Paulo School of Law-FGV for institutional support; my friends Michelle Ratton, Sanchez Badin, and Rafael Duarte Villa for continuous encouragement; and Professor James Rasband from Brigham Young University for introducing water-related issues to my research agenda.

Post-doc researcher at the São Paulo School of Law-FGV.

D. de Castro (✉)
São Paulo School of Law (FGV), São Paulo, Brazil
e-mail: douggcastro@gmail.com

© The Author(s) 2018
P. Frankowski and A. Gruszczak (eds.),
Cross-Disciplinary Perspectives on Regional and Global Security,
https://doi.org/10.1007/978-3-319-75280-8_10

which did not bring the peace and prosperity as advertised by revolutionary forces, for instance, in Angola after formal independence, the three national revolutionary groups that fought against Portugal began fighting each other for control over government institutions (Visentini 2002). Counties in the continent received a large sum of money from former colonizers, aligned countries, and international institutions to build the necessary infrastructure for development. However, the instability of the ruling institutions persisted, and in some cases worsened due to external pressures brought by the structural changes in the international system due to decolonization processes and the oil crisis in the 70s and 80s.

In this context, natural resources were an essential key in one hand for internal development and for another one to the voracity of African rulers and their international partners in business to produce cash for themselves (Deegan 2008). The competing demands for African natural resources produced a high inequality in benefits distribution and the lack of priority for some uses such as the use of water in familiar farming (very strong and traditional in Africa) and domestic uses. In addition to anthropic causes mentioned, other sources of pressure as population growth, unsustainable and irrational use of water and an increase in pollution sources adds to the serious situation of water stress in Africa.

Direct consequences of high pressure and competing claims over water is an unprecedented increase in hunger and thirst rates, leading the continent to a state of food and water insecurity to an already full menu of all sorts of insecurities. In this vein, in the 80s and 90s we observe the proliferation of research agendas claiming the existence of a causal relationship between water scarcity and the occurrence of violent conflict between states because of local instabilities and water stress (Homer-Dixon 2006).

However, worth noting that such research agendas fail to provide empirical evidence to make a good case in proving the existence of such relation, even to the point that the formulated hypothesis are impossible to test due to its large and undetermined spectrum of study and the complexity involving international watercourses.

As a matter of fact, the tendencies we see in the political and legal international arenas point to the opposite, meaning that countries sharing scarce water resources tend to engage in cooperative behavior to resolve saliences related to water uses, which might be observed by the proliferation of water-related treaties and the insignificant number of violent conflicts (Wolf 1998).

Recent studies have shown that there are factors that contribute to deeper solutions to the challenges related to shared water and joint water management, thus contributing to increase of political stability and the perception of water security in the region. Among these factors, we might include (1) the intensity of the interaction between countries; (2) the linked issues in their relationship; (3) the norms and institutions in terms of water usage developed within the basin communities due practice; and (4) the unchanging physical reality of the international basin (Gulbenkian 2013).

The Okavango River Basin defies both logics: that Africa is a constant source of bad news and that water scarcity will lead states inevitably to violent conflicts. The Okavango case presents water conflicting uses and scarcity in an international basin formed by Angola, Botswana, and Namibia. Despite of expectations over water uses, political saliences and great challenges in terms of internal institutional design and political instability, countries engaged in cooperative behavior towards sharing the benefits of water in the region, which has led them to the institutionalize the cooperation by the formation of the Permanent Commission of the Okavango River Basin (OKACOM).

The central argument of this chapter is that as states deepen the cooperation process by institutionalizing water management systems will lead them to increase political stability in the international river basin to the point in which it forms a water security community as theorized by Deutsch et al. (1957) and Adler and Barnett (1998).

The theoretical framework in this chapter is built upon three dimensions that lead to the formation of a security community in the international basin: (1) political communication; (2) machinery of enforcement, and (3) popular habits of compliance. The formation of a security community in the international basin setting has a positive direct impact on water and food security in the region, which spills over to shared factors such as culture, economy or security concerns, thus leading to an increase in societal security as a whole (Adler 1997).

Our challenge in this chapter is to deliver a comprehensive analysis that revolves around objective and subjective interests to the formation of a security community. To this end, the application of the theoretical framework as proposed is subject to a clear methodological approach of deductive nature in which the Okavango River Basin case is tested.

The research technique used is the process tracing that will help the reader to understand the interaction of causal conditions between the initial moment of conflicting positions towards water usage in the basin to the formation of the OKACOM, and the identification of the three dimensions leading to the emergence of a security community.[1]

The structure of the chapter consists of presenting an introductory literature review that sets the context for the development of the theoretical framework that includes the issues of water scarcity; conflict and cooperation settings in a water basin context; and international and water security theories. The following part of the chapter consists of the conceptualization of a security community and the ideas revolving it in terms of objective and subjective interests. Upon establishing the theoretical dimension, the empirical part of the chapter unveils important evidences and implications for the formation of interests, norms and institutions, and instruments that the Okavango case brings to theory. Finally, the conclusion presents the findings, challenges, and directions for future research.

LITERATURE REVIEW: WATER, COOPERATION AND SECURITY

The international community tends to agree upon the fact that demands over water resources have been growing although that the quantity of water available in the planet is a constant variable (Barlow 2009; Gleick 1993).

It is precisely in the context of great pressure on the use of available water resources and the increasing recognition of its vital necessity for survival of all species that we observe the emergence of a growing literature and research agendas. The main goal of these agendas is to establish the linkage between water scarcity and violent conflict in an international setting (Alao 2015; Buzan et al. 1997; Lipschutz 1995). Furthermore, research agendas and political rhetoric exacerbates the issue by adopting the water war analogy to oil (mixing concepts of non-renewable resources with renewable ones), thus prompting countries to promote any measure, including war, to secure the access to sources of water (Shiva 2002; Brown 2006).

---

[1] To a comprehensive understanding of the process tracing technique and its variants we suggest D. Beach and R. B. Pedersen, *Process-Tracing Methods: Foundations and Guidelines*, University of Michigan Press, Ann Arbor, 2013.

Homer-Dixon (2001) recognizes that analysts in recent decades have argued that environmental anthropic pressures can seriously affect national and international security, making the debate strenuous and unproductive due to the vastness and complexity of the issues. In addition, he argues that no reliable research might be conducted because the potential causal relationship has multiple variables that could interfere in the model; however, even considering this fact, he argues that:

> On the basis of the preliminary research reported in this book, however, I believe that in coming decades the world will probably see a steady increase in the incidence of violent conflict that is caused, at least in part, by environmental scarcity. (Dixon 2001, p. 8)

The author infers the existence of a causal relationship that operates connecting environmental scarcity and violent conflict. The basic causal mechanism comprises: (1) the reduction of the physically controlled stocks of environmental resources as water and land for cultivation would cause conflict or wars between states over such resources; (2) the large population movements caused by environmental stress induce conflicts between groups, especially ethnic conflicts; and (3) the severe environmental scarcity simultaneously increase economic deprivation and destabilize key social institutions that causes civilian and insurgent uprisings.

The theory is tested by the author in the cases of Chiapas; Gaza; Pakistan; Rwanda and South Africa; however, the findings have not showed empirical evidences of the alleged causal relationship mainly due to the lack of methodology and systematization of the analysis and reporting, making the case studies in mere descriptions without analytical gain to the field (Bernauer et al. 2012).

Gleditsch (1998) summarizes the general criticism made to this research agenda: (1) The lack of scientific rigor as to the limits of the terms, especially regarding the term environmental conflict; (2) The researcher engages in a mere exercise of controversy instead of engaging in an analysis; (3) Important variables are neglected in the model; (4) The model is so extensive and complex that it is impossible to be tested with accuracy; (5) Future events are postulated as empirical evidence; (6) It fails to establish the national and international limit of the conflict; and (7) There is no consensus on the appropriate level of analysis.

The fact that most of the rivers and lakes are shared by two or more countries exacerbates the perception of potential conflicts given the variety of interests on them, which does not necessarily mean that these disputes will lead countries to engage in violent conflict.

Therefore, it is necessary to understand the dynamics in the basin as for water uses and perceptions. In a previous study made by the author, the complex interdependence theory has been applied to the basin settings.[2] Usually the theory is applied to the economic domain but given the characteristics of the international basins it is suitable to be applied (most the literature uses the term dependency among basin states, but fail to expand the application of such concept if meaning interdependence). According to Keohane and Nye (2011), the basic characteristics of the complex interdependence are (1) multiple channels that connect societies; (2) absence of hierarchy among political issues; and (3) low risk to resource to military capabilities to resolve issues. As the states find themselves in an interdependent relationship, states will fell the sensitivity (actions promoted in one will provoke effects in the other) and vulnerability (impossibility or high costs to adapt to the effects).

Therefore, the basic causal mechanism inferred to be present in the international basin settings is **water projects upstream cause scarcity → deterioration of water quantity/quality (sensitivity) → impossibility to adapt to negative effects (vulnerability) → cooperation**. As the reader notices, this study goes beyond to the point of a simple process of cooperation over water resources in the international basin. As the Okavango case shows, the cooperation process reaches a further distance by the institutionalization of norms and interests into a legal framework and the creation of a permanent commission to manage water resources jointly.

Although tendencies show that water scarcity most likely will lead states to cooperation, anthropic pressures over water resources brings implications to national and international security. Concerns about security implications in environmental changes reached the United Nations Conference on Environment and Development (1991) and General Assembly in which economic, social humanitarian and environmental instabilities have converted to non-military threats to peace and security (Trottier 2001).

---

[2] In http://www.teses.usp.br/teses/disponiveis/8/8131/tde-01122014-184436/pt-br.php.

As stated by Ullman (1983), global challenges that international community is facing points towards the need of a broader concept of security to encompass environmental threats to peace. In this same sense:

> The assumptions and institutions that have governed international relations in the postwar era are a poor fit with these new realities. Environmental strains that transcend national borders are already beginning to break down the sacred boundaries of national sovereignty, previously rendered porous by the information and communication revolutions and the instantaneous global movement of financial capital. The once sharp dividing line between foreign and domestic policy is blurred, forcing governments to grapple in international forums with issues that were contentious enough in the domestic arena. (Mathews 1989, p. 162)

For this reason, Ullman (1983, p. 133) proposes a new conceptualization of security that takes care of the new reality facing international community. He argues that:

> A more useful (although certainly no conventional) definition might be: a threat to national security is an action or sequence of events that (1) threatens drastically and over a relatively brief span of time to degrade the quality of life for the inhabitants of a state, or (2) threatens significantly to narrow the range of policy choices available to the government of a state or to private, nongovernmental entities (persons, groups, corporations) within the state.

According to Villa (1999), changes in international perceptions of security happened in two dimensions. In the state dimension the need of creating structures capable of presenting global responses to environmental challenges and other transnational able to provide ampler diagnosis about environment, development and security. Thus, around the world we observe an unprecedented proliferation of conferences and international organizations, which exist in the legal and political conceptual legal space between state sovereignty and legal obligations (Soares 2003; Gleick 1993; Lipschutz 1995).

Thus, concerns with environmental issues extrapolate to the global and regional arenas given to the complexity and interdependence of issues. This is what Sheenan (2005, p. 104) explained by saying that:

Damage to the environment is often described as a planetary problem, the realities are somewhat different and problems tend to be regional rather than global. Most of the global pollution problems, for example, require joint action only by the highly industrialized states. Most "global" environmental crises have uneven effects and involvements. Some countries are far more at risk than others from the effects of specific environmental problems. Some countries are far more blame than others for causing those problems. Some countries are far better placed than others in financial or technological terms to deal with the problems.

Therefore, a new political phenomenon has emerged that promoted the securitization of the environment, which for Buzan and Graeger (1996, p. 111) *describes a way of handling environmental issues where threats to the environment are seen as urgent and immediate, requiring a quick response at top political level.*

In this sense, considering that the condition of water stress is objective, the concept of securitization as debated by Buzan and Graeger (1996) applies to water. Water is a referent object of securitization as state and non-state actors perceive scarcity as a threat to security, thus, worth to engage into the political discourse of securitization. For that end, the determination of a condition of water insecurity should contain indexes of quantity and quality of water, along with a cross-examination of the pretense scarcity vis-à-vis the communal uses of the water in the region or basin.[3]

SECURITY COMMUNITY: A PROPOSED THEORETICAL FRAMEWORK TO WATER SECURITY

As posed by McBride (2006, p. 10) one of the basics assumptions about the living in a community is that ... *communal experience is very rarely without obstacles, struggle, or disappointment.* Any social interaction is

---

[3] It is not our purpose in this work to extend discussions about this matter, considering that our main claim is that the Okavango River Basin has reached a point far beyond conflictual uses and lack of institutionalized cooperation in the regions, however, for the sake of providing ground to our claims, the water stress condition we are talking about is reached: less than 2500 cubic meters per person/annum; below 0.7 of the UN Water Stress Index (http://www.unep.org/dewa/vitalwater/article69.html); and according to standards set by UN Water Quality Index for the each use of water (http://www.unep.org/gemswater/Portals/24154/publications/pdfs/gwqi.pdf).

subject to conflict and need the mediation of social forces and constraints that keep communities holding together. Life in communities gives raise to social conflicts but also to cooperative behavior, thus, cooperation as a political process does not presuppose the absence of conflicts (Axelrod 2006).[4]

Cooperation is a political stance, thus, as such the cooperation over-water resources is called hydropolitics, which is defined as the authoritative allocation of values in society with respect to water (Turton 2002). This perspective shows that state actors might initiate the process of water securitization taking water as a referent object to national interests, opening up the door for participation of non-state actors. This tends to lead to a more rational and equitable utilization of the shared water resources, and the construction of norms and realities by communities making water a source of integration instead of a source of conflict escalation (Lowi 1995).

Most importantly, this movement makes states and non-state actors to count on a network of national and international institutions to help them to settle arising conflicts peacefully by providing technical and legal support to help them to reconcile the use of a common good as the river (Ostrom 1990; McCaffrey 2007). The engagement of state and non-state actors to manage the expectations over the shared water brings the sense of community, which is built upon the existence of four basic elements: (1) membership; (2) influence; (3) integration and fulfillment of needs; and (4) shared emotional connection (Anderson 2010). This is exactly what Ostrom (1990, p. 247) had in mind upon reporting the case of the fishermen in Alanya, Turkey:

---

[4]The basic assumption on how cooperation works is provided by the market theory, which, according to Macpherson (1961, p. 490): *Taking for granted a society in which there was division of productive labor and exchange of products and of labour, it had only to be assumed (1) that every individual rationally tried to maximize his gains (or minimize his real costs), and (2) that there was a freely competitive market for the resources, materials and energies needed to produce things, and for the things produced.* C. B. Macpherson, Market Concepts in Political Theory, *The Canadian Journal of Economics and Political Science/ Revue Canadienne D'Economique Et De Science Politique*, Vol. 27, Issue 4 (1961), pp. 490–497. https://doi.org/10.2307/139435. This means that cooperative behavior to securitize water takes into consideration rationality of the actors (state and non-state) and the maximization of gains as water is essentially a systemic good in which any disruption in part of the system provokes a implication in the whole system (see systems theory).

Although this is not a private-property system, rights to use fishing sites and duties to respect these rights are well defined. And though it is not a centralized system, national legislation that has given such cooperatives jurisdiction over local arrangements has been used by cooperative officials to legitimize their role in helping to devise a workable set of rules. The local officials accept the signed agreement each year also enhances legitimacy. The actual monitoring and enforcing of the rules, however, are left to the fishers.

Therefore, our theoretical framework departs from a constructivist epistemology in which reaching a higher degree of peace is an incremental process within the international system conducted by social forces (Wendt 1999).

Deutsch et al. (1957) builds the security community upon constructivist approach, providing a testable theory upon the tenets of structures and agents in the international system at the same time that he recognizes the construction of social aspects such as culture, ideas and values that influences the development of "isles" of peace.

This points out to the international basin as an "isle" of cooperation and security in terms of water. This is true due to two main interdependent conditions. First, the boundaries of a water basin are more or less defined. Second, social interaction within the boundaries in the basin are inevitable, thus, becoming more important to settle saliences faster than other aspects of the political life, as there is an expectation that *social problems can and must be resolved without resort to large-scale physical force* (Tusicisny 2007).

The research problem for Deutsch et al. (1957) is not why war happens but why it does not happen more often. In addition, he questions why for some states war is an incentive and for others have been eliminated in their relationship (United States and Canada for instance). However, beyond these questions, what matters most to Deutsch et al. (1957) is to establish the ontology of a political community, which for him is *a social group with a communications process, the existence of an enforcement engineering, and habits of compliance* (p. 3), and to understand how some relationships become a community.

In addition, the integration process is:

> [...] a matter of fact, not of time. If people on both sides do not fear war and do not prepare for it, it matters little how long it took them to reach

this stage. But once integration has been reached, the length of time over which it persists may contribute to its consolidation. (Deutsch et al. 1957, p. 3)

The next theoretical movement made by Deutsch et al. (1957) is to bring security to the political community approach, which according to him is a phenomenon build within the community, thus, security becomes inherent or dependent to the community setting for its existence or maintenance, thus a group of people become integrated. Integration in his words is *the attainment, within a territory, of a "sense of community" and of institutions and practices strong enough and widespread enough to assure, for a long time, dependable expectations of "peaceful change" among its population* (Deutsch et al. 1957, p. 2), and not a response to the fear of anarchy in the international system.

The development of a security community is subject to the existence of four fundamental factors according to Deutsch et al. (1957), namely: (1) common values; (2) the need to setup a network of communication; (3) capacity to anticipate other's behavior; and (4) transnational region of states.

Therefore, the presence of these factors leads states to a strong feeling that members of the community will not fight each other physically but will settle theirs disputes in a peacefully way. This happens because the formation of a security state by both institutionalized settings and the construction of norms and identities that lead them to develop common propositions to make communication as effective as possible.

Deutsch et al. (1957) classifies security communities as pluralistic and amalgamated. In a pluralistic community, states retain legal independence of separate governments. An amalgamated community is a merge among independent units to form only one with a common government. Clearly, an international basin as the unity of analysis of this chapter is a pluralistic security community over water resources for several reasons but mainly because is *a more easily attainable form of integration population* (Deutsch et al. 1957, p. 12).

Although promising, the theory was viewed during the Cold War as a dream by realists, which claimed that states were concerned of their own survival under the existing bipolar order kept under balance due to the mutually assured destruction (MAD) logic in which the UN seemed to be short in fulfilling its promises (Barnett and Finnemore 2004). The theory resurfaced with renewed interest after Cold War as the world experienced an unprecedented proliferation of institutionalized forms of cooperation.

Within this context, Adler and Barnett (1998) started to investigate under what conditions security communities may emerge, adding a more refined approach by incorporating the cognitive elements of shared practices, and identification of self-images. A security community is a social construction because interaction provides the emergence of collective identities that depends on communication, discourse, interpretation, and material environments (Adler 1997). Shared definitions created by identities promotes internalized norms that allow people from different countries to know each other and respond collectively to common concerns, thus, security communities emerge as states start to behave according to norms developed by shared values and identities (Adler 1997).

As a social process based on the construction of shared identities, the empirical observation of a security community comprises three phases: nascent, ascendant, and mature. In the nascent phase, the security community shows the minimal core properties. In the ascendant phase, the population in a sovereign State keeps dependable expectations of peaceful changes. In the mature phase, which is the case of the Okavango River Basin, there is the generation of mutual aid behavior. In addition, according to Adler and Barnett (1998, p. 30) there is [...] *a system of rule that lies somewhere between a sovereign state and a regional, centralized ... government; that is, it is something of a post-sovereign system, endowed with common supranational, transnational, and national institutions and some form of a collective security system.*

The existence and functioning of the OKACOM, Southern Africa Hydropolitical Complex, and Southern African Development Community make this empirical claim possible by presenting sufficient evidence of the climax of a communitarian approach, thus, precluding the arguments regarding the impossibility of existence of a security community due to internal political instabilities, especially considering water-related issues (Nathan 2004).

Building a relationship that links ideational factors at the State and population dimensions strengths the concept of the security community (even though not intended explicitly). It makes the interests of state and non-state actors to converge by promoting political communication and machine enforcement thru the institutionalization of the cooperative behavior (signing treaties, and forming international institutions that makes civil society able to participate in the water management).

Upon these considerations, the interaction between the concept of security community and the systemic setting in the water basin forms an important theoretical framework to be tested. This approach expands the reach of the security community theory, which up to now is applied only to military security issues, such as the OTAN after Cold War, or to show evidences of the existence of a cognitive security community in applying the Western security system to Australia.

Therefore, attaining water security in the basin mitigates the security dilemma (Jervis 1978) and brings stability due to peaceful changes made by the *population* that depends on the historical uses of the water (Deutsch et al. 1957).

THE OKAVANGO RIVER CASE: BACKGROUND CONDITIONS AND EMPIRICAL TESTING

Introduction

Before initiating this part of the chapter, we think necessary to present briefly the justification for choosing the Okavango case. According to George and Bennett (2005, p. 19), case selection is part of the strategy and objectives of the researcher, being necessary to comply with two basic requirements:

> Primary criterion for case selection should be the relevance to the research objective of the study, whether it includes theory development, theory testing or heuristic purposes, and cases should be selected to provide the kind of control and variation required by the research problem. This requires that the universe or subclass of events be clearly defined so that appropriate cases can be selected.

For that matter, the case selection follows a strategy in which water scarcity[5] and processes of cooperation conditions are present, therefore, providing the necessary variables for study. The observation on how variable

---

[5]The term is operational considering the lack of adequate quantity or quality to supply the historical demands or uses in the basin to accommodate conflicting uses, preferences, and expectations.

correlate, and, more importantly, testing the theoretical framework in search of the causal conditions, implications, and institutions in a constant physical and geographical context of the international basin. Thus, the aim in this section is to present minimal and sufficient evidences that under certain conditions an international basin becomes a water security community.[6]

Therefore, upon these considerations the case selection criterion is the typical case one, that for Seawright and Gerring (2008, p. 299) is:

> The typical case study focuses on a case that exemplifies a stable, cross-case relationship. By construction, the typical case may also be considered a representative case, according to the terms of whatever cross-case model is employed. Indeed, the latter term is often employed in the psychological literature. Because the typical case is well explained by an existing model, the puzzle of interest to the researcher lies within that case. Specifically, the researcher wants to find a typical case of some phenomenon so that he or she can better explore the causal mechanisms at work in a general cross case relationship.

The Okavango River is considered a typical case because fulfills the initial and outcome condition, meaning that it is in a semi-arid region in which there are competing uses for water (scarcity condition) and reached a high level of institutional cooperation with the OKACOM (cooperation condition). The case is worth studying because the countries in the basin present social, economic and political instabilities that did not preclude them to find peaceful solutions to shared water challenges. In addition, the basin and its ecosystem is one of the last pristine areas in the world and the largest endoreic[7] river system in Southern Africa (Turton 2002; Turton et al. 2003).[8] In addition, the case presents the analytical power

---

[6] As stated earlier in the chapter, part of the methodological strategy is finding the four fundamental factors as theorized by Deutsch et al. (1957) *that* leads to the formation of a security community: (1) common values; (2) the need to setup a network of communication; (3) capacity to anticipate other's behavior; and (4) transnational region of states.

[7] Discharge happens in the sands of Kalahari Desert rather than in the ocean as most rivers do.

[8] On a side note, the case interests the author as part of a research agenda he is part of that investigates the implications of the Brazilian investments made in Angola and the participations of transnational companies in the process. The research group counts with institutional support by the Sao Paulo School of Law (FGV) and Rio Grande do Sul Federal University (UFRGS).

to show the interaction between ideational factors, social, political and economic dimensions, and institutions in the basin that lead to the formation of the security community.

Physical Dimension

The Okavango river basin area is 323.192 km², being the fourth longest river system in southern Africa, and running for 1100 km from central Angola, as the Kubango, through Namibia to the Kalahari in Botswana. The river rises in the headwaters of the Cuito and Cubango tributaries in the highland plateau of Angola at an elevation of 1.780 meters. It derives its principal flow from 120,000 km² of sub-humid and semiarid rangeland in Cuito-Cubango province of Angola before concentrating its flow along the margins of Namibia and Angola and finally spilling into the Okavango delta at an elevation of 980 meters. Several rivers become one as the water moves south and east, branching again when it reaches and ends in the Okavango Delta, one of the largest freshwater inland wetlands on the planet.[9]

In the next section, we will verify the internal context of each country in the basin regarding context and water usage/allocation to next start an analysis of how these countries are handling their internal issues compared to international obligation assumed by entering into agreement to manage the river jointly.

State Actors and Security Issues

In Angola, the fight for independence last more than one year; however, formal independence did not bring peace to the country, as the three national revolutionary groups that fought against Portugal began fighting each other for control of government institutions (Visentini 2002). The country started to reproduce the effects of the Cold War in its borders. The former USSR and Cuba supported MPLA. South Africa supported UNITA. Zaire supported FNLA, which received also the support from China, Portuguese and British mercenaries, and South Africa. The United States initially supported FNLA but soon started to help UNITA as well, thus, keeping a division strategy in Angola (Whitaker 1970).

[9]For a detailed description of the physical and geographical aspects of the basin, see: http://www.okacom.org/knowing-the-river.

The civil war started right after independence and lasted until 2002, which left the country with a great need to resume the developing goals, especially in terms of infrastructure to distribute water and electricity (Pachova et al. 2008).

Angola is an upstream country that after civil war was in need to develop water-related projects for reconstruction, not to mention the great number of internal displaced people (IDP) that settle in the Province of Cuando-Cubango, thus increasing the risks of affecting the hydro-environmental integrity of the region (Turton et al. 2003). This wave of IDP's along with the already existing people in the region increases the pressure over water as the *current use of the basin's water resources is limited to water supplies to small regional centers and some small scale floodplain irrigation.*

Despite of challenges, *upstream basin offers good conditions for the development of agricultural projects, with great potential for hydroelectric and agro-industrial projects* (Turton et al. 2003). For that matter the provincial government of Cuando-Cubango has launched a plan of action to tackle: (1) agriculture and food security; (2) water and sanitation; (3) resettlement; (4) health and nutrition; (5) education; (6) protection of IDP's; and (7) de-mining (Pachova et al. 2008).

As of Botswana, it is a water-stressed country surrounded by deserts although receives large part of the river discharge forming the delta that as stated by Turton et al. (2003, p. 109):

> The presence of a vast body of water in a predominantly dry area has created a unique environment. From the natural environment and human settlements to a diverse animal and plant species, the Okavango Delta supports an ecosystem with entities that are highly dependent upon water.

The Okavango Delta is essential for population settlement that is spread all the way from Mohembo to Namibia's border, which villages depend on heavily on agriculture and livestock. Due to its pristine status, part of the delta has a unique ecosystem in which tourism activities supported by government in terms of making efforts to keep it as the prime tourist attraction with a low-volume/high-cost tourism policy is the main activity in terms of supporting the region economically (Turton et al. 2003 and Pachova et al. 2008).

As a downstream country, Botswana suffers great impact of upstream activities, especially from water development projects in Namibian that intend to divert water to other arid regions in the country as it's the only country's source for water.[10]

Considering that the delta is integrally in the country's territory, Botswana might use the waters with no regard to other riparian countries as interests for development and intense water uses are common in the region, especially after liberation movements. However, there is no observation of the absolute territorial integrity doctrine in the country's behavior in regards to the basin (Scudder 1993). Botswana has declared the Okavango Delta a Ramsar site, thus assuming the legal obligation to protect the site as state in Article 3 of the Ramsar Convention (1971).[11] For that to happen, the country has engaged in a very active process of communications and involvement of state and non-state actors to meet this obligation, which according to Turton et al. (2003, p. 110) *the government recognizes the need to consult the different stakeholders. These range from citizens in the settlements around the delta, local and central government authorities, and different NGOs working in the delta.*

Namibia is a water-stressed state with most of its economic development located in the dry central portion of the country that needs to transfer water from the Okavango to arid regions.[12]

Between 1970 and 1974 the country has experienced a 7% population growth per annum in the central region that depend on heavily over water resources for small agriculture and livestock projects (Turton et al. 2003). For this reason, the government has proposed the Eastern National Water Carrier to transfer water from the Okavango to the Grootfontein-Omatako River to supply water to central area of Namibia, which in practice has insignificant impact on Okavango's runoff. Furthermore, according to Turton, Ashton and Cloete (2003, p. 112):

[10] In http://www.greencrossitalia.it/ita/acqua/wfp/pdf/greencrosswfp_okavango.pdf.

[11] Article 3. (1) The Contracting Parties shall formulate and implement their planning so as to promote the conservation of the wetlands included in the List, and as far as possible the wise use of wetlands in their territory. (2) Each Contracting Party shall arrange to be informed at the earliest possible time if the ecological character of any wetland in its territory and included in the List has changed, is changing or is likely to change as the result of techno-logical developments, pollution or other human interference. Information on such changes shall be passed without delay to the organization or government responsible for the continuing bureau duties specified in Article 8. In http://portal.unesco.org/en/ev.php-URL_ID=15398&URL_DO=DO_TOPIC&URL_SECTION=201.html.

[12] Idem 8.

The 1993 study about the water supply to the central area of Namibia confirmed the results of the 1973 water master plan and the fact that Namibia would eventually have to obtain access to a reasonable and equitable share of the waters of the Okavango River to sustain further growth in the economy of the central area.

Another proposed use of the river is hydropower production in Popa Falls, which is the only feasible location for it. However, Nam Power canceled the plans presented in 2003 due to operational constraints and great impact in tourism activities. Nowadays no plan for use of the river for this purpose is under consideration.

As seen as in this description on the internal status quo of the water availability, uses and expectations, the conditions for securitization are present, thus if applied the model proposed by Buzan et al. (1997, p. 165) to the basin we will have the details of Securitization at different levels of analysis as presented in Table 1.

Therefore, at this point the proposed theory in this chapter starts to show initial empirical evidences. The local sources of insecurity over water resources that might have effect over the region are either weaker or being managed internally by each riparian country. This fact has no effect whatsoever in the water security in the region, confirming what we have stated before that internal instabilities should not preclude the advance of a more stable water regime (Nathan 2004).

First, we observe that riparian countries find themselves in a position to create and enable a positive environment as far as water management goes in their territory, which according to AMCOW (2012, p. 10) involves *developing and implementing the policy, planning, and legal framework needed for guiding and coordinating water resources management, development, and use.* The status of the countries in the Okavango basin is given in Table 2.

Second, some indicators that have direct impact on water security and are part of an important dimension of water resources is the food security. Agriculture is one of the anthropic activities with high volume of water consumption and source of pollution (Clapp and Cohen 2009).

Reaching food security is a situation in which *all people, at all times, have physical, social and economic access to sufficient, safe and nutritious food that meets their dietary needs and food preferences for an active and healthy life* (FAO 2015). Thus, a state of security in this matter encompasses food availability, economic and physical access to food, and food utilization and stability over time.

Table 1 Securitization at different levels of analysis (*Source* Made by the author based on Buzan et al. (1997, p. 165) and Pachova et al. (2008))

Dynamics/ Sectors	Military	Environmental	Economic	Societal	Political
Global					
Regional		Ramsar site integrity			OKACOM's effectivity
Local	Civil war/power disputes (Angola)	Drought (Namibia and Botswana); Unilateral water projects (Angola and Namibia)	Socio-economic development	Internal displaced persons (Angola); intergroup disputes (Namibia and Botswana)	Water resources development policies

Table 2   Local water management overview (*Source* AMCOW 2012)

	Water law	*Decentralized management*	*Institutional framework form management*	*Water management education*
Angola	Implementation advanced	Implementation started	Under development	Not relevant
Botswana	Fully implemented	Implementation started	Implementation started	Implementation started
Namibia	Developed, not implemented	Implementation started	Implementation started	Implementation started

Table 3   Food security indicators (1990 and 2011) (*Source* Made by the author based on FAO-Food Security Indicators (October 15, 2014))

Country/ Indicator	*Angola*	*Botswana*	*Namibia*	*Africa*
Average dietary energy supply adequacy (%)	79–115	100–97	93–92	107–116
Average protein supply (gr/caput/day)	35–53	68–64	58–59	59–65
Arable land equipped for irrigation (%)	2.7–1.9	0.4–0.7	0.8–1.0	6.0–6.0
Population with access to improved water sources (%)	42–54	92–97	67–92	55–69
Population with access to sanitation facilities (%)	29–60	39–64	24–32	34–39

As we observe in the graphic below, indicators related to food itself show an improving rate over the years. It would be expected to have the same increasing in terms of irrigation, however, it did not happen and as in Angola even the percentage of land with irrigation has decreased. This shows that countries in the basin are prioritizing other water usage by importing products with high water consumption (FAO 2015) at the same time that indicators related direct to water are improving steadily of the years (Table 3).

Water security is:

the capacity of a population to safeguard sustainable access to adequate quantities of acceptable quality water for sustaining livelihoods, human well-being, and socio-economic development, for ensuring protection against water-borne pollution and water-related disasters, and for preserving ecosystems in a climate of peace and political stability. (UN-Water 2013, p. 1)

As observed in the graphic above, the selected indexes provide a positive outlook in terms of access and use of available water resources. However, considering the fact that countries are in an arid region, it is an important matter to investigate how the available water resources support this demand. This is important because Botswana needs to transfer water to other parts of the country to meet the demands in regions with high water stress and Namibia that depends on water to keep environment at the Delta balanced for tourism and to meet the Ramsar obligations.

The graphic below indicates a compatibility with FAO's indicators in terms of food production and water use for it. In addition, in terms of water availability per capita the countries in the basin are in a very good standard if compared to United States or in a better situation if compared to some countries in Europe (UN-WATER 2013) (Table 4).

Therefore, for the purpose of our theory, findings indicate that in terms of internal water security Angola, Botswana and Namibia possess high standards although different expectations for using water according to national interests, thus, different sources of insecurity (Fig. 1).

Now we turn our attention to the regional level of analysis to test our theory considering that we are limited to the spatial dimension of the Okavango River Basin case. However, we do not exclude implications on the international level as Botswana has engaged into the Ramsar

Table 4 UN-Water indicators (*Source* Made by the author based on the UN-Water Federated Water Monitoring System (FWMS) & Key Water Indicator Portal (KWIP) Project)

Country/ Indicator	Angola	Botswana	Namibia	U.S.
Total renewable water resources (M3/inhab/yr)	7.108	6.108	7.844	9.666
Freshwater resources withdraw (%)	0.48	1.59	1.62	15.57
Municipal water withdrawal as a percent of total withdrawal (%)	45.27	40.72	25.35	13.68
Industrial water withdrawal as a percent of total withdrawal (%)	33.95	18.04	4.86	46.11
Agricultural water withdrawal as a percent of total withdrawal (%)	20.78	41.24	69.79	40.22

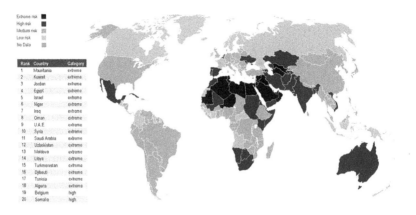

Fig. 1 Water security index

Convention, thus, committing itself to international scrutiny in terms of obligations assumed in the convention, including the need of participation of non-state actors, especially ONGs and epistemic community.

International and Regional Context—The Formation of a Water Security Community in the Basin

Principles regarding international shared water resources such as duty to not cause harm; equitable and rational use; and duty to inform and share information for instance have been developed over the years by state, international organizations and non-state actors. The contribution for the formation of said principles is made by court and arbitral decisions as the River Oder International Commission; the diversion of water from the Meuse River; the Gabcikovo-Nagymaros case; the Lake Lanoux case; the Trail Smelter case; the Gut Dam case, and the work of epistemic community such as the Institut de Droit Internacional and International Law Association through extensive debates and resolutions, which in terms of shared water is the Helsinki Resolution on the Uses of the Waters of International Rivers (McCaffrey 2007; Salman 2007; Delappenna and Gupta 2009).

The principles developed over the years were consolidated in the Convention on the Law of the Non-Navigational Uses of International Watercourses (1997), which was adopted by most of Southern African

Development Community (SADC),[13] but most importantly by the Okavango riparian states.

In the SADC framework, we observe in the 1980's an increasing number of freshwater agreements between Southern African states, having most of the agreements focus on cooperation, joint management and conflict prevention and resolution, the underlying rationale for these efforts has shifted in line with global trends, from economic development to sustainable development, thus incorporating environmental as well as social issues. In this sense the Protocol on Shared Water courses in the Southern African Development Community (2000), Article 3.7.a:

> Watercourse States shall in their respective territories utilize a shared water course in an equitable and reasonable manner. In particular, a shared watercourse shall be used and developed by Watercourse States with a view to attain optimal and sustainable utilization thereof and benefits therefrom, taking into account the interests of the Watercourse States concerned, consistent with adequate protection of the watercourse for the benefit of current and future generations. (SADC 2000)

The origins of the OKACOM are in the plans of Namibia to increase water supply in the arid central region. For that purpose, after independence Namibia started to negotiate with riparian states in order to secure that goal at the same time ensuring sustainable and rational use.

In September 1990 Angola and Namibia decided to reaffirm effectivity of the old agreements on the Cunene River between Portugal and South Africa, which re-establish the Permanent Joint Technical Commission. Following the same strategy, in November 1990 Namibia and Botswana established the Joint Permanent Technical Commission. Thus, all three Okavango River countries were represented in bilateral organizations.

As the need for water increased in the basin area due to development projects, the Namibian government suggested to bring the two commissions together to debate common issues and possibly to create a

---

[13]The Southern African Development Community (SADC) was established in August 1992 and presently consists of fourteen member states: Angola, Botswana, Democratic Republic of Congo, Lesotho, Malawi, Mauritius, Mozambique, Namibia, Seychelles, South Africa, Swaziland, Tanzania, Zambia and Zimbabwe. In http://www.sadc.int/english/about/history/index.php.

tripartite commission to address common issues. The meeting happened in Windhoek in June 1991 in which lead to the creation of the OKACOM in 1994. The institutional design of the OKACOM includes the formation of ad hoc and/or permanent working groups (so far OKACOM has created groups on biodiversity, hydrology, and institutional matters); national unities of coordination; and the OKASEC (OKACOM Secretariat). This structure provides the traction to OKACOM to accomplish the purposes as intended by riparian countries that is:

> To anticipate and reduce those unintended, unacceptable and often unnecessary impacts that occur due to uncoordinated resources development. To do so it has developed a coherent approach to managing the river basin. That approach is based on equitable allocation, sustainable utilization, sound environmental management and the sharing of benefits. (OKACOM 2016)

Under OKACOM's supervision and advisory capacity the riparian countries established a network that exchange information about environment, social, and economic aspects in the basin that addresses the challenges and solutions in it. As stated by Turton et al. (2003, p. 115):

> The first major achievement of OKACOM was to develop a proposal for a Project to execute an environmental assessment of the Okavango basin and to develop an integrated water resource management strategy by June 1995. It was envisaged that the process to develop the strategy would provide comprehensive information about the state of the environment in the whole Okavango basin, and that an assessment of the prevailing situation would show the potential for the future development of the basin in each watercourse state. Such developments would require water from the Okavango watercourse system.

The development of a water management strategy in international watercourses depend on three basic principles: sovereignty over water resources in each state's territory; equitable and reasonable use; and duty not to cause significant harm. The application of these principles should be preceded by a previous agreement to resolve water conflicts in a peaceful fashion, which in the case of the Okavango river the parties decided freely from interventions to take advantage of the existing bilateral institutions and treaties to form a multilateral institution to deepen cooperation among the riparian countries to make sure arising disputes would be resolved amicably (Turton et al. 2003).

As Angola, Botswana and Namibia continue to develop as part of their national and regional strategy, the pressure over water resources should increase, as well as the potential for conflicts. However, the fact that the OKACOM is already in place shows the recognition of the interdependence among the countries, thus, the need to keep the institutionalized strategy to sustain a balance between social, economic and environmental security in the basin as pressures arise (Swatuk 2005). As posed by Turton et al. (2003, p. 117) the strategy is being built as the *activities that have taken place so far—and will take place in future—are already building confidence, mutual understanding and trust between the parties through the exchange of information, joint planning and the development of a shared vision for the future.*

To reinforce this trend, the 2009 Okavango River Transboundary Diagnosis presents a clear picture of the social, economic and environmental situation in the basin. Despite of the challenges that local communities face in terms of the water usage, the report provides recommendations that indicate no serious threats to water security in the region or to countries, especially considering the existence of the OKACOM as the joint management structure to deal with water issues, which includes[14]:

1. Increase in human capital through literacy programs, basic education, community awareness (food security, conservation and environmental preservation and risk of disease);
2. Increased technological capital through small introduction rural technologies to the increase in household income and diversification activities (aquaculture, beekeeping, ...);
3. Expansion and improvement of the network of social services, especially in terms of education and health;
4. Expansion and improvement of technical assistance, especially with regard to medical (along the flow analysis environmental were often cited pests and diseases in animals) and rural extension;

---

[14]Adapted by the author from the Portuguese version. In http://www.oka-com.org/site-documents/tda-background-reports/tda-portuguese-documents/diagnostico-transfronteirico-bacia-do-okavango-analise-socioeconomica-angola/view.

5. Increasing access to safe drinking water, taking into account the two systems predominant—urban consumption and rural consumption;
6. Creation of local energy systems, using renewable sources (Solar and hydro);
7. Improvement of housing conditions;
8. Expansion and improvement of road infrastructure, with a view to increase circulation;
9. Urban requalification of urban development support centers tertiary activities (services, tourism, ...);
10. Bet on tourist infrastructure of excellence associated with the ecotourism and the safety and quality criteria internationally recognized;
11. Environmental Governance, including the awareness of governments and Administrations on projects with impact on the variation of water flow and polluting sources of rivers (taking into account the views urban growth and agro-farming projects);
12. Local legislative framework, focusing on soil conservation and forest and the management of water resources.

The 2011 OKACOM Annual Report supports this approach and sustains that achieving success in managing water uses in the region is possible by building local and regional partnerships within state and non-state actors, and other initiatives such as the funding from Global Environment Facility among others. In addition, the 2011 Cubango-Okavango Basin Transboundary Report brings important conclusions in terms of deepening even more the cooperative process to achieve optimal levels in the basin:

1. Establishing a shared vision for the entire basin, development of decision frameworks levels national and basin-wide, and strengthening of local institutions and the entire basin (decision making);
2. Strengthening the management and regulation of natural resources at local, national and basin-wide (Implementation);
3. Establishment and strengthening of regulatory monitoring programs (analysis and evaluation);
4. Development of an information management system at the basin level and clogging the knowledge shortages (Data and information);

5. Development of a system to support decision making and a common framework for planning (Analysis and advice).

The water-related treaties that riparian countries are part of and the reports and recommendations made by the OKACOM reflect the joint and holistic approach that informs and direct the commission's work and reflects what the countries intended to in institutionalizing the cooperation among them. They support international substantive obligations of sustainable and rational use, and duty to cooperate and not to cause harm; and procedural obligations to share information and previous consultation (Kiss and Shelton 2007).

This points out to a systemic approach to deal with water in the Okavango river basin that incorporates the most advanced principles and rules in terms of governance of shared natural resources, which provides security and political stability in the region. Therefore, the evidences presented in this section indicates the presence of the elements that support the formation of a security community in the Okavango basin.

An addition piece of evidence towards the confirmation of the hypothesis is provided by the research agenda conducted by the Oregon State University called Basins at Risk. It records that in the Okavango basin 3 events are reported in which 100% are positive, meaning that it scores high on water-related treaties and management and low in conflicts.[15]

Final Remarks

The examination of the Okavango River case in light of the security communities' theory points out to the viability of our hypothesis that the international river basin settings forms a security community as theorized by Deutsch et al. (1957).

The current studies about security communities are linked to high politics issues, mainly to military matters, and the empirical testing conducted using the NATO or European Union. Security is very complex and multi-causal phenomena; in order to be studied appropriately is necessary to break it down in small pieces in which theories are tested, and conditions, implications and causal forces are identified.

[15] In   http://www.transboundarywaters.orst.edu/research/basins_at_risk/bar/BAR_appendix4.pdf.

The strategy of breaking down to water security and applying the grand security communities' theory to the international river basin we found a plausible explanation on why states tend not to apply the natural resources scarcity rationale to water, thus cooperation over water is the most expected outcome even when scarcity is present.

The Okavango River case is emblematic in this sense as riparian communities depend on the river heavily for social, economic and environmental uses. Angola, Botswana and Namibia share a common history of being former colonies of European countries that have become independent recently, thus in need to become independent economically wise as well by developing internally.

In recognizing the importance and interdependence of water-related issues to development, riparian countries choose after independence to re-enact treaties signed by former colonizers to have in place a legal framework to regulate their relationship regarding shared water. Not satisfied to, riparian countries decided form bilateral commissions to manage water between them, which ultimately led to the OKACOM formation.

The work record of OKACOM presented in this chapter express the most contemporary values in terms of water management in the international watercourses, being necessary to clarify that it constitutes minimal evidence to the theory, meaning that a continuous research program is necessary to find more implications and additional supportive evidences.

There are sufficient evidences to support that the four formative elements of a security community are present in the Okavango case, which a summary is presented in Table 5.

This chapter concludes claiming that sufficient empirical evidences were found to support the application of the theory of security communities to the international basin as a viable research program deemed to be pursued.

Table 5 Water security community theory vs. empirical evidences

WSC *indicator*	*Evidences*
Common values	Importance of water for development
Network of communication	Discussion to re-enact old treaties and formation of bilateral commissions
Capacity to anticipate behavior	OKACOM
Transnational regions of states	Riparian communities—expectations in enjoying water uses while respecting others

REFERENCES

Adler, Emanuel. 1997. Imagined (Security) Communities: Cognitive Regions in International Relations. *Millennium—Journal of International Studies* 26 (2 June 1): 249–277. https://doi.org/10.1177/03058298970260021101.

Adler, Emanuel, and Michael Barnett, (eds.). 1998. *Security Communities.* Cambridge, UK and New York: Cambridge University Press.

Alao, Abiodun. 2015. *Natural Resources and Conflict in Africa: The Tragedy of Endowment* (Reissue Edition). Rochester, NY: University of Rochester Press.

AMCOW. 2012. *Status Report on the Application of Integrated Approaches to Water Resources Management in Africa.*

Anderson, Mary. 2010. *Community Identity and Political Behavior.* New York: Palgrave Macmillan.

Axelrod, Robert. 2006. *The Evolution of Cooperation* (Revised Edition). New York: Basic Books.

Barlow, Maude. 2009. *Blue Covenant: The Global Water Crisis and the Coming Battle for the Right to Water* (Edição: Reprint). New York: The New Press.

Barnett, Michael, and Martha Finnemore. 2004. *Rules for the World: International Organizations in Global Politics.* Ithaca: Cornell University Press.

Bernauer, Thomas, Tobias Böhmelt, and Vally Koubi. 2012. Environmental Changes and Violent Conflict. *Environmental Research Letters* 7 (1): 015601. https://doi.org/10.1088/1748-9326/7/1/015601.

Black, Maggie, Jannet King, and Candida Lacey. 2009 *The Atlas of Water: Mapping the World's Most Critical Resource,* 2nd ed. Berkeley: University of California Press.

Brown, Lester R. 2006. *Plan B 2.0: Rescuing a Planet Under Stress and a Civilization in Trouble* (Exp. Upd. Edition). New York and London: W. W. Norton.

Buzan, Barry, Ole Weaver, and Jaap Wilde. 1997. *Security: A New Framework for Analysis.* Boulder, CO: Lynne Rienner.

Clapp, Jennifer, and Marc J. Cohen, eds. 2009. *Global Food Crisis: Governance Challenges and Opportunities.* Waterloo, ON: Wilfrid Laurier University Press.

Deegan, Heather. 2008. *Africa Today: Culture, Economics, Religion, Security.* London and New York: Routledge.

Delappenna, Joseph, and Joyeeta Gupta. 2009. *The Evolution of the Law and Politics of Water.* New York: Springer.

Deutsch, Karl W., Sidney A. Burrell, Robert A. Kann, and Maurice Lee Jr. 1957. *Political Community and the North Atlantic Area.* New Jersey: Princeton University Press.

FAO, IFAD, and WFP. 2015. *The State of Food Insecurity in the World 2015.* Meeting the 2015 International Hunger Targets: Taking Stock of Uneven Progress. Rome: FAO.

George, Alexander, and Andrew Benett. 2005. *Case Studies and Theory Development in the Social Sciences* (Fourth Printing Edition). Cambridge, MA: MIT Press.

Gleditsch, Nils Petter. 1998. Armed Conflict and The Environment: A Critique of the Literature. *Journal of Peace Research* 35 (3 May 1): 381–400. https://doi.org/10.1177/0022343398035003007.

Gleick, Peter H. 1993a. *Water in Crisis: A Guide to the World's Fresh Water Resources*, 1st ed. New York: Oxford University Press.

Gleick, Peter H. 1993b. Water and Conflict: Fresh Water Resources and International Security. *International Security* 18 (1): 79–112.

Graeger, Nina. 1996. Environmental Security? *Journal of Peace Research* 33 (1 February): 111.

Homer-Dixon, Thomas. 2001. *Environment, Scarcity, and Violence*. Princeton, NJ: Princeton University Press.

Jervis, Robert. 1978. Cooperation Under the Security Dilemma. *World Politics* 30 (2): 167–214. https://doi.org/10.2307/2009958.

Just, R.E. 2002. *Conflict Prevention and Resolution in Water Systems* (Illustrated Edition). Cheltenham, UK and Northampton, MA: Edward Elgar Publishing.

Keohane, Robert, and Joseph Nye. 2011. *Power and Interdependence*, 4th ed. Boston: Pearson.

Kiss, A., and D Shelton. 2007. *Guide to International Environmental Law*, 1st ed. Boston: Brill.

Lipschutz, Ronnie D. (ed.). 1995. *On Security*. New York: Columbia University Press.

Lowi, Miriam R. 1995. *Water and Power: The Politics of a Scarce Resource in the Jordan River Basin*. Cambridge, UK and New York, NY: Cambridge University Press.

Mathews, Jessica Tuchman. 1989. Redefining Security. *Foreign Affairs* 68 (2 Spring): 162–177.

McBride, Keally D. 2006. *Collective Dreams: Political Imagination and Community*. University Park, PA: Penn State University Press.

McCaffrey, Stephen C. 2007. *The Law of International Watercourses*. Oxford: Oxford University Press.

Nathan, Laurie. 2004. Security Communities and the Problem of Domestic Instability. Working Paper No. 55, Crisis States Research Centre, London.

OKACOM. Relatório de Análise Diagnóstica Transfronteiriça Da Bacia Hidrográfica Do Cubango-Okavango: Permanente Das Águas Da Bacia Hidrográfica Do Rio Okavango Comissão—The Permanent Okavango River Basin Water Commission | OKACOM | Commissão Permanente Das Águas de Bacia Hidrografica Do Rio Okavango. Accessed 28 Mar 2016. http://www.okacom.org/site-documents/tda-final-reports/relatorio-de-analise-diagnostica-transfronteirica-da-bacia-hidrografica-do-cubango-okavango-permanente-das-aguas-da-bacia-hidrografica-do-rio-okavango-comissao/view.

Ostrom, Elinor. 1990. *Governing the Commons: The Evolution of Institutions for Collective Action*. Cambridge and New York: Cambridge University Press.

Pachova, Nevelina I., Mikiyasu Nakayama, and Libor Jansky (eds.). 2008. *International Water Security: Domestic Threats and Opportunities*. Tokyo and New York: United Nations University Press.

SADC. 2000. Protocol on Shared Watercourses in the Southern African Development Community (SADC) 1995 (revised 2000). http://www.orang-esenqurak.org/UserFiles/File/SADC/SADCprotocol_Revised.PDF.

Salman, Salman M.A. 2007. The Helsinki Rules, the UN Watercourses Convention and the Berlin Rules: Perspectives on International Water Law. *Water Resources Development* 23 (4 December): 625–640.

Scudder, T. 1993. *The IUCN Review of the Southern Okavango Integrated Water Development Project*, 1st ed. Gland, Switzerland: Union Internationale pour la Conservation de la Nature et de ses Ressources.

Seawright, Jason, and John Gerring. 2008. Case Selection Techniques in Case Study Research A Menu of Qualitative and Quantitative Options. *Political Research Quarterly* 61 (2 June 1): 294–308. https://doi.org/10.1177/1065912907313077.

Sheehan, Michael. 2005. *International Security: An Analytical Survey*. Boulder, CO: Lynne Rienner Publishers.

Shiva, Vandana. 2002. *Water Wars: Privatization, Pollution and Profit*. London: Pluto Press.

Soares, Guido Fernando Silva. 2003. *Direito internacional do meio ambiente: emergência, obrigações e responsabilidades*. São Paulo: Atlas.

Swatuk, Larry A. 2005. Political Challenges to Implementing IWRM in Southern Africa. *Physics and Chemistry of the Earth, Parts A/B/C*, Integrated Water Resources Management (IWRM) and the Millennium Development Goals: Managing Water for Peace and Prosperity 30 (11–16): 872–880. https://doi.org/10.1016/j.pce.2005.08.033.

Trottier, Julie. 2001. Water Wars: The Rise of a Hegemonic Concept. In *Exploring the Making of the Water War and Water Peace Belief Within the Israeli–Palestinian Conflict*. Paris: UNESCO International Hydrological Programme. http://armspark.msem.univ-montp2.fr/bfpvolta/admin/biblio/Trottier.pdf.

Turton, A.R. 2002. Hydropolitics: The Concept and Its Limitations. In *Hydropolitics in the Developing World—A Southern African Perspective*, ed. Turton, A.R. and Henwood, R. Pretoria: African Water Issue Research Unit.

Turton, Anthony, Peter Ashton, and Eugene Cloete, eds. 2003. *Transboundary Rivers, Sovereignty and Development: Hydropolitical Drivers in the Okavango River Basin*. Pretoria, South Africa and Geneva: African Water Issues Research Unit.

Turshen, Meredeth. 2016. *Gender and the Political Economy of Conflict in Africa: The Persistence of Violence.* New York: Routledge.

Tusicisny, Andrej. 2007. Security Communities and Their Values: Taking Masses Seriously. *International Political Science Review* 28 (4 September 1): 425–449. https://doi.org/10.1177/0192512107079639.

Ullman, Richard H. 1983. Redefining Security. *International Security* 8 (1): 129–153.

UN-Water. 2013. *Water Security & the Global Water Agenda: A UN-Water Analytical Brief.* Hamilton, ON: UN University.

United Nations. 2006. *Water a Shared Responsibility: The United Nations World Water Development Report 2.* Paris, France and New York: Berghahn Books.

Villa, Rafael Antonio Duarte. 1999. *Da Crise do Realismo à Segurança Global Multidimensional.* São Paulo: Annabllume, 146.

Visentini, Paulo Fagundes. 2002. *As revoluções Africanas.* São Paulo: UNESP.

Gulbenkian Think Tank on Water and the Future of Humanity. 2013. *Water and the Future of Humanity: Revisiting Water Security.* New York: Springer.

Wendt, Alexander. 1999. *Social Theory of International Politics.* Cambridge, UK and New York: Cambridge University Press.

Whitaker, Paul M. 1970. The Revolutions of "Portuguese" Africa. *The Journal of Modern African Studies* 8 (1): 15–35.

Wolf, Aaron T. 1998. Conflict and Cooperation along International Waterways. *Water Policy* 1 (2): 251–265.

CONCLUSION: DRIFTING APART REGIONAL SECURITY ORDERS

In the introduction to this volume we suggested analysis of regional security through the perspective of three intertwined factors, which altogether allow to explore contemporary problems. Thus the aim of this book has been to explore and analyze whether there are underlying patterns and relationship between ideas and interests for regional security in the context of particular challenges and problems. In so doing we set out to find out the extent to which ideas may constrain and limit specific interests, and create scope conditions for ongoing interactions between stakeholders. The change nature of governing security structures in regions in the twenty-first century was underlined when more NGOs and non-state actors began pushing the states with new array of security instruments on offer. Nevertheless this important step in the process of building the world society, somehow based on the exclusion of territory as crucial element (Larkins 2010) should be analyzed through the framework of responsibility for actions, when the states are still entities who bear the burden when things go terribly wrong. Still we have to deal with containers of sovereignty (Agnew 2010), when territory delimits, structures and sometimes facilitates security measures. Yet, we also must notice that good number of actors raise their voices on challenging

© The Editor(s) (if applicable) and The Author(s) 2018   239
P. Frankowski and A. Gruszczak (eds.),
Cross-Disciplinary Perspectives on Regional and Global Security,
https://doi.org/10.1007/978-3-319-75280-8

solutions and frameworks for the world security (Abrahamsen and Williams 2011). By its very nature, international security is unpredictable, and with diverse functions in relation to societies and linkages between sectoral level governing structures and the macro-regional level. Relying on findings provided by our contributors our account explains the uneven progress of security building in different regions and areas, and suggests that cross-disciplinary perspective is the most promising path to understand security nowadays (Bourbeau 2015b).

At the outset of this book posited that there is a casual relationship between ideas, interests, and institutions. Regional case studies provide a rich stream of evidence of the ways in which ideas interact with institutions, and have impacted interactions regarding incoming challenges. Direct or indirect casual links between interests and institutions aside, there is also evidence of self-sustaining ideas, non-contested, arising as a response to states' inability to regulate dynamics of contemporary international security. Thus, by analyzing the factors leading to regional projects, and the first group will include a "vision of the world", whose supporters, without ambitions to transform the global order into a regional order, appeal first and foremost to the values and ideas that underlie regional arrangements. Because the basic normative purpose of states and nations is to avoid war, and provide security this is part of the traditional research program of science and international relations. However, by the regionalization of particular challenges we can expect different a set of ideas that may limit the possibility of conflict within the existing value system, to propose new ideas, to a new concept of politics that is beyond the catalog of existing solutions, or to focus on anti-ideologies that will avoid conflict. The most common model of new regional security arrangement in an ideology-based approach, where new ideas are added to existing ideas, not undermining existing values, but complementing them with new ideas that over time replace the ideas underlying the regionalization project. Replacing regional ideas can be evolutionary or violent, depending on the possibility and frequency of the political window, ideas can remain for years only in theoretical considerations. It is important, however, to accept the fact that ideas are not a stable part of political constructions (Baumgartner 2014) and the constant reference to a specific idea as a key concept always allows for understanding and clarifying political reality.

Ideas for regional security never appear suddenly, but they evolve as a certain vision of the world, changing their character according to place, time, and political circumstances. Therefore ideas for security should be considered in the context of incremental changes (Carstensen 2011), which, when combined, can lead to unexpected results. They are also not separated from general reflection on the state of politics and should not be considered as self-contained concepts (Risse-Kappen 1994). Replacing the idea of security is possible, and following Kingdon (Kingdon 2003), it happens when a "policy window" appears, and when ideas that have been on the margins appear to be mainstreamed into the political conception. Certainly the possibility of a window of politics merges with the emergence of focal events, such as political or economic crises affecting several states in the region. Nevertheless, it should be borne in mind that focal events, although they are an opportunity for ideas, are affected by the impact of such events on the perception of political processes. When the political window opens, but the solution is not ready and the idea is not ready and the "policy window" closes. Therefore, any security ideas, in order to be the actual source of political power must appear in due time. This could be the case of monetary regulations (Riedel, this volume) or space security (Słomczyńska, this volume).

The second group of factors, *interests*, refers to a rationalist approach to political processes taking place on a regional scale. Any asymmetry (economic, military, political or territorial) existing within the geographical region should translate into a regional system that supports or suppresses this asymmetry. However, if one analyzes individual regional systems as well as those concepts that have failed to be particularly important, the existence of core states that uphold the regional idea and without which any integration around the idea would be impossible. This postulate appears in Peter Katzenstain's ideas, which considers that the emergence of a regional project is primarily a result of political will (Katzenstein 2005, p. 9); economic factors are less important.

The basic premise of this volume is the analysis of the concept of shaping regional security through the prism of ideas, considered as the appropriate level of articulation of political interests. We tried to answer the following two questions: What is the role of ideas as a political constructs in shaping regional orders, and what risks are involved adopting particular ideas to achieve political objectives? In order to answer these questions chapters have been divided into three parts, the first of which is a reflection on the specificities of ideas and the place of specific concepts in regional arrangements. The second part of every chapter has been devoted to the characteristics of some regional interests contributing to the formation of a regional security, when main purpose is to increase the broad sense of security. The third part presents reflections on institutions, with particular reference to interactions. Regional systems and regionalism, as well as sovereignty, are constructs, forms of a social contract whose contents and ideas are subject to evolution and change. The authors in this volume share the view that the concepts of regional security nowadays have two meanings: (1) instrumental and (2) normative. In the first case, it is a form of projection of power or an attempt to undermine the regional hegemonic ambition from imposing its own conception of regional solutions. At the same time, regional security can be based on positive or a negative ideas. Nevertheless, any assumption that is possible to distinguish strictly exogenous or endogenous factors as predominating in the concept of regional security does not lead to useful conclusions. Moreover, quest for similarities between large-scale regional and multinational frameworks is not and cannot be an effective research program. By searching for similarities, there are no clear criteria for comparing complex systems, such as states (but also sub-national entities) operating in regional agreements. Normative element of regional security is an attempt to construct a system of norms and values distinct from existing and enforced regional solutions based on factor. Economy is a key for the emergence and existence of robust regional agreements (see Meissner this volume), but also law (Kleczkowska this volume) and environmental challenges are driving factors for cooperation (Castro this volume).

Findings

When ideas and norms are important for security institutions, one should not forget about material factors for stability and peace. Cottrell suggests that international security institution, to be resilient, should be based on materially defined power. Therefore powerful players can create working institutions to preserve such kind of order that promotes interests of most powerful actors. Thus, any shift in institutional order comes from changes in the distribution of power, and institutions, in fact, are not independent actors. Even some of them may stray from the original path, and develop own authority, they are not replaced by new actors but incrementally layered (Cottrell 2016, pp. 24–25).

Institutional design might reflect power strategies or challenges important for particular region or states involved into security institutions. Nevertheless our contributors were asked to look over existing regional security arrangements from different perspectives, with emphasis on functional elements, and opportunities to create predictable patterns of behavior, with limited amount of possible conflicts over solutions, and dense interactions with stickiness of structure. Hard cases, as examples of working institutions, are easy to explore and explain through given perspectives and assumption that institutions can be tested and validated only when security is at stake. However, by focusing on interactions, changed security perceptions, and mitigating effects of institutions, and problem solving rather than power seeking actors our contributors analyze the operational implications of institutional patterns. Therefore relationship between ideas and interests on the one hand, and implications for regional orders could be analyzed by the content of legitimization strategies based on international law (Kleczkowska), quest for autonomy (Meissner) and influence (Reich), human rights (White, Cichecka), perception of threats (Blessing), federal virtues (Frankowski) environmental challenges (Castro), global problems (Słomczyńska) or market/monetary justifications (Riedel). All those strategies, whether procedural or substantive contents have been used to reach desired goal, by far, are supported by cognitive bias towards unknown security claims. Therefore logic of security, and legitimacy provide in particular arrangements, configures possible contestation of security, or in other words, impose the limits of conflicts over challenges and problems. Such logic, by putting forward uncontested meanings, as natural and necessary, develops and embeds understanding of problems and challenges, and what is more important, limits possibilities for resistance. It also offers positive notion of security, when regional institutions have been depicted as set of instruments, positioned in lager institutional array, intelligible and acceptable without restraints. Yet, subjective elements of regional security, such as inevitable question of power distribution, in the sense of being able to undermine ideas like stability, coexistence, and sovereignty must be explored in more depth to understand the reality of security. When some challenges seem to be distant and irrelevant for the public, the very idea of security, as an absence of threats, provided by variety of institutions, and resilience of such arrangements are in the centre of this book. Institutions, procedural or legal, to be resilient, and able to maintain their structure, deal with conflicts, must be robust. However such robustness reflects not only in being resilient to disturbances, but also open to opportunities that might emerge. Thus resilient institutions should be essentially flexible, and able to reorganize when necessary (Bourbeau 2015a, p. 174).

QUESTIONS FOR FUTURE RESEARCH

The question of security on the regional level explores three ways in which ideas, interests, and institutions may be reimagined to offer new perspective on contemporary security. However all three elements should be treated as equally important and intertwined. By focusing on ideas, where construction of our perceptions comes from material and non-material sources, some questions cannot be recognized properly. For example, by emphasizing the notion of human rights, common goods or rule of law, one may overlook the fact that industrialized market economies offer valuable ways to think about ideas supported by economic and rational strategies. Therefore resistance to reality, when simple negation or ignorance of externalities beyond control is valued more than practical solutions does not translate into robust institutions and stability in the region. Institutions, by nature, resist to big or even incremental changes, but the most important threat occurs when institutions are unable to adapt and change in response to a threat to the system. Systemic resistance, supported by inflexibility of preferences and conservative stance, results in inability to provide security. On the other hands, when interests are valued more than ideas and institutions, taking ideas *à la carte*, to justify interactions and institutions, results in a lack of support for predictable institutions in a longer term. Surely, material elements of power are important, and any blueprint for institution should recall it, but making institutions out of the blue, without embedded and widely supported ideas is ill-considered strategy as well. Finally, established institutions are unlikely to change in a sense that they are necessary flexible to respond to ongoing or coming crises. Is it a failure of institution as such or was it ill-conceived from the very beginning and prone to failure by nature? Answer to these questions, obvious after the every failure, appear quite often, and do not offer any lesson-learned recipe for future actions. Thus not every failure results from wrong assumptions or imprecise calculations, but from plethora of different factors which are beyond the control of institution as such. However real problems for institution created for security lay in their frameworks, mostly due to the fact that as mentioned in the introduction institutions appear always for someone and for some purpose. There is no clear preference for egoistic activity for any institution, but some of them may pursue their interests in accordance with the overarching principle of institutional robustness and coherence, when security challenges remained unaddressed. Thus the role of ethic and self-interest in institutions remain crucial to analyze contemporary security, and some our contributors (White, Castro) elucidate it. Another challenge for future research that seems to be problematic is the level of analysis, i.e. what is truly regional or global problem, and how to deal with regional integration for security as opposed with high politics, when national interests prevail. This is to a certain extent reflected in chapters on space security, EUROscepticism, integration in South America and paradiplomacy (Słomczyńska, Riedel, Meissner, and Frankowski). Yet again, level of analysis is a question on pooling of sovereign powers, when governments are unwilling and sometimes unable to share their power. Within the particular framework of security institutions in Latin America (Kleczkowska, Meissner), some ideas serve as an interpretive device, when in Africa results of such interpretation could be mixed (Castro, Blessing). This brings us to the level of individual, and the need for finding the right balance between global, regional, national security and individual rights. The idea that institutions could be, per se, exceptional and accurate, by defending global and universal norms is misleading. Role of individuals (Cichecka) or group of individuals, not necessarily bounded by institutions, networked and acting beyond traditional politics, should be scrutinized further (Rosenau 2008). For the triad of idea, interests, and institutions, individuals as actors important for global security, are equally important. It highlights also the importance of domestic politics (Frankowski), when security issues could be de-politicized and resolved in a technical manner by individuals and networks instead of focusing on solely political institutions. Finally, apart from providing the basic framework for analysis of given facts and norms, one factor remains still beyond any control of security institutions. When spatial, ethical, or normative aspects are, for sure, political, how to analyze properly temporal aspects of any institution? Norms, ideas, values of current generations might not necessarily adhere to rules created in the past, and belief in nation, state, cooperation, institutions, as virtues of contemporary world order, may diminish. Therefore institutions, that have been created and established for current problems, and reflect contemporary structure of world politics, produce laws and rules that might be hard to change. The very structure of UN Security Council is a clear example.

Therefore analysis of long-lasting institutions, which privilege certain norms and objectives, and provide apparently cohesive force for regional orders, in comparison with new ones, allows to measure their benefits, legitimacy, and effects for regional security. Such findings from multilevel and comparative analysis, conducted in cross-disciplinary manner, help to understand the world beyond the lenses of particular paradigm and field of science, because security studies is an area, where law, international relations, economics, psychology, and natural sciences overlap.

Paweł Frankowski
Artur Gruszczak

BIBLIOGRAPHY

Abrahamsen, Rita, and Michael C. Williams. 2011. *Security beyond the State: Private Security in International Politics.* Cambridge and New York: Cambridge University Press.

Agnew, John. 2010. Still Trapped in Territory? *Geopolitics* 15 (4): 779–784. https://doi.org/10.1080/14650041003717558.

Baumgartner, Frank R. 2014. Ideas, Paradigms and Confusions. *Journal of European Public Policy* 21 (3): 475–480. https://doi.org/10.1080/135017 63.2013.876180.

Bourbeau, Philippe. 2015a. Resiliencism and Security Studies: Initiating a Dialogue. In *Contesting Security: Strategies and Logics,* ed. Thierry Balzacq, 173–188. London and New York: Routledge.

Bourbeau, Philippe (ed.). 2015b. *Security: Dialogue across Disciplines.* Cambridge: Cambridge University Press.

Carstensen, Martin B. 2011. Ideas Are Not as Stable as Political Scientists Want Them to Be: A Theory of Incremental Ideational Change. *Political Studies* 59 (3): 596–615. https://doi.org/10.1111/j.1467-9248.2010.00868.x.

Cottrell, Patrick. 2016. *The Evolution and Legitimacy of International Security Institutions.* Cambridge: Cambridge University Press.

Katzenstein, Peter. 2005. *A World of Regions: Asia and Europe in the American Imperium.* Ithaca: Cornell University Press.

Kingdon, John W. 2003. *Agendas, Alternatives, and Public Policies,* 2nd ed. New York: Longman.

Larkins, Jeremy. 2010. *From Hierarchy to Anarchy: Territory and Politics before Westphalia.* New York: Palgrave Macmillan.

Risse-Kappen, Thomas. 1994. Ideas Do Not Float Freely: Transnational Coalitions, Domestic Structures, and the End of the Cold War. *International Organization* 48 (2): 185–214.

Rosenau, James N. 2008. *People Count!: Networked Individuals in Global Politics.* Boulder, CO: Paradigm Publishers.

INDEX

© The Editor(s) (if applicable) and The Author(s) 2018   247
P. Frankowski and A. Gruszczak (eds.),
Cross-Disciplinary Perspectives on Regional and Global Security,
https://doi.org/10.1007/978-3-319-75280-8

9 783319 752792